Jack
Jo

FOLDS, FAULTS AND FOSSILS
EXPLORING GEOLOGY IN PEMBROKESHIRE

15 May 2012

Happy Birthday
Reg.

Jack & Colette

Folds, Faults and Fossils

Exploring geology in Pembrokeshire

John Downes

First published in 2011

ISBN: 978-1-84524-172-8

Cover design: Eirian Evans

Published by Llygad Gwalch,
Ysgubor Plas, Llwyndyrys,
Pwllheli, Gwynedd, Wales, LL53 6NG,

www.carreg-gwalch.com

To my wife Pamela

Acknowledgements

I would like to thank the many Open University colleagues and students who have contributed ideas and comments during the preparation of this book; also Professor Bill Fitches for his helpful advice, Toni Pearson for checking the script and Kevin Wilkinson for his practical help in the field.

Contents

List of colour photographs (between pages 49 and 64)

Introduction

This field guide has been written for students, amateur geologists, walkers and those readers who simply want to discover and understand the geological wonders of the Pembrokeshire coastline. It is based on observations of major features such as rock formations, folds, faults and coastal landforms. The origin of these features is clearly explained in the context of their field relationships. Chapters 2–11 are set out according to the age of the rocks starting with the oldest Precambrian outcrops and finishing with the deposits and landforms of the Pleistocene Ice age. Each chapter also deals with a particular area where there are rocks belonging to the same geological period. A glossary is provided to help explain some of the more technical terms that are in bold type in the text.

Most of the localities have been researched and recorded in academic publications (see the Bibliography) but here I have attempted to bring geology alive to the enthusiastic amateur observer by concentrating on key features. Indeed, to be able to practice geology in the field, in an area such as Pembrokeshire, is one of the most rewarding and enjoyable experiences of life, providing a glimpse of the treasures of the earth, often in the company of the 'salt of the earth' ... your fellow explorers. Details of access to each locality are correct at the time of writing but you should be aware that ownership of land changes, and rights of way may be diverted or restricted from time to time, particularly on Ministry of Defence land. Nevertheless, since the whole of the Pembrokeshire coast is a National Park, the coast path is normally open all the year round. You may find the coastal bus services useful when planning walks. These operate daily during the summer season and timetables are available in Tourist Information Centres and in the free newspaper 'Coast to Coast' produced by the Pembrokeshire Coast National Park; see *www.visitpembrokeshirecoast.com*

You should also read the Geological Fieldwork Code, printed at the end of this guide. It is designed to ensure both your safety and the preservation of the geological environment. Some localities are designated Regionally Important Geodiversity Sites [RIGS]; some are Geological Conservation Review sites [GCR] and some are Sites of Special Scientific Interest [SSSI]. These administrative bodies help to conserve and protect geological sites. Organisations such as the National Parks Authority, the National Trust, or the Local Authority also play an important role in landscape conservation.

For many years I tutored courses for The Open University where the contributions of Earth Science students from all walks of life have so often enriched enigmatic discussions concerning the origin of the rocks. It is in this spirit of enquiry that we need to approach geology in the field. Moreover, it is important to recognise that more often than not there is no neat and tidy answer to the riddle of the rocks. Even the experts often disagree and rarely commit themselves fully one way or another; some preface their answers with expressions such as 'on the one hand there is the possibility that ... whilst on the other it may be that ...' In fact, it is often the case that more than one event in the past has produced what we see today. Perhaps our best guide must still be the principle of uniformitarianism as proposed by the Scottish philosopher James Hutton in the eighteenth century. His thesis was that the present is the key to the past; in other words such contemporary activity as erosion by rivers or glaciers, the deposition of sands on a beach or the eruption of volcanoes involves processes that have operated for millions of years in the making of our Earth. Hutton succinctly expressed his thoughts on the origins of the rocks when he declared, 'There is no vestige of a beginning ... no prospect of an end.'

Wales has a rich history of geological research particularly relating to rocks of the Palaeozoic era and many of the divisions used in the classification of geological time are named after Welsh places or peoples. In the early nineteenth century, pioneer workers established the general sequence of Welsh rock formations. Professor Adam Sedgwick defined the Cambrian system in north Wales in 1835 whilst his contemporary Roderick Murchison researched the areas of rocks that he classified as being of Silurian age. Later in 1879 Charles Lapworth proposed a new system called the Ordovician that covered strata between the two previously designated systems. The names of these periods of geological time are derived from early Celtic tribes. Moreover, many of the subdivisions of the geological classification originate in Welsh localities where the particular rocks were first identified. In Pembrokeshire, the St David's Series of the Cambrian and the Llanvirn Series of the Ordovician are recognised subdivisions in British stratigraphy. The boundary between the Cambrian and Ordovician systems is currently defined at the base of the Tremadoc Series, and this sequence of rocks that outcrops around the village of Tremadog in north Wales is now internationally recognised, so that strata of Tremadocian age can be identified as such wherever they occur across the world.

Finally, it is worth remembering that the geology of Pembrokeshire forms part of the natural heritage of Wales. The varied and beautiful scenery of the coastline is the result of millions of years of geological activity. The landscape has been sculptured from the underlying rocks and today both local people and tourists can enjoy the unrivalled views of mountains, valleys and sea cliffs that are an integral part of the Welsh countryside. The human heritage is also imprinted on the geological landscape. Prehistoric people utilised the local stone to build their cromlechs and stone circles, and in the Middle Ages the great Norman castles of Wales were established on rocky defensive sites. Later, Welsh miners and quarrymen worked the coal, slate and minerals that supported the Industrial Revolution and today many former industrial sites have been restored as heritage projects illustrating the role of economic geology in the history of Wales.

1
A brief geological history of south-west Wales

Drifting Continents

Plate tectonic theory is arguably the most revolutionary geological concept since Darwin's theory of evolution. In essence, it states that the surface of the earth is composed of a number of large plates that are constantly in motion in respect to one another. Magma continually rises up at the mid oceanic ridges, cools and solidifies and slowly forces the oceanic plates apart. As these plates move outwards they eventually collide with adjacent continental plates where they are forced down in a process known as **subduction**. This plate movement has been going on throughout the Earth's history causing oceans and continents to drift across the surface of the globe, so that the present configuration of land and sea is vastly different to that in Precambrian times.

During the late Precambrian, approximately 700–550 million years ago [Fig. 1.1], the northern regions of the British Isles (Scotland and Northern Ireland) together with Greenland and North America were located on the passive margin of the continent of Laurentia. The southern part of Britain lay on the margins of the sub continent of Avalonia, which was initially part of the super continent of Gondwana. Avalonia was separated from Laurentia by the **Iapetus Ocean** that was actively opening and was probably several thousand kilometres wide. However, by the end of the

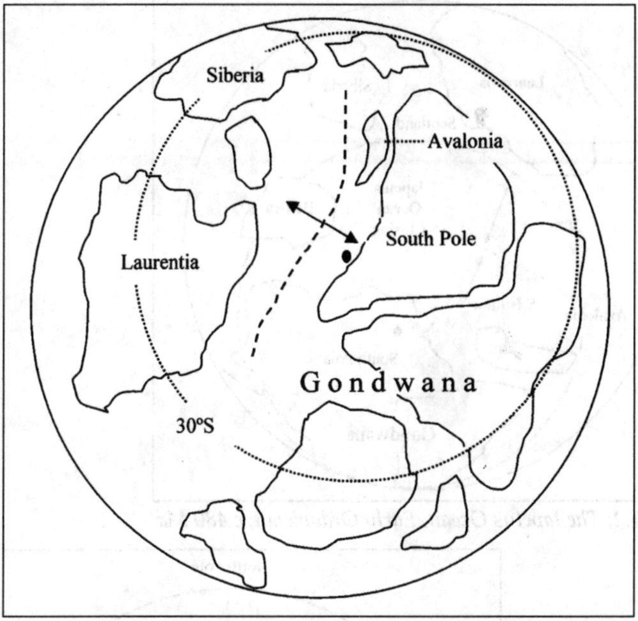

Fig. 1.1: Distribution of the continents, Late Precambrian, c.600 Ma
--------: Spreading ridge along which the Iapetus Ocean opened

Cambrian Period (490 Ma) the ocean began to close and by early Ordovician times [Fig. 1.2] the southern margin of the ocean floor began to be subducted below Avalonia, triggering considerable island arc volcanicity. The Iapetus Ocean continued to close until by the end of the Silurian period (418 Ma) the continents of Laurentia and Avalonia (together with Baltica) collided and the two parts of Britain were united along the Iapetus suture line [Fig. 1.3]. The result of this collision was the formation of the Caledonian mountains as the ocean sediments were compressed, uplifted and folded. From the late Precambrian to the end of the Silurian Period, Avalonia had moved from around 60° S of the equator to 20° S; a testimony to the power of plate movements.

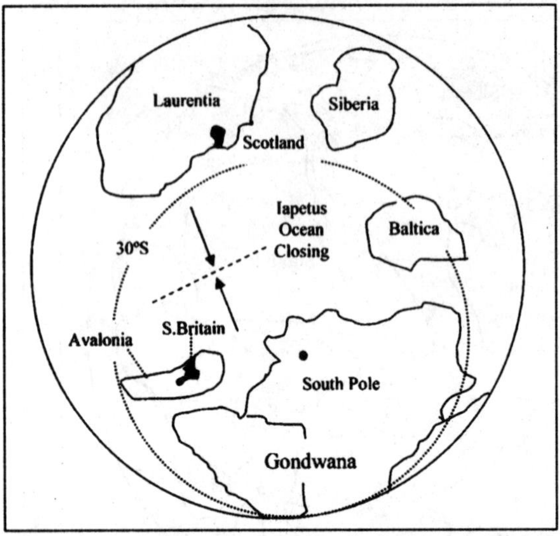

Fig. 1.2: The Iapetus Ocean, Early Ordovician, c.480 Ma

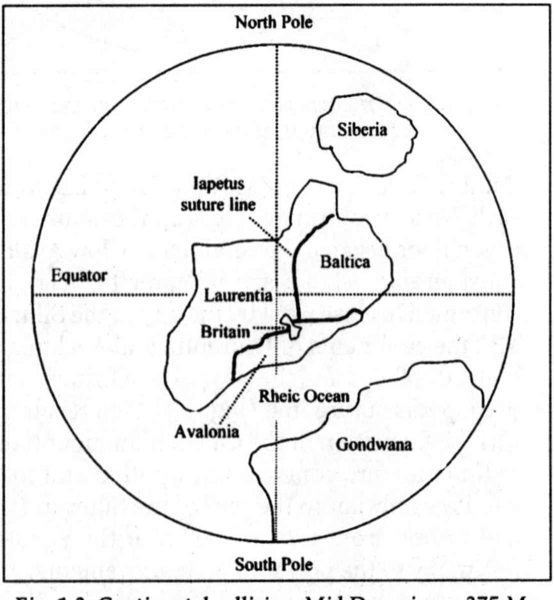

Fig. 1.3: Continental collision, Mid Devonian, c.375 Ma

By Devonian times, most of Britain was a mountainous landmass that was being actively eroded in an arid environment. Huge amounts of erosional debris were swept down from the highlands and deposited as alluvial and gravel fans by heavily braided rivers. However, at this time the **Rheic Ocean** had opened up to the south and shallow shelf seas covered what is now South Devon and Cornwall where marine limestones and sandstones were laid down. By the beginning of the Carboniferous period (354 Ma) the Rheic Ocean had transgressed northwards and almost surrounded the Wales-Brabant landmass that extended from Wales across Central England to Belgium. Then, by the late Carboniferous, the ocean began to close and vast river deltas and coal-forming swamps developed along the margins of the highland. By the beginning of Permian times (300 Ma), the Rheic Ocean had completely closed as the micro-continents of Iberia and Armorica united with Avalonia and a zone of intense folding and deformation advanced northwards. The leading edge of this movement is known as the **Variscan Front** and it extended roughly E–W across southern Ireland and southern Wales to the Thames estuary. The great northern landmass had become joined to Gondwana and one vast super continent known as Pangaea had been formed.

The Geological Evolution of south-west Wales

Today there are only a few **inliers** where Precambrian rocks are exposed in England and Wales; for the most part the ancient metamorphic basement of Avalonia has a thick cover of younger materials. The only outcrops of high grade metamorphic schists and gneisses of Precambrian age occur in the Monian Complex of Anglesey, in the Wrekin area of Shropshire and in the Malverns. Using radiometric dating these rocks are known to be between 670 to 650 million years old.

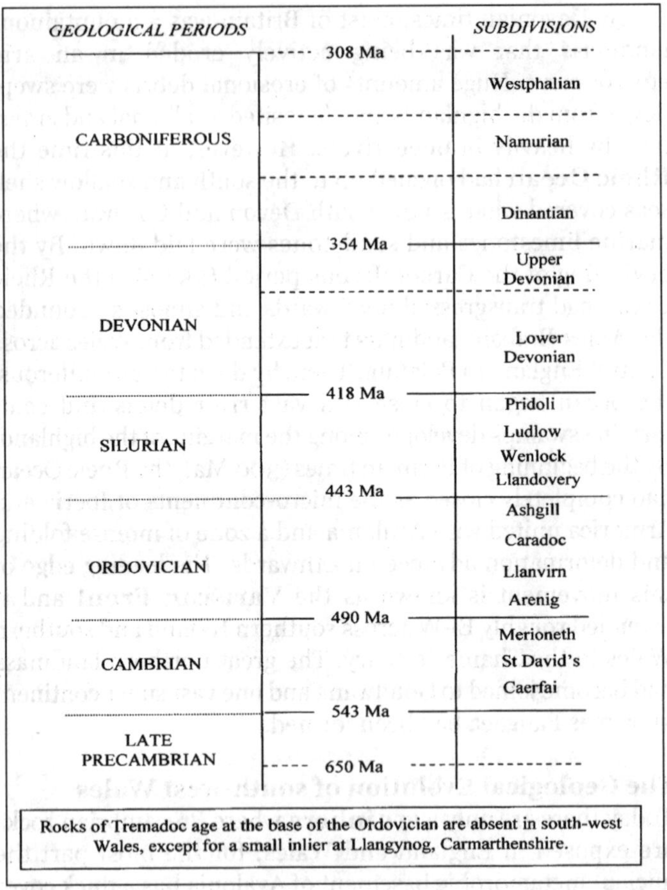

Fig. 1.4: Stratigraphical column for south-west Wales

The oldest rocks in Pembrokeshire have been dated approximately 643 Ma [Fig. 1.4]; these occur as a faulted slice of an igneous intrusion that extends E-W through Johnston to the southern side of St Bride's Bay. In the St David's peninsula, the volcanic sequence is somewhat younger, around 610-575 Ma and this is intruded by the St David's **granophyre**.

During Cambrian times (543-490 Ma) marine conditions existed over much of Wales. **Turbidite** mudstones were deposited on the continental slopes of the subsiding Welsh Basin, as seen in the Harlech Dome, whilst in North Pembrokeshire, in the shallow shelf seas on the margins of the basin, conglomerates and flaggy sandstones were laid down. Also mudstones rich in the fossilised remains of trilobites and brachiopods give an indication of the abundance of marine invertebrate life that developed during the Cambrian. The well-known large trilobite *Paradoxides* is present in the Middle Cambrian shales of the St David's peninsula.

By the Ordovician period (490-443 Ma) igneous activity was widespread across Wales as shown by the volcanic rocks of Rhobell Fawr and Cadair Idris in north Wales and the spectacular coastal exposures of the Strumble Head **pillow lavas** in north Pembrokeshire [Fig. 1.5]. The 'spotted' **dolerites** of Mynydd Preseli that were probably the source of some of the Stonehenge bluestones, and the massive layered **gabbros** of St David's Head are examples of igneous intrusions. Many early Ordovician volcanoes were associated with island arc development on the edge of the Welsh Basin and vast quantities of **pyroclastic** ash and volcanic debris were deposited in the surrounding seas. At the same time, marine sedimentation was continuing to lay down thick muds that became sandwiched between ash layers on the sea bed. The mudstones contain the remains of marine organisms including the well-known 'tuning fork' graptolites that are found in the shales at Abereiddi.

In central Wales – around Aberystwyth, for example – there are great thicknesses of turbidite sandstones and

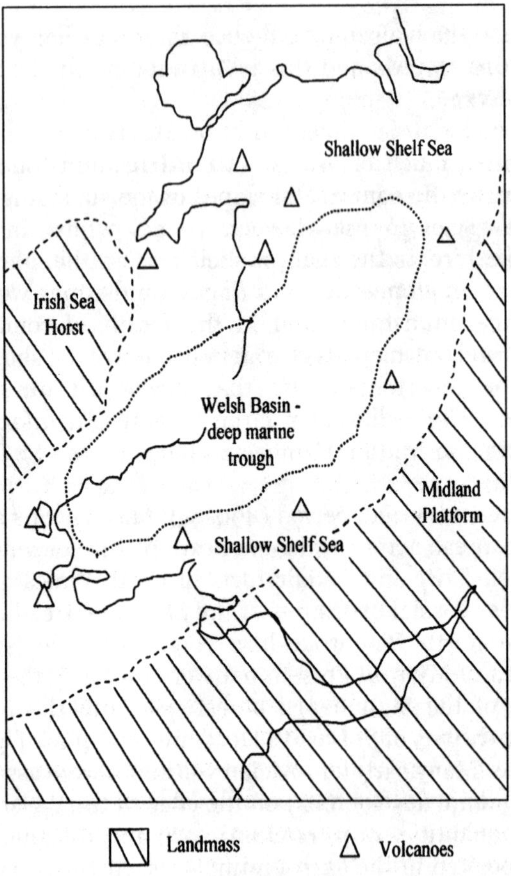

Fig. 1.5: The Welsh basin, Mid Ordovician, c.466-443 Ma

graptolitic shales that were deposited within the deep waters of the Welsh Basin during the early part of the Silurian (443-418 Ma). However, Pembrokeshire was located on the southern margins of the basin, and here the Skomer Volcanic Group represents the products of volcanism that occurred in shallow shelf seas. The lavas are interbedded with sandstones and mudstones that contain a variety of **brachiopods**, **graptolites** and corals. This classic Silurian sequence is well-exposed at Marloes Sands where in the 1960s pioneering research was carried out on brachiopod communities to demonstrate how they could be used as marine depth indicators.

The **Caledonian Orogeny** or mountain-building episode began in the early Ordovician in Scotland as the

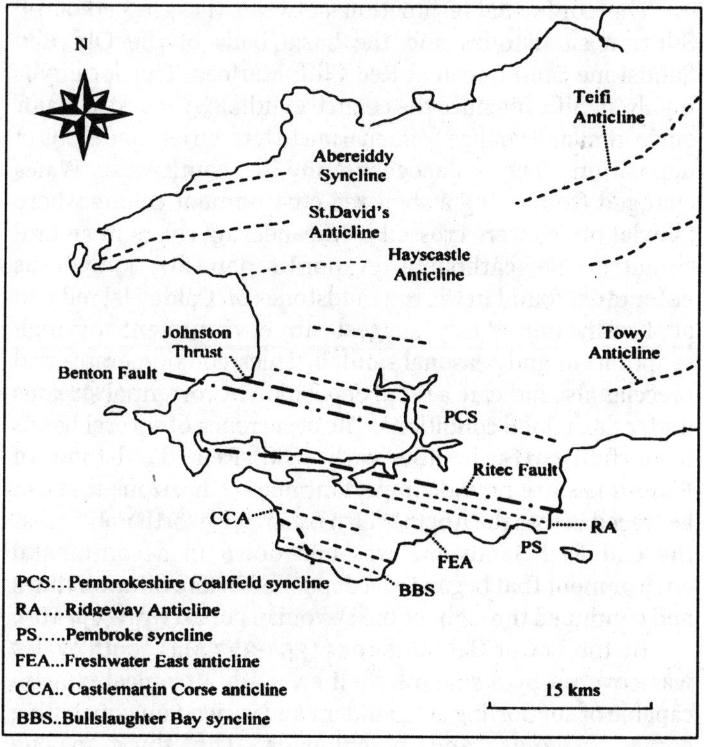

Fig. 1.6: Major geological structures in Pembrokeshire

Iapetus Ocean was closing, but the main deformation phase in southern Britain occurred from the end of Silurian to Mid Devonian times. This produced the characteristic NE-SW trending folds such as the Towy and Teifi **anticlines** in Central Wales. In North Pembrokeshire, the trend is seen in the Hayscastle and St David's anticlines and the Abereiddy **syncline** [Fig. 1.6]. Further south, the Benton and Ritec faults were active during the late Silurian and early Devonian controlling sedimentation in the tectonic basins between the faults.

The conformable junction between the grey coloured Silurian sandstones and the basal beds of the Old Red Sandstone can be seen at Red Cliff, Marloes. This locality is highly significant since the change in lithology marks a major environmental change from marine to terrestrial conditions of deposition. The palaeogeography of south-west Wales changed from being a shelf sea environment to one where alluvial plains were crossed by meandering rivers in an arid climate. The carbonate evaporite deposits known as **calcretes**, found in the red mudstones on Caldey Island and at Freshwater West, suggest an environment of high evaporation and seasonal rainfall. Thick conglomerates and breccias also indicate a rapid deposition by torrential streams under flash flood conditions. The occurrence of several bands of airfall **tuffs** in the early Old Red Sandstone of Pembrokeshire provide important marker horizons that can be traced across the Anglo Welsh basin. It is worth noting that the Old Red Sandstone was laid down in a continental environment that began to be deposited in late Silurian times and continued throughout the Devonian period (418-354 Ma).

By the Lower Carboniferous (354-327 Ma) south Wales was covered by a shallow shelf sea with a tropical climate capable of supporting an abundant and varied fauna including corals, crinoids, and brachiopods. The thick marine limestones of south Pembrokeshire and the Gower form

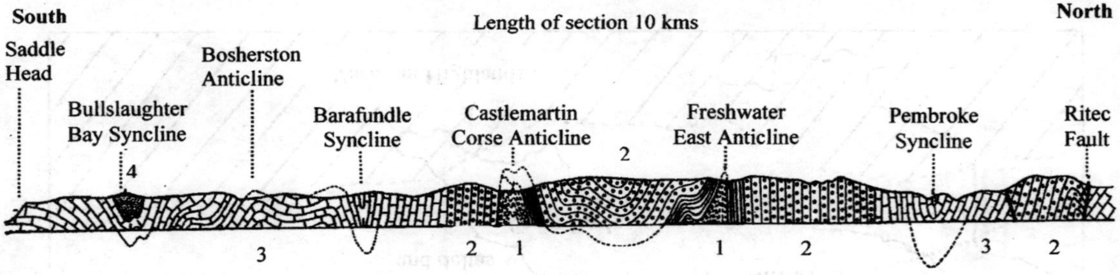

1. Ordovician/Silurian 2. Old Red Sandstone 3. Pembroke Limestone Group 4. Marros Group

Adapted from British Regional Geology, South Wales (1970) p.107.

Fig. 1.7: Variscan folds in the Pembroke Peninsula

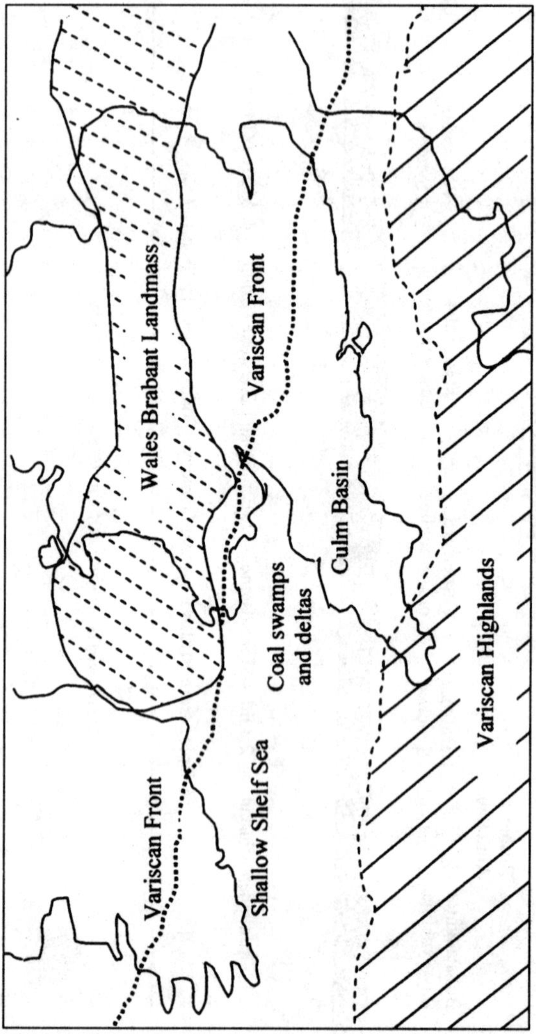

Fig. 1.8: Upper Carboniferous Palaeogeography

majestic cliffs and the rocks often show features of karstic weathering such as limestone pavements and swallow holes. Collapsed caverns and fault zones sometimes contain **gash breccia** deposits formed of red coloured sands and clays containing limestone **clasts**. The Pembroke peninsula classically demonstrates the influence of Variscan earth movements where a series of complementary folds are aligned E–W [Fig. 1.6]. Fold structures such as the Bullslaughter syncline, the Pembroke syncline and the Ridgeway anticline form distinctive topographical features [Fig. 1.7].

During the Upper Carboniferous (327-290 Ma) the seas were invaded by vast deltas as rivers advanced southwards from the Wales–Brabant landmass [Fig. 1.8]. Thick sandstones interbedded with shales were laid down in repeated cycles of sedimentation. Where swamp conditions prevailed on the delta plains, tropical forests provided the raw material for coal seams. The Pembrokeshire coalfield with its E–W axial trend is a westerly extension of the main south Wales coalfield. The coalfield has a gentle synclinal structure but it is crushed and crumpled along its southern margin where Precambrian igneous rocks have been thrust northwards over the coal measures [Fig. 1.9]. Coastal exposures of these strata often demonstrate complex **thrust faults** and folds; this is the direct result of the northward advance of the Variscan Front during the earth movements that took place at the end of the Carboniferous period.

There are no rocks younger than Upper Carboniferous in south-west Wales, except possibly the gash breccias that may be of Triassic age. The next major episode in the evolution of the landscape occurred about 5 Ma ago during the Pliocene period when marine erosion bevelled the region, cutting indifferently across the underlying geological structure. This marine platform has now been uplifted to about 65 metres above sea level and is well seen on the St David's peninsula

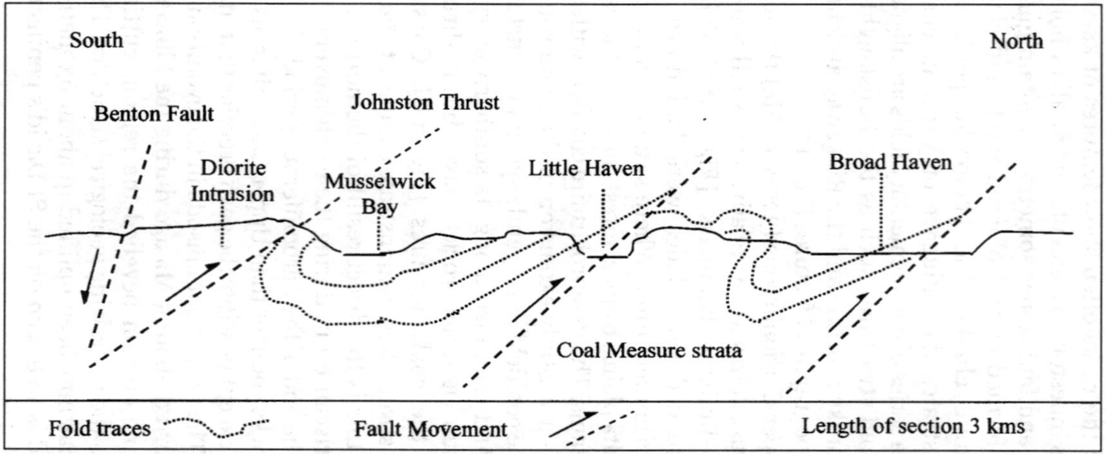

Fig. 1.9: Simplified section across the southern side of the Pembrokeshire coalfield in St Bride's Bay

where the erosional remnants of Carn Llidi and other igneous outcrops stand above the platform level.

About 140,000 years ago during the Upper Pleistocene, the landscape of south-west Wales came under the influence of the Irish Sea ice sheet that moved south-east across the relatively low coastal areas of Pembrokeshire depositing glacial clays and boulders. During a warmer interglacial period sea levels increased and formed wave cut platforms, beaches and cliff lines. Today, we see these features as raised beaches standing several metres higher than the present sea level. A further invasion of Irish Sea ice in late Devensian times resulted in the formation of **proglacial** lakes, deposits of **fluvioglacial** sands and gravels and meltwater channels in the Fishguard-Cardigan area. As the ice receded, much of the region experienced **periglacial** conditions, but when melting occurred in the surface layers above the frozen subsoil, the lubricated top soil moved down coastal slopes to create thick layers of unstratified 'head'. This mixture of stones and sandy clay is commonly seen on the top of cliffs masking the underlying solid rocks. Less than 10,000 years ago a more temperate phase began and rising sea levels created drowned river valleys or rias such as Milford Haven. Finally, we should be aware that the processes of weathering, erosion and deposition are continuing to shape and mould the topography of south-west Wales to this day.

2
Precambrian and Cambrian rocks in the St David's peninsula

St David's peninsula offers a superlative blend of Celtic history and geology. Coetan Arthur, a Neolithic burial chamber, overlooks the rugged coastline near St David's Head and stands witness to prehistoric settlement in the area. By the sixth century a monastic community had been established in the small sheltered valley of Afon Alun and the building of the present St David's Cathedral (*Eglwys Gadeiriol Tyddewi*) began on the monastic site circa 1180, making use of the local Caerbwdy sandstone [see Locality 4]. The most celebrated medieval builder was Bishop Henry de Gower, who was also responsible for the construction of the neighbouring Bishop's Palace. This magnificent architectural gem, with its distinctive arcaded parapet, was home to a succession of bishops, who enjoyed an opulent lifestyle, in stark contrast to the frugal monastic figure of St David. However, the Reformation brought an end to the power of the medieval bishops and by the sixteenth century decay and destruction had taken its toll on the building. Yet even today the cathedral and the ruins of the Bishop's Palace are seen against a backdrop of fields and woodland on the north-west side of St David's. This is the smallest city in Britain, with a population of around 2,000, but nevertheless it remains the ecclesiastical capital of Wales.

Physically the 'Land of St David's' or Dewisland is dominated by the dark igneous intrusion of Carn Llidi, an isolated hill mass that rises steeply above the surrounding plateau surface. The cliffs around the peninsula display some magnificent geological sections through some of the oldest rocks in Wales. In the extreme south-west, overlooking Ramsey Sound, the coastline is cut into late Precambrian volcanics (610-575 Ma). These rocks are composed of pyroclastic debris interbedded with lava flows, but they have been subjected to intense **tectonic** forces, which makes it difficult to recognize the original rock structures. Furthermore the volcanics have been subsequently intruded by a suite of **felsic** igneous rocks including the St David's granophyre [Fig.

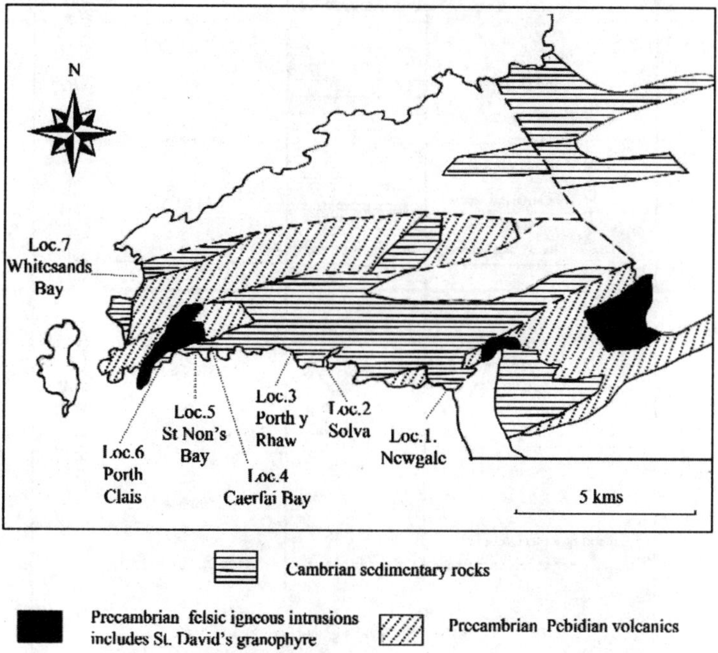

Fig. 2.1: Precambrian and Cambrian outcrops in the St David's peninsula

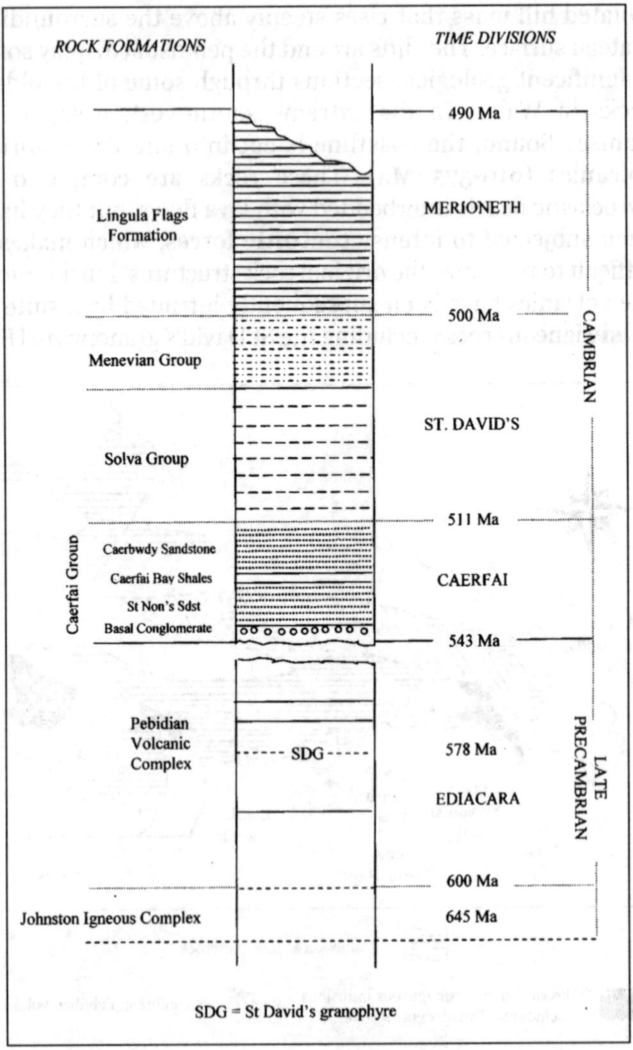

Fig. 2.2: Stratigraphical column for the Precambrian and Cambrian of the St David's peninsula

2.1]. Finally, the region underwent uplift and erosion before the deposition of the Cambrian strata in the shelf seas on the southern margin of the Iapetus Ocean.

In 1836 Professor Adam Sedgwick, the eminent Cambridge geologist, took the young Charles Darwin on an expedition to north Wales. Here Darwin made geological observations that were to prove so valuable when he undertook his voyage in the *Beagle*. At this time Sedgwick was studying rocks that he would later assign to what he defined as the Cambrian System. Since then strata of this age have been found in the St David's peninsula where they are seen to rest **unconformably** on the eroded Precambrian surface [Fig. 2.2]. Along the south coast of the peninsula the Cambrian rocks dip steeply south on the flank of the St David's anticline, the core of which is formed of the underlying Precambrian volcanics. The axes of this fold and the adjacent Hayscastle anticline, are aligned NE–SW. These folds and the associated faults are the product of the Caledonian earth movements.

However, despite a long history of upheaval and erosion, the topography of the St David's peninsula is best described as a plateau dissected by small river valleys and numerous inlets. This is because it was eroded by the sea some 5 million years ago in Pliocene times, producing a marine platform which now has a mean height of 60 metres above sea level. (This surface can also be recognised in the Pembroke peninsula; see Chapter 8.) There are several hills rising above the plateau level, which geographers refer to as **monadnocks**. They are the erosional remnants of high land that has been levelled by the sea. Carn Llidi, formed of highly resistant igneous rock, is a good example of a monadnock.

The following localities have been chosen to illustrate some of the most accessible and geologically interesting parts of the coast from Newgale in the east to Whitesands Bay on the far western side of the St David's peninsula.

1. Newgale (*Niwgwl*) [SM 847224]

This small seaside village at the northern end of St Brides Bay stands where the northern boundary of the Pembrokeshire coalfield is faulted against the Cambrian strata of the St David's peninsula. You can reach Newgale by following the A487 from Haverfordwest. Cars can be parked in the village opposite the café, but during the tourist season it is probably better to use the car park on Pinch Hill [SM 851216]. It is necessary to walk over the shingle storm beach to reach the cliffs at the northern end of Newgale Sands. The storm beach blocks the entrance of Brandy Brook and the water percolates through the pebbles emerging on the beach as a series of gushing springs. The shingle embankment serves as a natural sea defence structure stretching for about 2 kms to the south and rising some 5 metres in height.

You may like to spend a little time collecting a variety of well-rounded pebbles from this locality. The sea polishes the pebbles and so you can easily see the rock textures especially when the surfaces are wetted. Many of the pebbles are derived from local sources of igneous rocks such as St David's Head and Ramsey Island. Quartz, flint and jasper are common minerals forming the pebbles, some of which must have been transported by ice sheets across Cardigan Bay during the Pleistocene Ice Age.

Now walk over to the cliff face where sandstones and conglomerates of the Middle Solva Group [Fig. 2.3] can be seen to dip at 45° S. Marine erosion has removed some of the outer sandstone layers, particularly where intersecting joints are exposed. On the north side of the first headland the bedding is distorted in the direction of dip by a **monoclinal fold**, much brecciated in the hinge area. The strata are well-exposed in several small sea caves where the sandstones display interesting sedimentary structures. Look for examples of **graded bedding** within individual sandstone units where

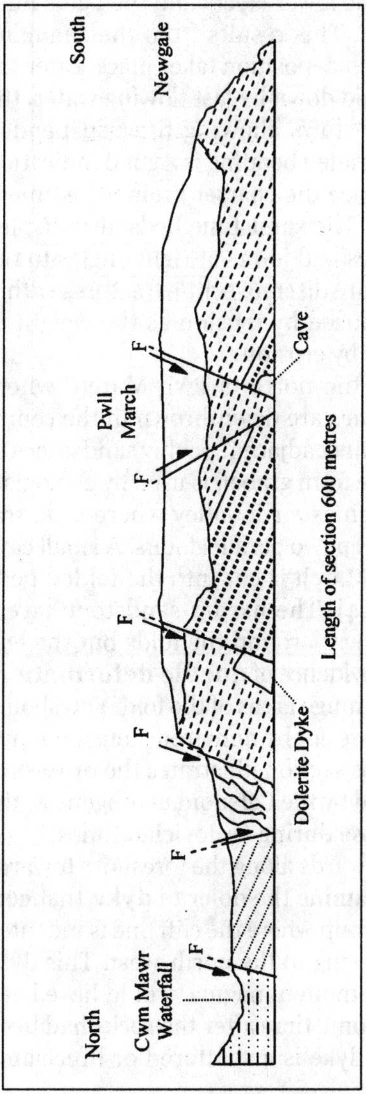

Fig. 2.3: Geological section from Cwm Mawr to Newgale

the grain size is coarse in the lower layers and then gets finer as you go up the sequence. This results from the changing velocity of the water in which deposition takes place. After the coarse material has been laid down by fast flowing water, the current velocity gradually slows allowing finer suspended material to be deposited. Graded bedding is a good indication of the 'way up' of strata since the coarser grained sediment will always be at the base. The sandstone beds also display well-defined bedding planes and joints at right angles to the bedding planes. The joints are discrete brittle fractures within the rock that may be produced by tension as the weight of overlying rocks is removed by erosion.

About 200 metres to the north is Pwll March, where Middle Solva grey sandstones are downthrown in the centre of a **graben structure** against adjacent pebbly sandstones of the Lower Solva Group. The term graben is used by geologists to describe a structure such as a rift valley where a central block is downthrown between two parallel faults. A small cave on the south side of Pwll March is cut into the folded beds within the graben [Fig. 2.4]. The harder sandstone layers maintain a constant thickness around the folds but the less resistant mudstones show evidence of **ductile deformation**, being squeezed in the open hinge areas of the fold. You should also notice that the layers are cut by numerous tension joints around the fold hinges. This section illustrates the process of crustal shortening produced by the Caledonian orogeny as the Iapetus Ocean began to close during Ordovician times.

Continue to walk northwards along the foreshore towards Cwm Mawr stopping to examine the dolerite **dyke** that cuts through the Lower Solva Group where the cliff line is indented by a major fault downthrowing to the north-west. This dyke that originally consisted of molten magma, would have been injected into the strata at some time after the rocks had been consolidated. Beyond the dyke is a shattered or brecciated

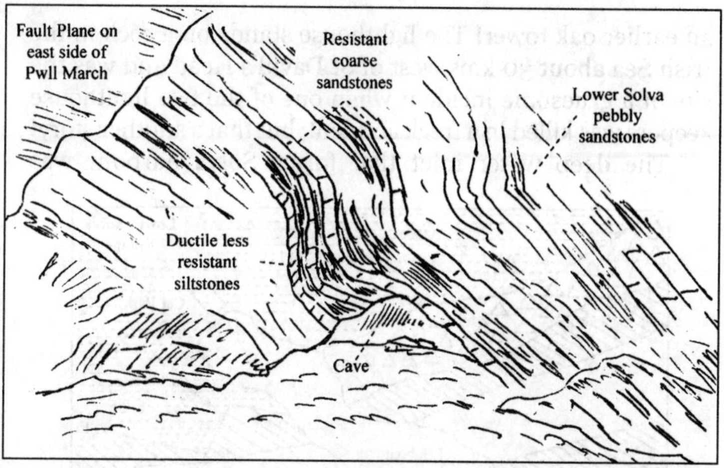

Fig. 2.4: Pwll March Cave

fault zone that separates the Middle Solva Group from the older St Non's Sandstone dipping at about 40° S. There is a faulted junction near the Cwm Mawr waterfall that separates the St Non's Sandstone from the purple Caerbwdy Sandstone that extends north towards Cwm Bach.

2. Solva (*Solfach*) [SM 806243]

This delightful sheltered harbour is located about 6 kms west of Newgale on the A487. In medieval times Solva was the main trading centre on St Brides Bay and by the nineteenth century there were thirty registered trading vessels. Today the sailing tradition is continued since the harbour provides a safe anchorage for yachts and small fishing boats. The village is a thriving centre for tourists in the summer season with a large car park conveniently situated adjacent to the Ship Inn. Take a little time to examine the blocks of Cornish granite at the entrance to the car park. These blocks were left over after the construction of the Smalls Lighthouse in 1861, which replaced an earlier oak tower! The lighthouse stands on a rock in the Irish Sea about 30 kms west of St David's Head and was the site of a gruesome incident when one of the two lighthouse keepers was killed in a freak accident; but that's another story!

The deep water inlet that forms Solva harbour was

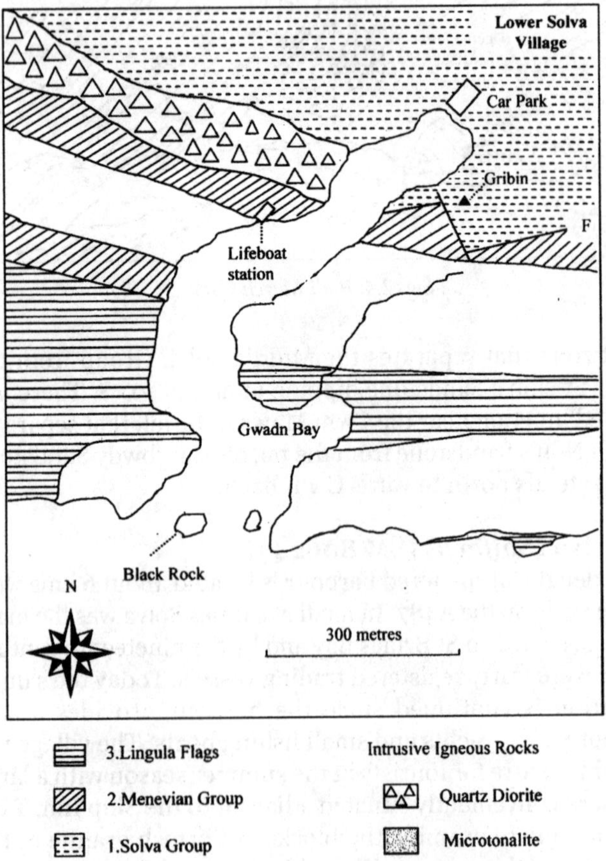

Fig. 2.5: The geology around Solva harbour

produced by Afon Solfach cutting down to a lower sea level during the late Devensian glaciation (10,000–120,000 BP). A subsequent post-glacial **eustatic** rise in sea level has created the present day Solva ria or drowned valley. You will notice that the harbour has a dog leg shape since the upper section is orientated NE–SW along a fault zone whilst the outer section has a N–S trend [Fig. 2.5].

You can walk from the car park, cross the bridge near to the pub, and follow the track up to the Gribin [SM 806241] where the purple sandstones and shales of the Middle Solva Group form a craggy outcrop. Then walk south-west along the ridge crossing exposures of igneous rocks that can be examined in more detail at the lifeboat station. Continue along the path to the headland where the Lingula Flags outcrop at the summit [SM 801238]. These thin bedded medium grained sandstones and interbedded shales are dipping at 75° S. (See Locality 7 for a fuller description of these flagstones.) The **strike direction** is E–W, which can be traced across to the east side of the adjacent Gwadn Bay The latter has a shingle bar that almost completely blocks the drainage from the marshy Gwadn valley. Look towards the entrance to Solva harbour and you will see that the outer headlands are formed of a dark resistant igneous intrusion. Return to the car park by taking the path down to the old lime kilns. These were supplied with coal and limestone by sailing vessels in the nineteenth century. The limestone was then burnt to produce quicklime, mainly for agricultural use.

You may like to take refreshment in the village before following the track along the west side of the harbour until you reach the old lifeboat station [SM 801241]. Strongly cleaved Menevian mudstones can be seen behind the boathouse. They belong to the same zonal horizon that has yielded the large trilobites at Porth y Rhaw (see Locality 3.) Walk around to the front of the old lifeboat station to view a

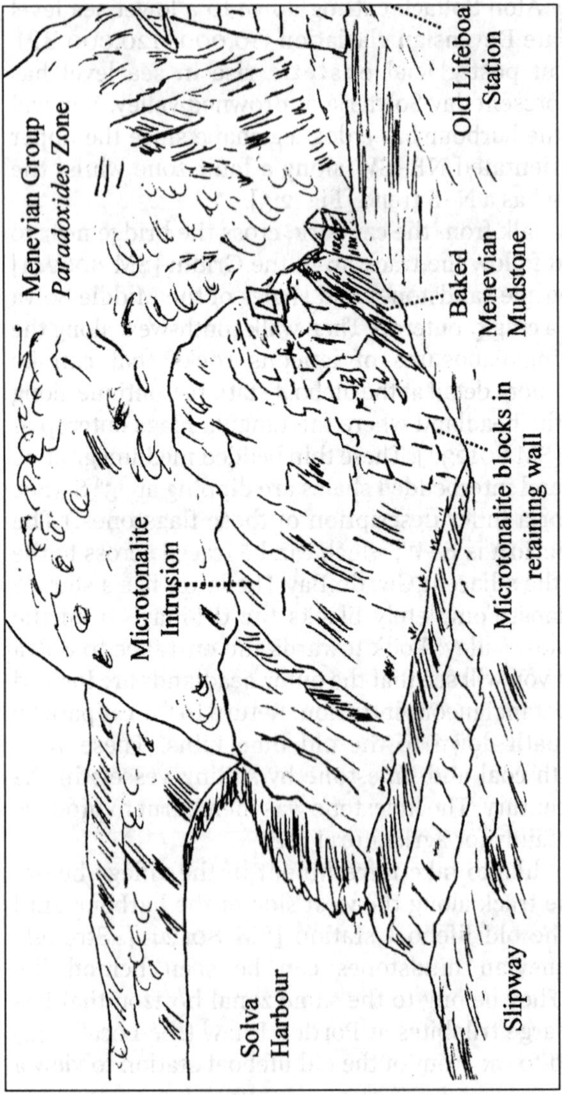

Fig. 2.6: Solva old lifeboat station section

microtonalite intrusion that is considered to be of Ordovician age [Fig. 2.6]. This medium-grained igneous rock has a distinct flow texture and contains large crystals of plagioclase feldspar. The mudstones dip at about 70° S and have been baked by **contact metamorphism** where they are adjacent to the intrusion. Here a chilled margin developed along the boundary of the hot igneous intrusion as it was cooled by the relatively cold mudstone.

3. Porth y Rhaw [SM 786242]

This wild and beautiful inlet is located about 2 kms west of Solva. You can get to it from Nine Wells on the A487 but please take care as you approach the bend into the valley at Nine Wells, as there is a sharp turn into the driveway leading to Tŷ'r Pwmp cottage where there is a small car park. Walk down the track to the coast, stopping at the old quarry at SM 788246 where a sill of quartz dolerite is in contact with the Lingula Flags dipping at about 50° S. The latter are downfaulted against the Solva Group about 100 metres to the south. Near the bridge carrying the coast path over the stream [SM787243], the Solva beds pass conformably into Menevian strata that are well-exposed around the inlet of Porth y Rhaw, where the beds are dipping at 80° S. At low tide it is possible to examine the dark mudstones on the eastern cliff that belong to the *Paradoxides davidis* zone. It was in these rocks that in 1862 John W Salter, a palaeontologist with the Geological Survey, first discovered a rich trilobite fauna containing fragments of a specimen of *Paradoxides davidis* that was almost 60 cms long. You can see a complete specimen of this distinctive trilobite in the National Museum of Wales in Cardiff. The Menevian sediments must have been laid down in calm relatively shallow water under reducing conditions since the beds contain much disseminated pyrite and phosphatic material. However, towards the end of Menevian

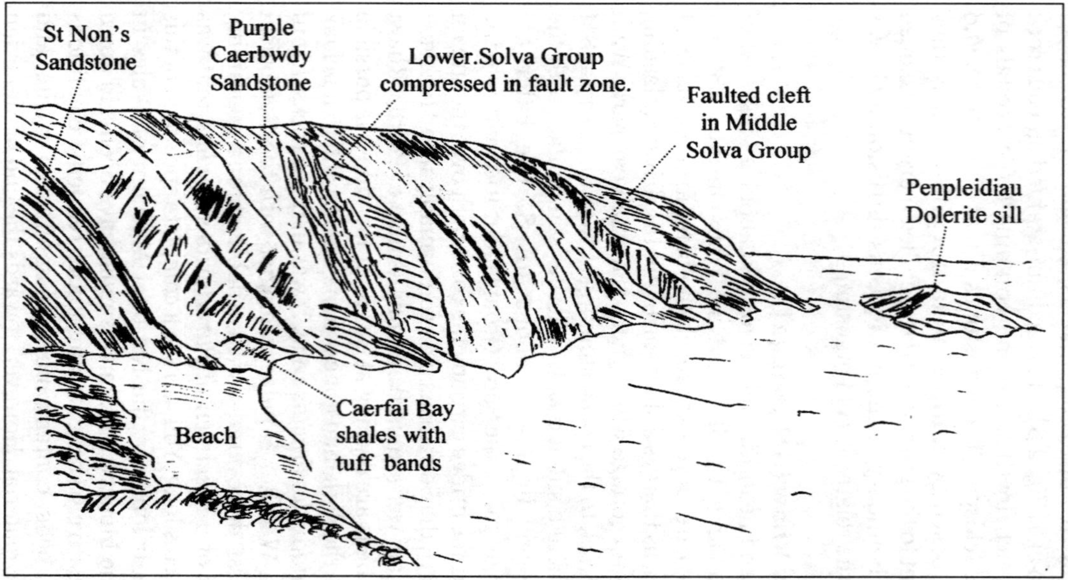

Fig. 2.7: Caerfai Bay, east side

times coarse sandstones were deposited as a result of turbidite flows and these rocks, which contain the brachiopod *Orthis hicksii*, can be seen on the eastern headland of Porth y Rhaw.

4. Caerfai Bay [SM 760244]

This locality lies immediately south of St David's and can easily be reached from the A487 by taking the signposted minor road down to the coast, where there is a car park and picnic area overlooking Caerfai Bay. Walk down the cliff path and steps that are cut through the St Non's Sandstone near the base of the Cambrian succession. (The basal conglomerate is best seen at Locality 5.) The sandstone beds weather to a greenish colour due to the presence of chlorite and epidote. Major bedding planes can be seen to dip at around 50° S. You should be aware that there is a major fault zone running ENE–SSW through the bay that produces the crushed rocks immediately to the west of the beach steps. The fault **breccia** lies between two parallel **wrench faults** that are clearly seen at beach level. At low tide walk along the eastern side of the bay (see photo on page 49) and notice that the green sandstones change to a red-purple colour as the first recess is approached. Here the relatively soft red cleaved mudstones known as the Caerfai Bay Shales have been deeply eroded by the sea [Fig. 2.7]. The original bedding is marked by a sequence of volcanic tuff bands, each less than 10 cm thick. The light coloured tuffs are generally coarse-grained and display sharp erosional bases, together with **load casts** where the slightly denser volcanic ash has sunk down into the underlying mud, forming bulbous depressions. Sedimentary structures such as graded bedding and cross-lamination within the bands indicate that the volcanic ash was deposited under water. The tuffs, which can be traced along the coast to Newgale, are the only evidence of vulcanicity during Cambrian times in Pembrokeshire.

The purple-coloured Caerbwdy Sandstone outcrops for 150 metres to the south of the red cleaved mudstones. The sandstone is medium grained, micaceous, felspathic and massively bedded. There is a cave at SM 761242 where the Caerbwdy sandstone passes conformably into the vertical Lower Solva Group where the rocks appear to be considerably compressed alongside a steep reverse fault complex.

In order to explore the higher Cambrian beds of the headland, you will find it easier to go back to the steps at the head of the bay and then follow the cliff path southwards. The purple sandstones of the Middle Solva Group are exposed in the deep faulted cleft at SM 762240, where a major bedding plane dips steeply down to the sea on the north side. The

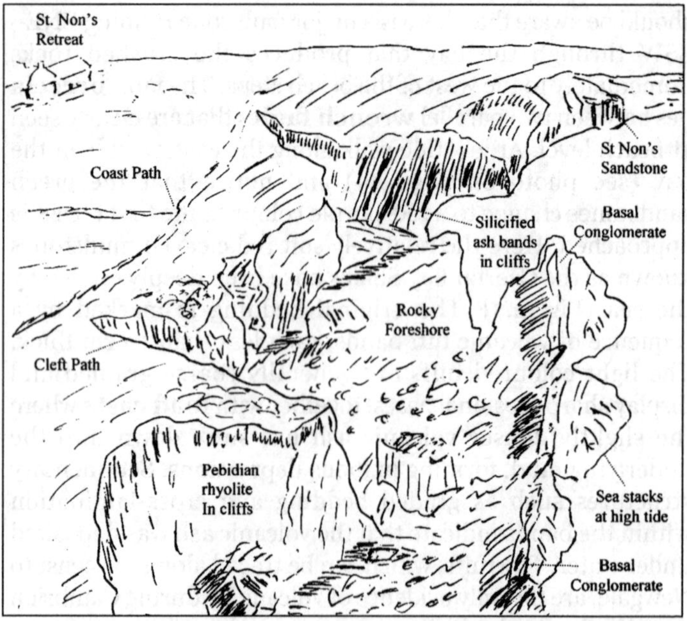

Fig. 2.8: View eastwards across St Non's Bay

headland itself and the small islands of Penpleidiau are formed of a well-jointed dolerite **sill** which rests on a narrow outcrop of Menevian mudstones. A sill is generally concordant with the surrounding strata since the molten magma was squeezed between the rock layers, unlike a dyke, which cuts discordantly through the beds. From the vantage point of the headland look across Caerbwdy Bay to the spectacular folds in the Caerbwdy Sandstone and Lower Solva Group.

Follow the coast path to the head of Caerbwdy Bay where there are several disused and overgrown quarries that worked the purple Caerbwdy Sandstone. These quarries were the source of much of the building stone for St David's cathedral. Recent restoration work on the cathedral in 1972 and 1998 resulted in the temporary reopening of some of the quarries.

5. St Non's Bay [SM 753243]

From the car park at Caerfai Bay you can follow the coastal path around Pen y Cyfrwy to reach St Non's Bay, or you may prefer to park in St David's and walk down Goat Street and take the narrow lane past the Warpool Court Hotel to St Non's Retreat. Nearby you will see the ruins of St Non's Chapel and the holy well. The chapel is traditionally held to mark the place where St David was born during a lightning strike.

About 150 metres west of the retreat, along the coast track, there is a steep path leading down into a narrow faulted cleft [SM 751242] giving access to the foreshore. The cleft is occupied by the stream flowing from St Non's Well, so you must be careful when descending the rocky path, particularly when it is wet and slippery. At the base of the cleft there are thick **rhyolites** adjacent to vertical bands of silicified ash (formerly referred to as halleflinta), each band being 10–20 cms wide [Fig. 2.8]. These rocks belong to the Pebidian Series of late Precambrian pyroclastics and lavas. An E–W ridge of Cambrian basal **conglomerate** runs along the seaward edge of the foreshore and at high tide this forms a line of sea stacks extending into the bay. This conglomerate is overturned (i.e. rotated through about 100° from its original horizontal position), which means that it now dips steeply north and so the oldest layers are exposed on top of the bed on the landward side. On the foreshore you will see that the conglomerate makes unconformable contact with the underlying Pebidian tuffs. The tuffs near the contact are purple in colour that may represent an original weathered surface. The basal conglomerate can be examined in some detail at low tide. The pebbles are composed of vein quartz, dark red quartzite, silicified tuff and granophyre set in a sandy matrix. These **clasts** have been derived from Precambrian rocks and show a preferred orientation resulting from tectonic forces. The conglomerate can be described as being clast-supported, since most pebbles are in contact with each other.

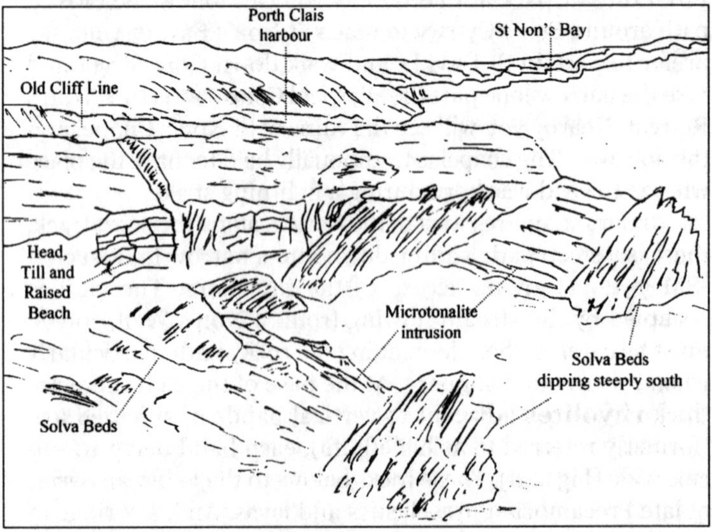

Fig. 2.9: View north-east across Ogof Golchfa, Porth Glais

6. Porth Glais [SM 741242]

Drive from St David's and continue for about 1.5 kms south-west along the lane through Lower Moor, thence to the National Trust car park near to the ford at the head of Porth Glais harbour. This tidal inlet is at the mouth of Afon Arun, and is another example of a ria or drowned valley. The Precambrian St David's granophyre is exposed in a small quarry behind a bungalow about 100 metres north of the ford, but this rock can be better examined in its coastal outcrops. Walk along the west side of the inlet towards the headland; from the track you can see the faulted junction between the Caerbwdy sandstone and the St Non's sandstone near the north end of the quay [SM 743240] on the eastern side of the inlet. Beyond the breakwater you will see the prominent bedding planes of the Caerbwdy sandstone dipping at about 80° S (see photo on page 49). This sandstone is relatively fine grained and has developed widely spaced cleavage at a high angle to the bedding; the result of uplift and compression during the Caledonian orogeny.

Continue along the coast path to Ogof Golchfa [SM 741237], which is a fault gully where there is a magnificent exposure of a microtonalite sill. This is a medium grained igneous rock, rich in plagioclase feldspar and quartz, that has been intruded into the steeply dipping Middle Solva beds. It is possible to clamber down to the foreshore to examine the contact zone between the 10 metre wide sill and the surrounding slates [Fig. 2.9]. The latter have been baked close to the intrusion and the feldspar crystals in the igneous rock increase in size towards the centre where the rate of cooling would have been slower.

Standing on the wave cut platform you will also notice several metres of a Quaternary drift sequence overlying the erosion surface of the upturned Solva beds. (See Chapter 11,

Locality 6 for more details.)

Continue westwards along the coast path that crosses the headland of Carreg Fran. This is located at the most southerly tip of the St David's granophyre intrusion. Granophyre is a medium grained felsic igneous rock containing mostly quartz and **alkali feldspar**, which usually show angular intergrowth. The western side of the intrusion is faulted against the Pebidian Volcanic Series. The latter are formed of sheared tuffs and ashes that are relatively less resistant to erosion than the granophyre. Hence the deep inlet known as Porthlysgi Bay is excavated in the softer volcanic material. You can examine the contact between the resistant granophyre intrusion and the volcanics in the eastern corner of the bay. This sheltered inlet is a marvellous spot in which to have a picnic lunch before returning to Porth Glais.

7. Whitesands Bay [SN 734272]

This is a popular holiday and surfing location on the western end of the St David's peninsula. You can easily reach it from the A487 Fishguard road out of St David's by turning left on to the B4583 that terminates in a large car park at Whitesands Bay. There are toilet facilities and a cafe/shop alongside the car park, but please be aware that the car park is often full by mid-morning at the height of the tourist season.

From the car park walk northwards along the coast path for about 200 metres then branch off left towards the first headland known as Trwynhwrddyn ('ram's nose'), which is formed of the Lingula Flags of Upper Cambrian age [Fig. 2.10]. The strata dip to the north-west at about 70° and are composed of sandstones, flagstones and mudstone. The rocks are riddled with quartz veins in places and these veins have strengthened the resistance of the headland to erosion. You may be able to see a variety of sedimentary structures including **cross-stratification**, graded bedding, and load casts that provide excellent 'way up' indicators in the rocks.

Caerfai Bay showing steeply dipping Lower Cambrian strata bevelled by the 65 metre Pliocene marine platform

Cliffs of Caerbwdy sandstone at Porth Glais

Columnar dolerite sill at Point St John with Ramsey Island in the background

Jointed Gabbro at St David's Head with Carn Llidi in the background

Trwyn Castell headland and the disused slate quarry workings at Abereiddi

Pwll Deri looking towards the microtonalite intrusion of Dinas Mawr headland

Pillow lavas on the cliffs above Porth Maen Melyn

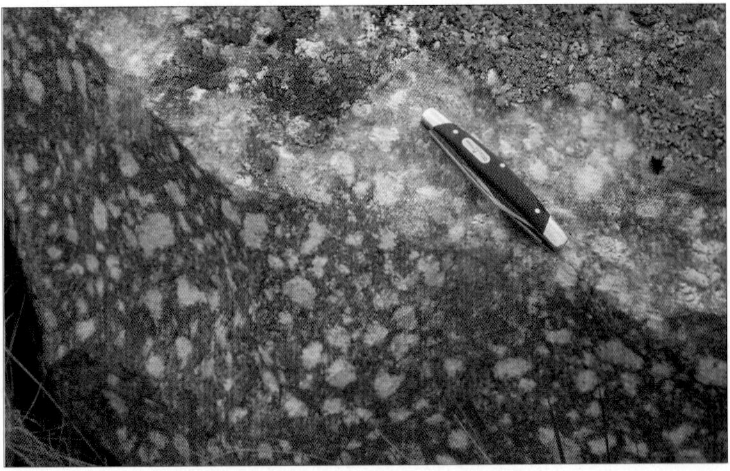

Block of 'spotted dolerite' on Carn Menyn, probable source of the Stonehenge bluestones

Frost-shattered dolerite tors on Carn Menyn, Preseli

Flooded workings in Rosebush slate quarries

Anticlinal fold showing axial planar cleavage on the foreshore at Parrog

Cliffs formed of turbidite sandstones and mudstones at Ceibwr Bay

Harmonic folding in the cliffs of Pen-yr-Afr

View looking towards Gateholm Stack from Marloes Sands. Steeply dipping Silurian sandstones on the foreshore

The Three Chimneys at Marloes Sands
formed of vertical beds of ferruginous sandstone

Rook's Cave tuff band near Manorbier.
The 70 cms thick light coloured tuff is seen in the centre

Old Red Sandstone basal conglomerate near Gravel Bay

Townsend Tuff bed at Little Castle Head

The Green Bridge of Wales, a natural arch in Carboniferous Limestone near Castlemartin

Elegug Rocks, erosional sea stacks in Carboniferous Limestone

Huntsman's Leap, a faulted inlet or geo in the limestone cliffs near St Govan's Head

St Govan's Chapel at the foot of limestone cliffs

Stackpole Head with St Govan's Head in the background

Vertical beds of Carboniferous Limestone on Lydstep Head showing saddle and ridge topography

Caldey Island showing a promontory of Carboniferous Limestone in the north and cliffs of Old Red Sandstone in the foreground

Cross cutting channel deposits in Middle Coal Measures at Wiseman's Bridge

Soft sediment deformation in Lower Coal Measures at Waterwynch Bay

Haroldston Chins landslip in the Telpyn Point Sandstone Formation

View looking north from Druidston Haven towards Rickets Head where the cliffs are formed of Upper Coal Measures

Upper Coal Measures dipping seawards at Rickets Head

Raised beach resting on a bevelled rock platform at Poppit Sands

Cliffs formed of Irish Sea boulder clay (glacial till) at Aber Mawr

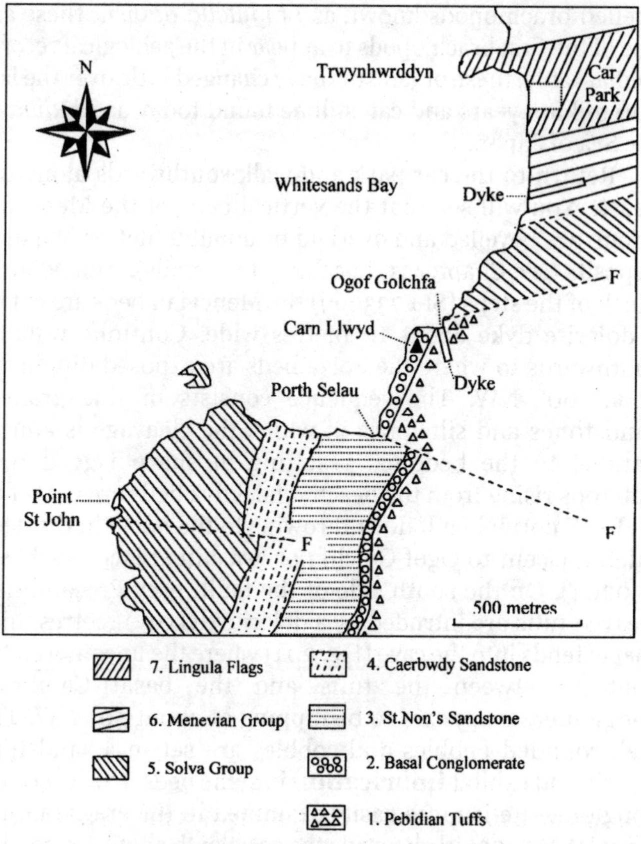

Fig. 2.10: The geology of Whitesands Bay

The cross-stratified sandstone beds can be easily recognised if you look at the cross-section parallel to the direction of dip, where they exhibit foreset beds lying at an angle to the bedding planes. The foresets are inclined in the direction of current flow when the sediment is laid down in shallow water. Some of the mudstone bedding planes contain small dark-shelled brachiopods known as *Lingulella davisii*; these are one of the first brachiopods to appear in the geological record. Remarkably, these organisms have changed little over the last 500 million years and can still be found today as *Lingula* in the Sea of Japan.

Return to the car park and walk southwards along the beach. You will see that the vertical beds of the Menevian Group are bevelled and overlaid by about 2 metres of a drift deposits (see Chapter 11, Locality 5 for details). Immediately north of the steps [SM 733269] the Menevian beds are cut by a dolerite dyke about 10 metres wide. Continue walking southwards to where the Solva beds are exposed dipping at about 60° NW. The sequence consists of fine grained sandstones and siltstones in which the cleavage is almost parallel to the bedding, resulting in sharp jagged rock outcrops rising from the beach. The Solva beds are cut off by an E–W normal fault downthrowing to the north in the deep inlet adjacent to Ogof Golchfa or 'washing place cave' [SM 730264]. On the south side of the fault, grey Precambrian cleaved tuffs are intruded by a dolerite dyke 20 metres thick that extends into the cave [Fig. 2.11] where the unconformable contact between the tuffs and the basal Cambrian conglomerate appears to be dipping at about 50° NW. The well-rounded pebbles and cobbles are set in a sandstone matrix and exhibit **imbrication** in some beds. However, this conglomerate is more easily examined in the crags of Carn Llwyd [SM 729263] alongside the coast path about 100 metres to the south. Unfortunately, you will have to return to the steps in order to reach the cliff top path and then walk southwards. Some of the clasts in the crags near to the cliff top bungalow near Porth Selau are up to 20 cms across composed of Pebidian tuff, vein quartz and dark red quartzite.

Another E–W fault downthrowing to the south, reaches the coast at Porth Selau and offsets the basal conglomerate

200 metres to the east. The view south-west across the bay shows a succession of Cambrian strata including the St Non's Sandstone, the Caerbwdy Sandstone and the Solva beds; all dipping north-west at approximately 50°. Continue along the path to the headland of Point St John [SM 719258] where a thick dolerite sill with columnar jointing can be seen resting on the steeply inclined sandstones and siltstones of the Solva beds (see photo on page 50). From this excellent view point you can look across to Ramsey Island and identify the two main peaks of Carn Ysgubor in the north and Carn Llundain in the south, formed of Ordovician gabbro and volcanic tuffs respectively.

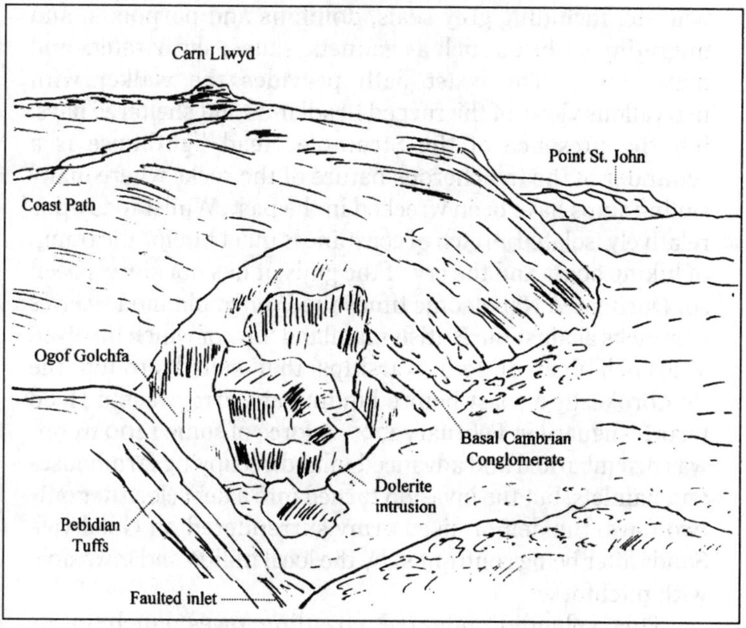

Fig. 2.11: View south-west over Ogof Golchfa, Whitesands Bay

3
Ordovician rocks on the north Pembrokeshire coast between St David's Head and Fishguard

The cliffs of north Pembrokeshire attract a rich variety of wildlife, including grey seals, dolphins and porpoises, and migrating seabirds such as gannets, skuas, shearwaters and many more. The coast path provides the walker with marvellous views of the rugged headlands and sheltered bays, but the presence of the Strumble Head lighthouse is a reminder of the treacherous nature of the rocks where many sailing ships have been wrecked in the past. Whilst today this relatively isolated stretch of coastline is quiet but for the tramp of hiking boots and the cry of the gulls, it has not always been so. During the Napoleonic times the French planned a series of attacks against the British mainland, one of which involved a French fleet of four warships that sailed around the Pembrokeshire coast before landing at Carregwastad Head near Fishguard in February 1797. A force of some 1400 troops was disembarked and advanced inland occupying farmhouses and hamlets, but the invasion turned into a debacle. After only two days, the demoralised army surrendered on Goodwick Sands after being confronted by the local militia and townsfolk with pitchforks!

This splendid indented coastline owes much to its geological structure. Differential marine erosion has ensured that the hard igneous rocks produce prominent headlands, whilst the softer sediments have been eroded to form bays. It is also significant that the strike of the rocks often runs transverse to the coastline. Together with the numerous faults that cut the coast, this structural trend tends to accentuate the indentations.

All the rocks that outcrop between Whitesand Bay and Fishguard are of Lower or Middle Ordovician age [Fig. 3.1]. The sediments are dominated by mudstones that were deposited in the deep waters of the Welsh Basin where the remains of graptolites accumulated on the muddy sea floor under **anoxic** conditions. The mudstones have subsequently been uplifted, folded and cleaved to form slates during the Caledonian earth movements. These tectonic upheavals imparted a NE–SW structural trend on the landscape that is evidenced by folds such the Llanwnda anticline that crosses the Pen Caer peninsula and the Abereiddi syncline.

During Mid-Ordovician times numerous volcanoes must have risen out of the seas of the Welsh Basin. Ramsey Island was a centre of volcanic activity where there are great thickness of lavas and tuffs. Around Strumble Head there are magnificent exposures of **pillow lavas** that were formed as lava flows were quenched by sea water. Intrusions of **mafic** igneous rocks are also to be found along the coast including the gabbros of St David's Head and Carn Llidi and the dolerites of the Pen Caer peninsula at Garn Fawr and Pen Anglas [Fig. 3.2].

The economic geology of this coast is nowhere better illustrated than at Porthgain [SM 815326], with its fascinating nineteenth-century industrial heritage in the form of huge brick-built hoppers overlooking the quayside. The hoppers were used to store crushed dolerite, an igneous rock that was quarried on the headland at Penclegyr and brought to Porthgain via an inclined tramway. When crushed, the

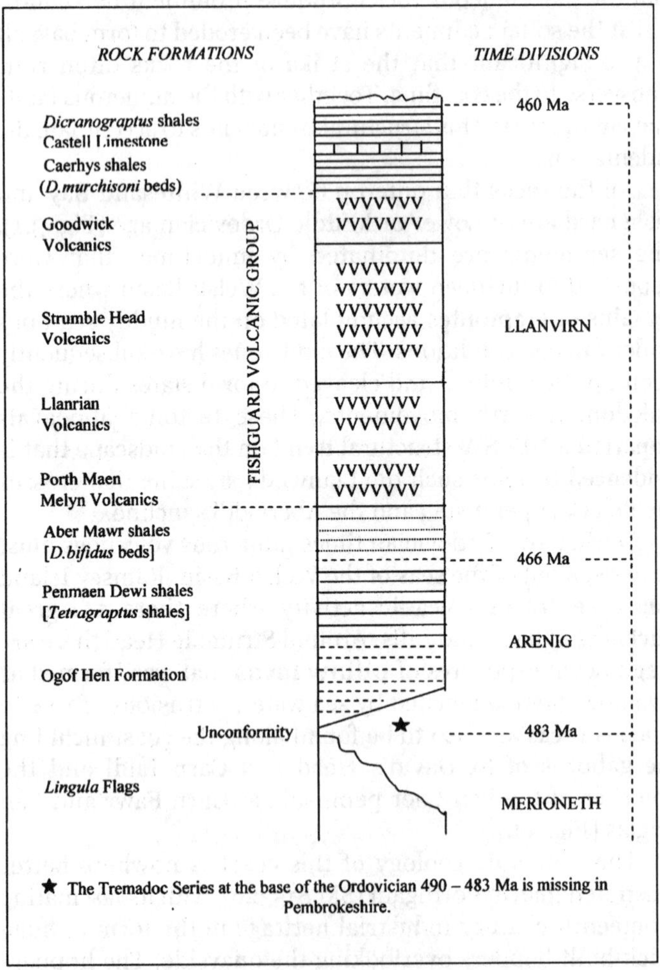

Fig. 3.1: Stratigraphical column for the Ordovician rocks on the coast between St David's Head and Fishguard

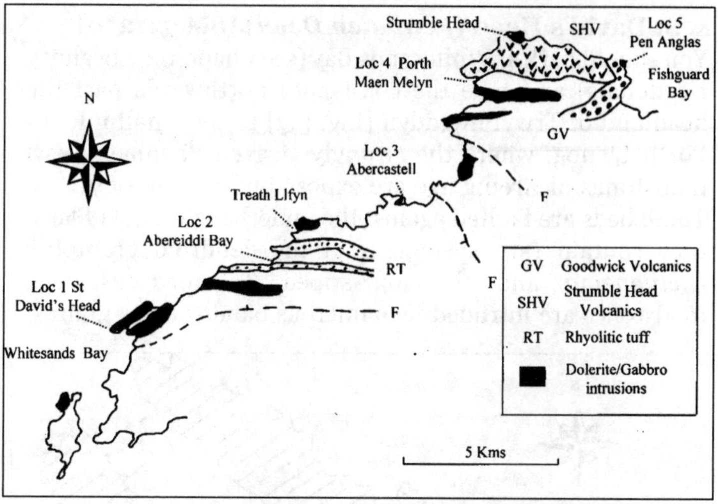

Fig. 3.2: Outcrops of Ordovician igneous rocks in north Pembrokeshire

dolerite became a valuable roadstone and was exported by sailing vessels operating from the small harbour. Porthgain was also important for brick manufacture and this industry was based on the use of cleaved mudstones that were quarried nearby. Coal was shipped in from south Pembrokeshire to fire the brick kilns and the lime kilns that stood near to the quayside. The slates were also used for roofing and building materials in the locality. The economic depression of the 1930s forced the closure of this once-booming industrial complex, although the village has survived to become a thriving tourist centre in modern times.

The following localities illustrate the typical features of both the mudstones/slates and the igneous rocks that can be seen along this section of the coast. The itinerary is described beginning at St David's Head and progressing north-eastwards towards Fishguard.

1. St David's Head (*Penmaen Dewi*) [SM 721279]

You should park at Whitesands Bay (see Chapter 2, Locality 7 for details) and take the coast path northwards past the headland of Trwynhwrddyn [Fig. 3.3] to the small inlet of Porth Lleuog, where the strongly cleaved Penmaen Dewi mudstones of Arenig age are exposed with a dip of 70° N. These beds are faulted against the underlying Lingula Flags; they contain rare specimens of the dendroid graptolite *Dictyonema* and the four-stiped *Tetragraptus*. The mudstones are intruded by numerous bands of fine grained

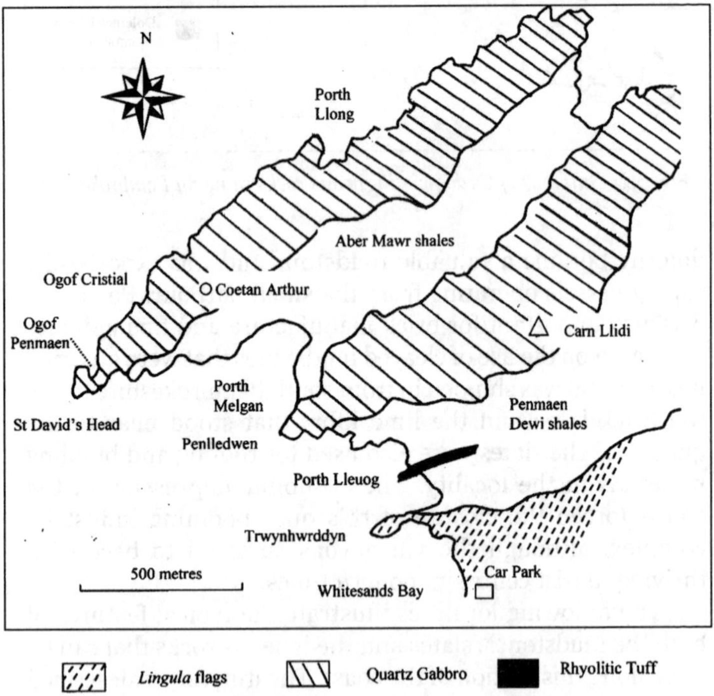

Fig. 3.3: The geology of the area around St David's Head

volcanic rock that are concordant with the bedding and in the middle of the bay a resistant rhyolitic tuff forms the prominent sea stack [Fig. 3.4].

Continue along the coast path as it climbs up to the next headland of Penlledwen and take time to admire the wonderful view north-westwards across Porth Melgan towards St David's Head. Penlledwen is the western extension of the quartz gabbro intrusion that forms Carn Llidi. You can examine several large boulders of gabbro on the headland and the junction between the baked Aber Mawr shales (Llanvirn age) and the gabbro intrusion can be seen near the footpath. Next walk down to Porth Melgan, which is cut into the less resistant shales. There are several large boulders of pegmatic gabbro on the foreshore with fresh faces that display well shaped pyroxene and plagioclase feldspar crystals. These large crystals, which you can see with the naked eye, are called **phenocrysts**, and they are set in a fine grained groundmass.

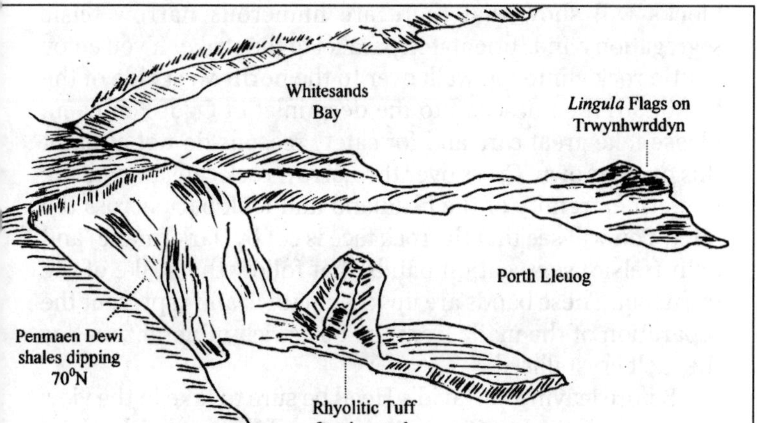

Fig. 3.4: View south across Porth Lleuog

They cooled slowly and grew to a relatively large size in the still molten magma before the whole intrusion cooled more rapidly and became a solid crystalline igneous rock.

The coast path continues towards St David's Head, crossing the baked shales along the southern margin of the St David's quartz gabbro intrusion. The gabbro intrusions appear to have been emplaced conformably into the Ordovician sediments. The Carnllidi gabbro dips steeply to the north-west, whilst the St David's gabbro dips steeply to the south-east, suggesting that they may be linked at depth. These intrusions are between 335 and 396 metres thick and are flanked by **hornfelsed** sediments forming a baked zone some 60 metres wide. The gabbros are composite differentiated sheets that are zoned parallel to the Caledonian trend of the intrusions.

The crags around the Iron Age fort on St David's Head clearly illustrate the NE–SW strike direction of the jointed gabbro (see photo on page 50), and careful examination of the blocks will show that there are numerous narrow felsic segregation bands orientated parallel to the strike. If you enjoy a little rock climbing, walk over to the north-west side of the headland, then descend to the deep inlet of Ogof Penmaen. Please take great care and for safety reasons do not attempt this on your own. Cross over the narrow rock causeway to the western extremity of the headland and look back across the inlet. You will see that the rock face is cut by dark (mafic) and light (felsic) segregation bands that follow the strike of the intrusion. These bands are up to 5 cm thick and represent the separation of the mafic from the felsic rich mineral zones as the melt crystallised.

Before leaving St David's Head be sure to take in the view of Ramsey Island to the south-west and the outer islands of the Bishops and Clerks, then follow the path along the cliff top towards Porth Llong. There are several small bays en route that display alternations of different varieties of gabbro but the mineralogy is complex. Suffice to say that there is a general coarsening of the rock texture inland where a pegmatic texture is developed. This is due to the slower cooling rate of the magma in the centre of the intrusion.

The Neolithic burial chamber of Coetan Arthur [SM 725281] stands on the moorland above the cliffs and is well worth visiting. It has a massive capstone of gabbro that has now partly collapsed. From here you can easily climb up to the summit of Carn Llidi or take the track back to Porth Melgan where the coastal route can be rejoined for the return journey to the car park.

2. Abereiddi Bay [SM 796313]

This locality can be reached from Croes Goch on the A487 Fishguard road, by following the signposted lane for about 3 kms down to the coast. You can park in the area overlooking the beach. There are toilet facilities and in summer the ice cream van provides welcome refreshments. Nevertheless, it would be a good idea to bring a packed lunch with you for sustenance on the walk to Traeth Llfyn, which is the bay to the north of Abereiddi.

Abereiddi Bay is eroded along the E–W axis of a syncline [Fig. 3.5] developed in the mudstones of Llanvirn age that are rich in graptolitic remains. The high fossilisation potential of these organisms in this locality is largely due to the fact that the bedding planes of the strata are close to the direction of cleavage. This means that the organic remains were not destroyed during the Caledonian earth movements that folded the rocks, since the cleavage was imposed almost parallel to the bedding rather than at a high angle to it.

You should walk from the car park down to the far southern corner of the bay where, at low tide, you will be able to examine the Abereiddi Tuff, formerly known as the

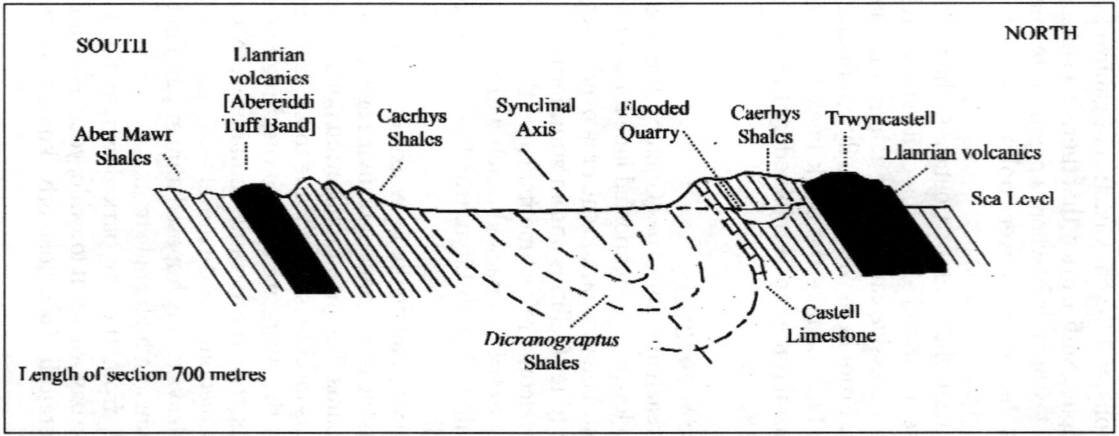

Fig. 3.5: Geological section across Abereiddi Bay

Murchisoni ash band. This unit is about 30 metres thick and dips steeply north towards the centre of the syncline, forming the sloping cliffs along the south side of the bay. The tuff contains **lapilli** of pumice generally about 2 mm in size, set in a coarse ash matrix. The overlying Caerhys Shale Formation is famous for its specimens of the graptolite *Didimograptus murchisoni* that are present on the bedding planes. The specimens can be easily recognised by their tuning fork appearance consisting of two branches or stipes that look rather like fret-saw blades! Please remember that this locality is designated as an SSSI and on no account should the rocks be hammered. Nevertheless, you can enjoy looking for the graptolites and photographing them on the rock surfaces, but do not despair because collecting is possible at the next stop!

Walk back to the car park, crossing the axis of the syncline, and make for the gate leading to the path up to the northern headland. You will see the old miners' cottages, now converted into holiday lets, in the marshy Abereiddi valley. The path follows the route of the old tramway. When you get to the cutting leading to the disused quarry, stop and examine the Castell Limestone. It is difficult to recognise as a limestone because it is really a hard calcareous mudstone. However, there is a well-developed cleavage in the interbedded shales, and this dips at a lower angle than the limestone bedding planes indicating that the strata is inverted. (Cleavage dips at a greater angle than bedding when the strata is the right way up.) In other words, you are standing on the northern limb of the Abereiddi syncline that has been overturned by the Caledonian earth movements [Fig. 3.5]. So appearances can be deceptive since the upturned beds are dipping at 70° N! Remember that **cleavage** has been produced by intense pressure on the mudstones during orogenesis and the platy minerals such as mica and chlorite have been realigned along the cleavage planes. This is, of course, why cleaved mudstones or slates split so easily along the cleavage planes.

Next enter the quarry across the wooden bridge. The sea has now flooded the lower part of the quarry, but the Caerhys Shale is well-exposed and faulted against the Castell Limestone on the south side of the quarry (see photo on page 51). Scree material in the quarry yields a fragmented fauna of graptolites, brachiopods, and trilobites. The steep northern face is cut into the resistant Abereiddi Tuff belonging to the Llanrian Volcanic Formation, which also forms the headland of Trwyncastell, marked by a stone tower.

The coast path leads over Trwyncastell headland to the next bay called Traeth Llyfn [SM 803320]. You will see that there is a deep gully following a fault line that cuts across the base of the headland. Follow the path past Carn Llwyd [SM 798317] where there are numerous small outcrops of a gabbro intrusion that extends along the cliff top. When you reach Treath Llfyn descend to beach level by the steps and walk over to the south side of the bay. Here the cliffs are formed of the Llanrian Volcanics, dipping at 80° N forming the north side of the Abereiddi syncline, hence they are inverted. Several of the beds of coarse ash contain lapilli ranging in diameter from 1–5 cm. The junction between the rhyolitic tuffs and the Aber Mawr Shale Formation can be seen in the south-east corner of the bay, but walking back towards the steps the shales become deformed and crushed. Continue north beyond the steps past a gabbro outcrop to where a metre thick tuff unit crosses the beach; this has a distinctive erosional base on the north side and a sharp erosional contact with the shales [Fig. 3.6]. There are several graded beds showing an overall fining upwards sequence indicative of an airfall deposit.

3. Abercastell [SM 853336]

This picturesque fishing village is off the beaten track but it is well worth a visit. You should leave the A487 Fishguard road at the Square and Compass Inn [SM 845311] and follow the

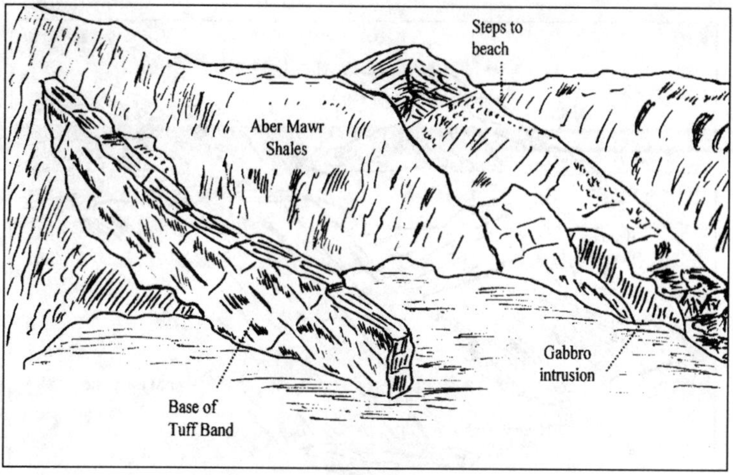

Fig. 3.6: Traeth Llyfn, north side

minor road to Trefin. Turn right in the village onto the narrow lane signposted to Abercastell, where you will find a small car park alongside the slipway.

Follow the coast path on the west side of the estuary. In several places the track is cut through outcrops of the Penmaen Dewi shales that display strong cleavage dipping about 70° NE. Follow the path up onto the headland until you are opposite Ynys y Castell. The north side of this island displays a large dolerite intrusion cross-cutting the bedded rhyolitic tuffs. Continue along the path towards Ynys Deullyn where the Aber Mawr Shale Formation is well-exposed in the steep sided faulted cleft that separates the island from the mainland. About 300 metres along the coast to the west there is a spectacular natural arch [Fig. 3.7] where the cleavage planes are dipping steeply north-west but the bedding planes can clearly be seen above the arch dipping at about 30° SE.

The next headland is Pen Castell-coch, the site of an Iron

Fig. 3.7: Natural arch west of Abercastell

Age encampment. This is a marvellous place to view the indented rocky coast stretching south-west towards Porthgain and beyond the summit of Carn Llidi rises above the plateau surface. The headland itself is composed of rhyolitic tuffs that can be well seen in the west facing cliffs, where they contain almost vertical beds of coarse lapilli separated by ash bands. Walk around Pwll Whiting to the promontory on the south side that is formed of a vertically bedded basaltic lava flow. Beyond this feature the cliffs of massive grey sandstones and conglomerates outcrop on the south side of Pwll Llong. These rocks belong to the Ogof Hen Formation of Arenig age, and so they are some of the oldest Ordovician beds in south-west Wales.

You can either retrace your footsteps back to Abercastell on the coast path or take the footpath from Pwll Llong across the fields to the Trefin-Abercastell road.

4. Porth Maen Melyn [SM 889393]

This small inlet lies on the coast south of Strumble Head and is a favourite location of mine, not only for the splendid geology but also for the spectacular wildlife including grey seals and a host of sea birds. You can approach from the A487 Fishguard road by taking the minor road to St Nicholas and thence to the coast at Pwll Deri. There is a small car parking

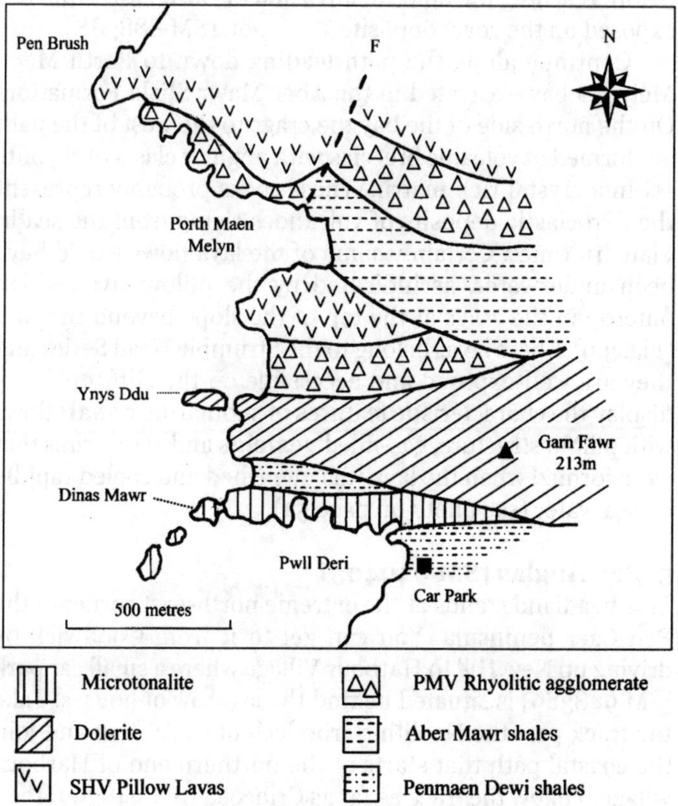

Fig. 3.8: The geology of Porth Maen Melyn

area on the east side of the road [SM 892388], which is cut out of the cleaved mudstones of the Penmaen Dewi Shale Formation [Fig. 3.8]. Walk down the track leading to the youth hostel and descend to Dinas Mawr [SM 888386], which is a headland formed of an intrusion of microtonalite (see photo on page 51). Follow the coast path in a northerly direction crossing another outcrop of the cleaved mudstones before reaching the dolerite intrusion of Garn Fawr, which is exposed on the coast opposite Ynys Ddu [SM 888388].

Continue along the path leading down to Porth Maen Melyn, a bay excavated in the Aber Mawr Shale Formation. On the north side of the bay the crags to the west of the path are formed of volcanic breccias with angular clasts of rhyolite set in a crystal rich matrix. These rocks probably represent the pyroclastic deposits of volcanoes rising from the sea in Llanvirn times. Certainly some of the lava flows would have been underwater, as indicated by the pillow lavas which outcrop in the crags at the top of the slope beyond the wall [Fig. 3.9]. These lavas belong to the Strumble Head Series and they are well-exposed and accessible on the cliff top. They display the characteristic features of submarine **basalt** flows with pillow-structure, gas-filled **vesicles** and glassy rims that were formed when the lava was quenched and cooled rapidly by sea water (see photo on page 52).

5. Pen Anglas [SM 949405]

This headland stands at the extreme north-east corner of the Pen Caer peninsula. You can get to it from Goodwick by driving up New Hill to Harbour Village where a small car park [SM 948389] is situated behind the last row of houses. Take the track past the Neolithic cromlech of Garn Wen and join the coastal path that starts at the northern end of Harbour village. Follow the track as far as Crincoed [SM 948399] then leave the main path and bear right towards Pen Anglas;

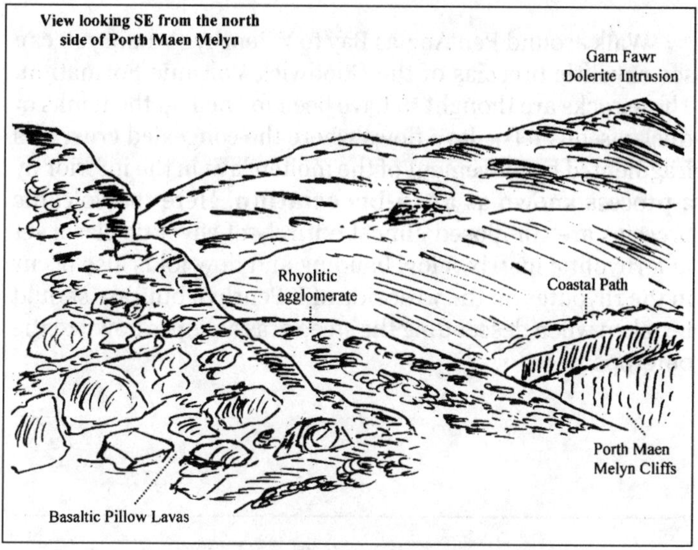

Fig. 3.9: Pillow lavas at Porth Maen Melyn

following the narrow path to the first beacon, which is a thick wooden pole on a concrete base. You should continue along the line of the stumps of several more beacons leading down to the headland that is surmounted by a stone pillar. Take great care when examining the rocks here because it is easy to slip into the sea from the steep sloping rock surface.

Pen Anglas is formed of a dolerite intrusion and on the north-east facing cliffs below the stone pillar, there are some excellent examples of columnar jointing [Fig. 3.10]. This inclined rock face shows sections through the columns demonstrating the polygonal cooling joints. Climb over the ridge to the south-west side of the headland where the long axes of the columns can be seen. These columns formed perpendicular to the surface of the intrusion, which is dipping at about 45° towards the north-east where the upper surface is exposed.

Walk around Pen Anglas Bay to Y Penrhyn where you can see rhyolitic breccias of the Goodwick Volcanic Formation. These rocks are thought to have been formed on the flanks of thick viscous felsic lava flows where the congealed crust was fragmented by movement of the molten lava in the interior by a process known as **auto-brecciation**. Here the volcanic breccias are composed almost entirely of rhyolitic clasts set in a rhyolitic matrix. Flow banding and flow folds also occur in the rhyolites on the west side of Y Penrhyn but care should be taken when descending the steep grassy slopes down to the outcrops.

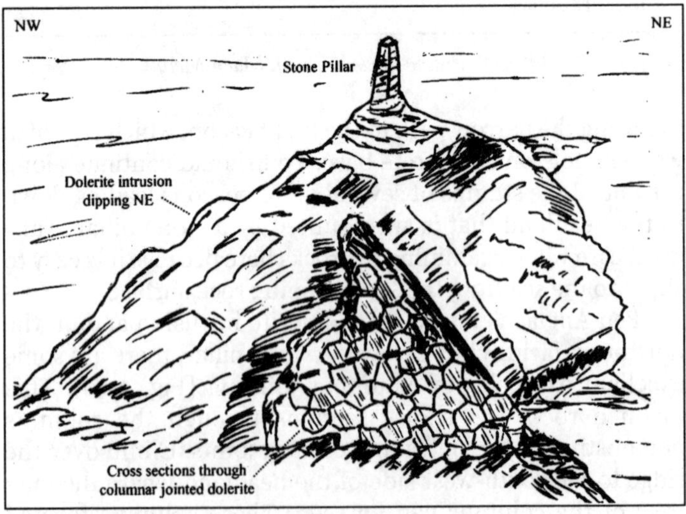

Fig. 3.10: Columnar dolerite at Pen Anglas

4
Ordovician rocks on Mynydd Preseli

Mynydd Preseli is a range of hills in north Pembrokeshire that rise to 536 metres above sea level on Foel Cwmcerwyn, the highest point in the county. Preseli has long been known as the reputed source of the Stonehenge bluestones. Myths abound as to the exact way in which these stones were transported from west Wales to Wiltshire. Neolithic argonauts may have hauled the stones overland to the coast and thence voyaged on log rafts across the Bristol Channel and onwards to Salisbury Plain. Folklore even suggests that Merlin the wizard had a hand in moving the bluestones! More down-to-earth geologists tend to favour a glacial transport theory. Nevertheless the association of Preseli with Stonehenge has created a long-standing interest in these rolling magical hills with their numerous prehistoric stone circles and cromlechs.

During World War II the Preseli area was used as a training ground for the military and it would still have been MOD property today, had it not been for a successfully organised campaign by Plaid Cymru to prevent the army's continued use of the hills. Now the public has the right to walk the many paths that criss-cross the landscape and to explore the fascinating geology and archaeology.

The hills are formed of rocks of Middle Ordovician age that strike approximately ENE–WSW following the Caledonian structural trend [Fig. 4.1]. There are several anticlines that plunge eastwards and other minor Caledonian

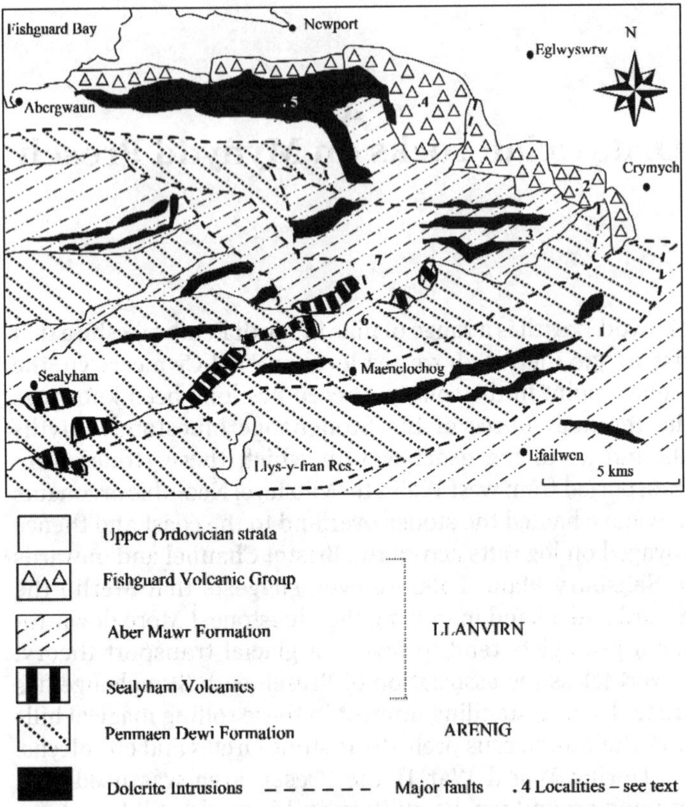

Fig. 4.1: The geology of Mynydd Preseli

folds affecting the strata. The area is also much disturbed by south-east-directed thrust movements, as for example on Foel Drygarn where the Fishgard Volcanic Group is overthrust by at least 800 metres over the underlying shales and in the neighbourhood of Rosebush, the Sealyham Volcanics are strongly displaced by thrusting [Figs. 4.2 and 4.3]. The numerous dolerite sills appear to be aligned along the strike

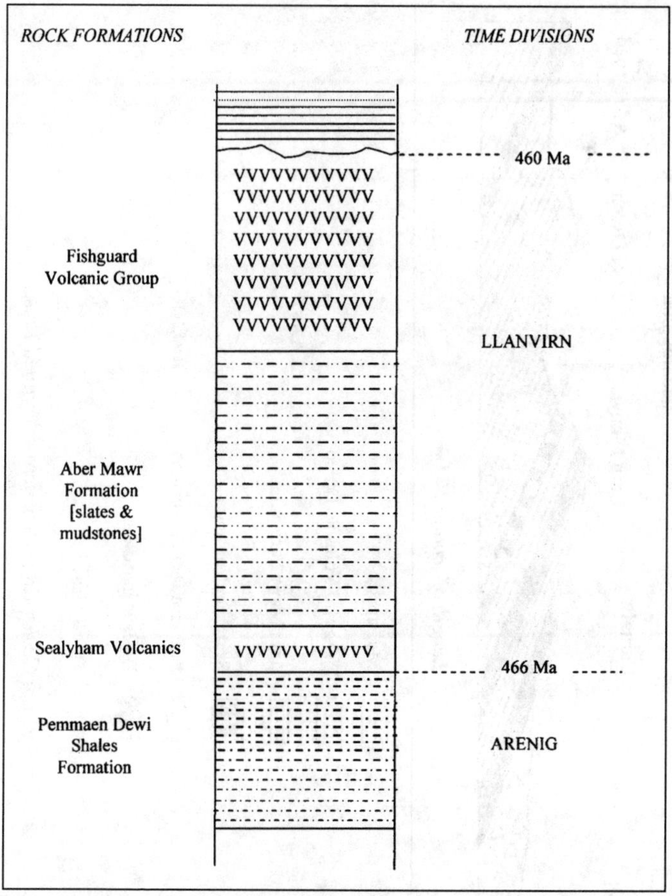

Fig. 4.2: Stratigraphical column for the Ordovician rocks of Mynydd Preseli

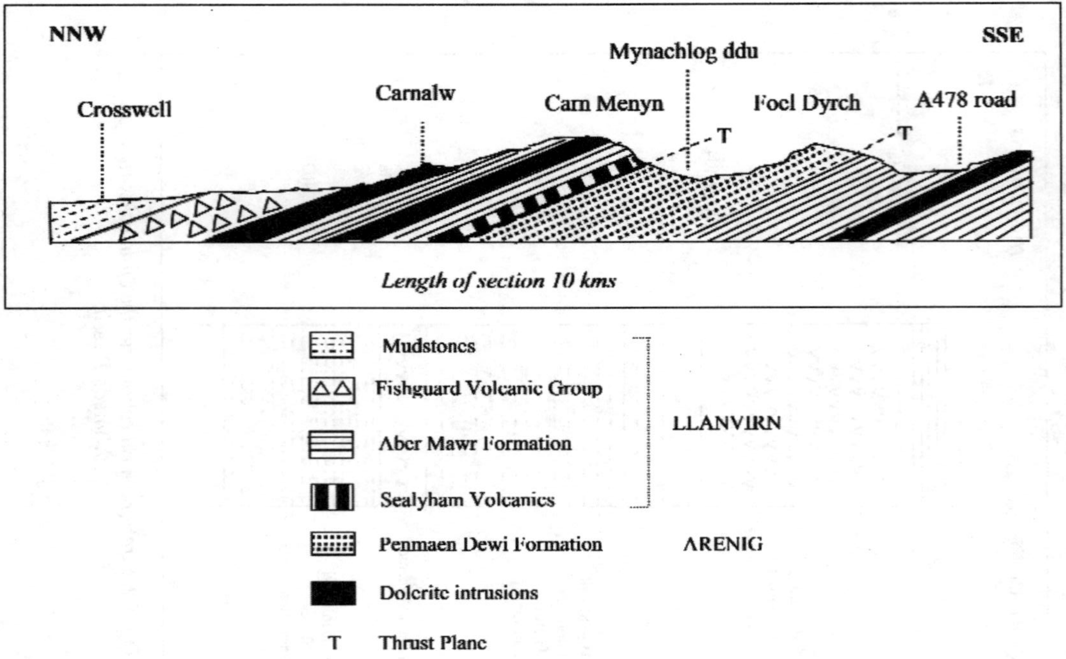

Fig. 4.3: Geological section across Mynydd Preseli

within the mudstones and shales that dip NNW over much of the Preseli area. The mudstones are often strongly-cleaved, producing good quality slates that were quarried extensively in the nineteenth century. The rocky crags or tors that form the summit of many of the hills owe their present development largely to periglacial weathering during the late Devensian.

You should try to visit some of the following places to get an understanding of the key features of the geology of Mynydd Preseli. Obviously to reach the higher localities you will have to do some rough uphill walking.

1. Tyrch Quarry [SN 157297]

This disused quarry is located on the slopes of Foel Dyrch about 5 kms south east of Crymych. It can be reached from the A 478 Narberth to Crymych road. Parking is available alongside the entrance to Carn Wen Quarry at SN 165288. Walk down the narrow lane leading to Pentre Glas. Here the track ends and you should ask permission at the farmhouse to cross the fields to the old quarry. The rocks exposed in the quarry face and on the old spoil heaps are mostly dark coloured mudstones of Arenig age. The dominant structural feature is a strong closely spaced cleavage that is orientated approximately NNE–SSW. This cleavage in the mudstones was produced by intense pressure at the end of the Caledonian orogeny.

The igneous intrusions that form craggy outcrops immediately to the north-east of the quarry are formed of dolerite, a dark, medium grained igneous rock. Unfortunately the contact between the igneous intrusion and the mudstones is not exposed in Tyrch Quarry or in the immediate surrounding area. The dolerite is probably part of the same Mid-Ordovician igneous suite that forms many of the sills that outcrop along the crest of Mynydd Preseli.

2. Foel Drygarn [SN 158336]

You can approach this locality from the southern outskirts of Crymych, where you must take the minor road signposted to Mynachlog-ddu and continue for about 1.5 kms to a small lay by at SN 166331. From here follow the well marked footpath north west to the summit of Foel Drygarn, where there are three Bronze Age cairns within the Iron Age fort. The dry stone ramparts almost completely enclose the area of the hill fort.

The igneous rocks that form craggy outcrops on the summit of Foel Drygarn are composed of interbedded rhyolite lavas and tuffs belonging to the Fishguard Volcanic Group. The tuffs represent pyroclastic deposits that contain vesicles that were originally gas-filled bubbles, and also small fragments ejected from a volcano, known as lapilli. There are examples of bedded splintery felspathic tuffs in the crags on the south west side of Foel Drygarn. The blue-grey rhyolite is well exposed on the eastern side of the hill where some lavas show evidence of flow banding.

3. Carn Menyn [SN 144325]

Carn Menyn is located about 1.5 kms south west of Foel Drygarn. There is a footpath connecting the two summits. However if you wish to approach by road then there is a small parking area at Glanrhyd [SN 152318], from where a footpath leads up to Carn Menyn. This is probably the best-known rock outcrop in Preseli since it is reputed to be the source of the Stonehenge bluestones (see below).

The igneous intrusions that form craggy outcrops or tors on the summit of Carn Menyn are sills of a dark, medium-grained rock [Fig. 4.4]. Examination of the rock shows it to be 'spotted' dolerite that is characterised by the presence of white plagioclase phenocrysts together with dark pyroxene crystals (see photo on page 52). The dolerite is intruded into the cleaved mudstones of Llanvirn age. The summit outcrop is characterised by many strong vertical fractures that result from tensional stress caused by contraction when the dolerite cooled and crystallised after being intruded into the country rock. Some of these contraction joints have the appearance of columnar jointing.

The physical appearance of the tors can be described as accumulations of large irregular blocks resting on the dolerite outcrop of Carn Menyn and surrounding summits (see photo on page 53). Large blocks litter the slopes having been detached from the main outcrop. Many researchers consider that the tors evolved under periglacial conditions during the late Devensian when the area is thought to have been just beyond the maximum ice limit. On the other hand, Linton (1955) proposed that the Preseli tors were formed by a two-stage process, involving deep tropical weathering during the Palaeogene followed by **mass movement** during the Pleistocene. The 'river of stones' known as Rhestr Gerrig is a line of boulders extending southwards from Carn Menyn that

Fig. 4.4: View of Carn Menyn tors looking westwards

provides evidence of downslope movement (solifluction) of wet thawed surface material above the permafrost.

Since 1921, when Herbert Thomas presented his paper to the Society of Antiquities on the source of the Stonehenge bluestones, it has been generally accepted that Mynydd Preseli was the source area of these stones. More recently in 1991, Richard Thorpe and others from the Open University matched the spotted dolerite of Carn Menyn (and several similar localities nearby) to some of the 'bluestones' of Stonehenge using petrographic and geochemical analysis. What has long been contested is how the stones actually reached Stonehenge from south-west Wales. It has been proposed by archaeologists that these bluestones were transported by Neolithic people across Pembrokeshire to Milford Haven and thence by raft across the Bristol Channel, and finally overland to Salisbury Plain. By contrast, most geologists have long been of the opinion that the stones were carried as erratics by the earliest advance of the Irish Sea ice that crossed the Preseli and extended eastwards up the Bristol Channel towards Salisbury Plain.

4. Pentre Ifan [SN 098368]

This is probably the most famous Neolithic cromlech in Pembrokeshire [Fig. 4.5]. It can be approached by signposted minor roads either from the A487 near Nevern or from the B4329 at Brynberian. The structure dates from around 3,500 BC and the existing stones formed the portal to the main communal burial mound which was c.36 metres long. The massive upright pillars and the capstone are composed of agglomeratic tuff (volcanic ash) from the Fishguard Volcanic Group that outcrops in several localities in the surrounding area.

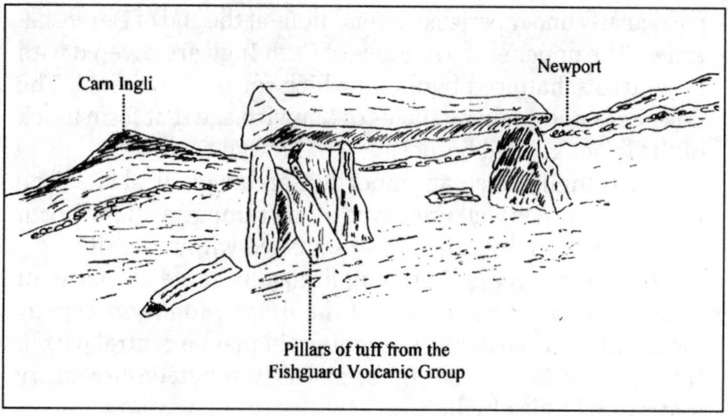

Fig. 4.5: The Neolithic Cromlech of Pentre Ifan

5. Carn Ingli [SN 063373]

Carn Ingli rises to 347 metres above sea level and is the highest point in the western part of Mynydd Preseli. The summit is formed of rocky crags that dominate the skyline to the south of Newport. You can approach the locality along the narrow lane leading from Newport to Cilgwyn. After about 2 kms branch off to the right and continue for about 500 metres to a small lay by at SN 070374. From here a footpath leads directly to the top of Carn Ingli. About half way up the hill you will see two stone-built pillars standing on a flat grassy area. These pillars supported a cable drum that controlled the descent of rail wagons carrying stone down the incline to a crushing plant on the Cilgwyn road. The quarry closed in the 1930s and is now much overgrown.

Geologically, Carn Ingli is composed of a dolerite sill that strikes NE–SW and dips towards the north-west. The dolerite is strongly jointed and in places there is evidence of columnar jointing, the result of magma contraction during cooling. The fissures have subsequently been widened by freeze-thaw action, particularly under periglacial conditions at the end of Devensian times. The upper eastern slopes of Carn Ingli are covered with large frost-shattered boulders which form a blockfield. The dolerite is underlain by shales of Llanvirn age that form much of the lower ground bordering the Cilgwyn road.

Carn Ingli is also an important archaeological site. The Iron Age fort has well preserved stone ramparts on the north side and hut circles can be distinguished within the site.

In recent years Carn Ingli has become a place of pilgrimage for those readers of the *Angel Mountain* saga by local author Brian John. The mountain plays a central part in the story of Martha Morgan, an early nineteenth-century matriarch of Plas Ingli.

6. Bellstone and Rosebush Slate Quarries [SN 078300]

The B4329 Haverfordwest to Cardigan road is the best scenic route across Mynydd Preseli. At New Inn crossroads [SN 061301] take the B4313 signposted to Maenclochog, after 1.5 kms turn left into Rosebush village and park near to Y Tafarn Sinc. This pub, with its distinctive corrugated iron roof, was formerly called the Preseli Hotel. It was built in 1876 when the Maenclochog railway was opened to provide a link between the quarries and Clunderwen on the main line. The street of terraced cottages in the village provided accommodation for the quarrymen.

The slate quarries were excavated on the western flanks of Foel Cwmcerwyn immediately north of Rosebush [Fig. 4.6]. They are easily accessible along the track leading past the cottages. The first quarry to be opened in 1825 was Bellstone, the most northerly of the workings. A deep pit drained by an adit was used to extract some of the best slates. Bellstone closed in 1891. Rosebush quarry opened in 1842 and expanded rapidly after the opening of the railway from Clunderwen (which was later extended from Rosebush to

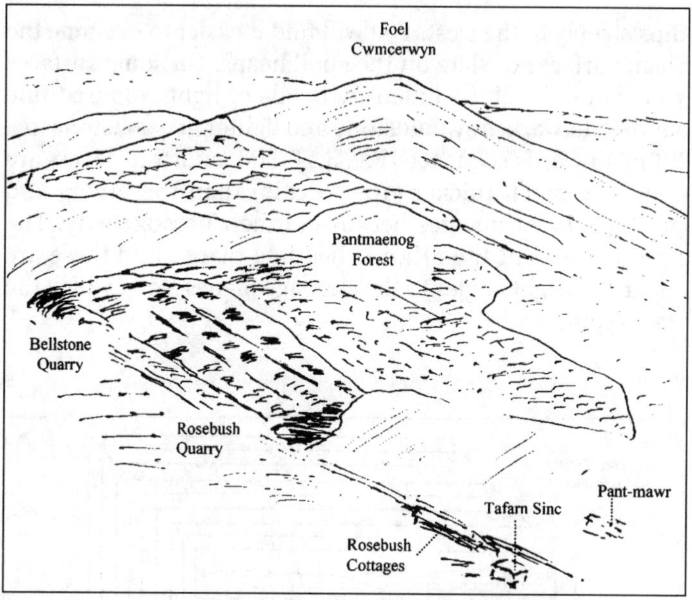

Fig. 4.6: Foel Cwmcerwyn and Rosebush quarries

Fishguard). The slate produced at Rosebush was of high quality and was used for roofing the Houses of Parliament. Today the only quarry buildings to have survived are the ruins of the locomotive shed and part of the dressing shed adjacent to the trackway. Some of the old quarries are now flooded (see photo on page 53).

The rocks at Rosebush were deposited as turbidites from debris-laden submarine currents that flowed down the shelf slope into the southern part of the Welsh Basin during late Arenig times. Numerous volcanic centres existed at this time and volcanic ash was laid down and interbedded with mud and sand in the surrounding seas. These sediments were later subjected to intense pressure during the Caledonian orogeny and now exhibit strong cleavage which strikes NNE–SSW and dips steeply to the west. You will find it easier to examine the clean surfaces of slate on the spoil heaps. On some surfaces you should be able to identify bands of light-coloured fine sandstone, dark grey mudstone and lighter grey siltstone in a fining upwards sequence [Fig. 4.7]. The mudstone layers are generally much thicker (10–50 cms) than the others and produce the best slates because of their homogeneity. The layers represent the original bedding planes and these are roughly at right angles to the cleavage planes along which the slates split.

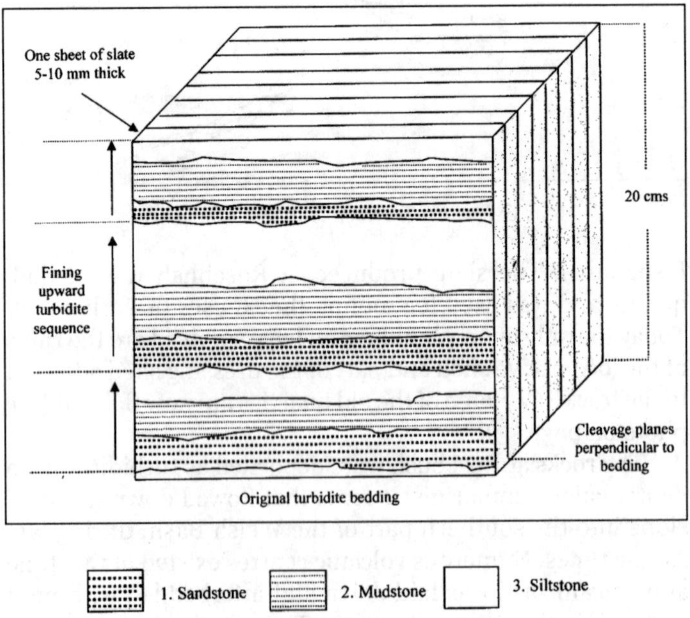

Fig. 4.7: Bedding and cleavage in a block of slate

7. Foel Cwmcerwyn [SN 095312]

The easiest way to reach Foel Cwmcerwyn is to park at Bwlch-gwynt [SN 075322] on the B4329, then follow the footpath eastwards towards Bwlch Pennant at the junction with the track from Rosebush Quarries. Continue along the boundary of the Forestry Commission land (Pantmaenog Forest) then turn south on the path leading up to the summit of Foel Cwmcerwyn. Alternatively, you can park in Rosebush village and take the track through Pant-mawr farm, famous for its cheese making. This route to the summit follows the eastern boundary of Pantmaenog Forest and provides good views of the crags of Carn Afr formed of a faulted slice of trachyte lava belonging to the Sealyham Volcanic Series.

On a clear day there are some excellent views from the summit of Foel Cwmcerwyn across Mynydd Preseli and the surrounding area. You should be able to identify the rocky tors of Carn Sian, Carn Menyn and Foel Drygarn orientated roughly ENE. The TV mast at SN 172306 provides a useful location marker [Fig. 4.8]. The view to the north west shows Carn Ingli and Afon Nyfer estuary at Newport. About 200 metres east of the triangulation pillar is Cwm Cerwyn, where the headwaters of the Eastern Cleddau rise. There is an overgrown disused slate quarry in the headwall of the cwm where strongly-cleaved mudstones of Llanvirn age are exposed. On the south east side of the quarry near to the original entrance there is a wedge of the Sealyham Volcanics composed of vesicular rhyolites and splintery tuffs that are faulted against the shales. A more accessible outcrop of the Sealyham Volcanics occurs at Garn Turne Rocks, 2 kms south east of Sealyham (see Chapter 12, Locality 2).

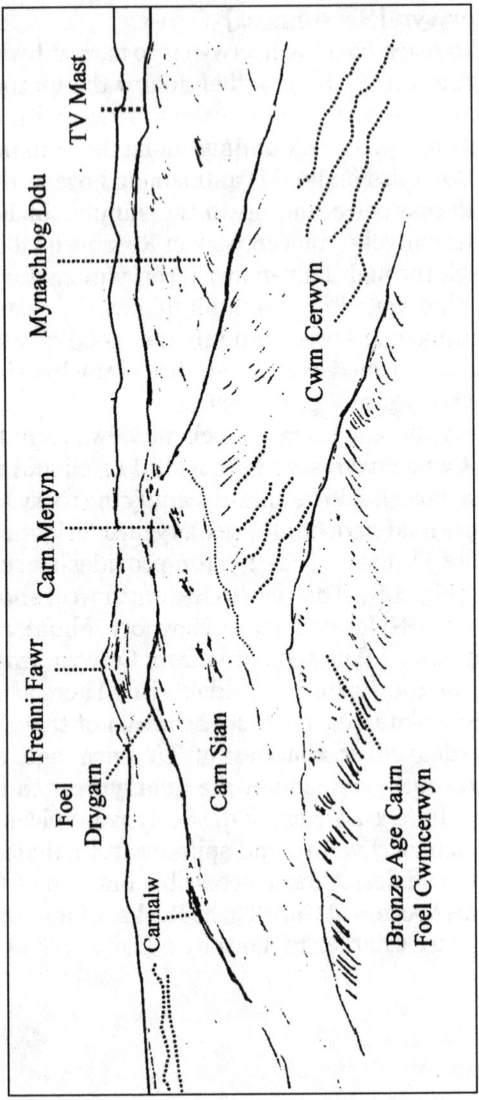

Fig. 4.8: View eastwards from Foel Cwmcerwyn

5
Ordovician rocks on the north Pembrokeshire coast between Fishguard and Cardigan

This remote stretch of coast in north Pembrokeshire is strikingly beautiful, but it is possible to get down to beach level in a only few places due to the high inaccessible cliffs. However, there are three spectacular river mouths along the coast [Fig. 5.1]. Fishguard (Abergwaun) is a lovely old-world fishing port and tourist centre. Afon Gwaun flows through a glacial overflow channel and out into the harbour in the Lower Town where the old cottages were used as the film setting for Dylan Thomas's *Under Milk Wood.* Halfway up the coast is Newport, on the estuary of Afon Nyfer, with the majestic backdrop of Carn Ingli rising above the old town. At the northern end of this stretch of coast is the Teifi estuary and the village of St Dogmaels built around its ruined twelfth-century abbey. Nearby Poppit Sands marks the end (or the beginning) of the Pembrokeshire coast path.

The whole of the coast from Dinas Head to Cemaes Head exposes Ordovician rocks of Caradoc age [Fig. 5.2]. It is thought that they were deposited as turbidite sediments in a submarine trough or graben aligned along the Fishguard–Cardigan Fault Belt. Lavas and tuffs of the Fishguard Volcanic Group form the basement of this faulted structure and these rocks reach

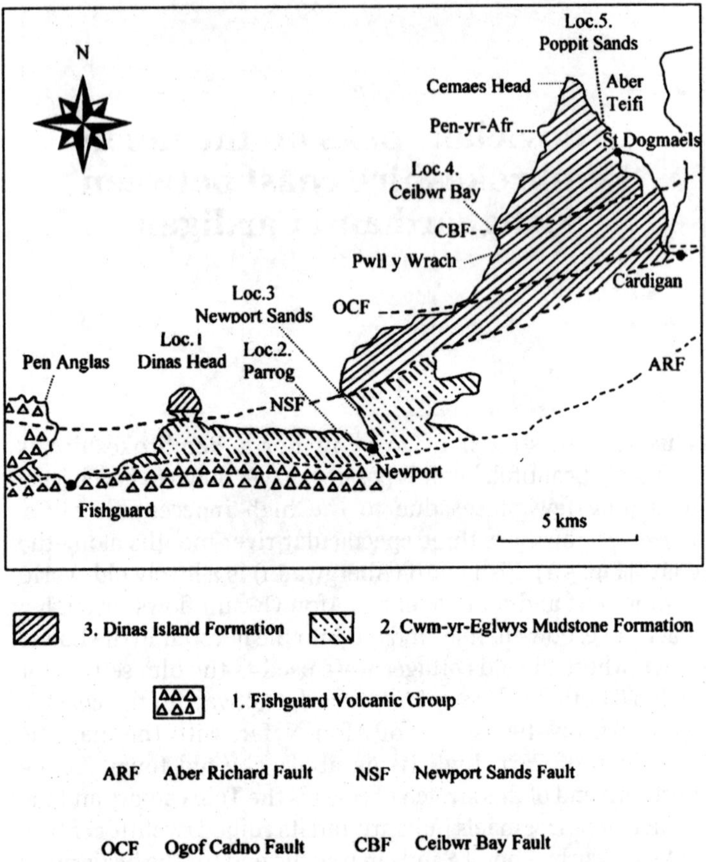

Fig. 5.1: The geology of the coast between Fishguard Bay and Cardigan

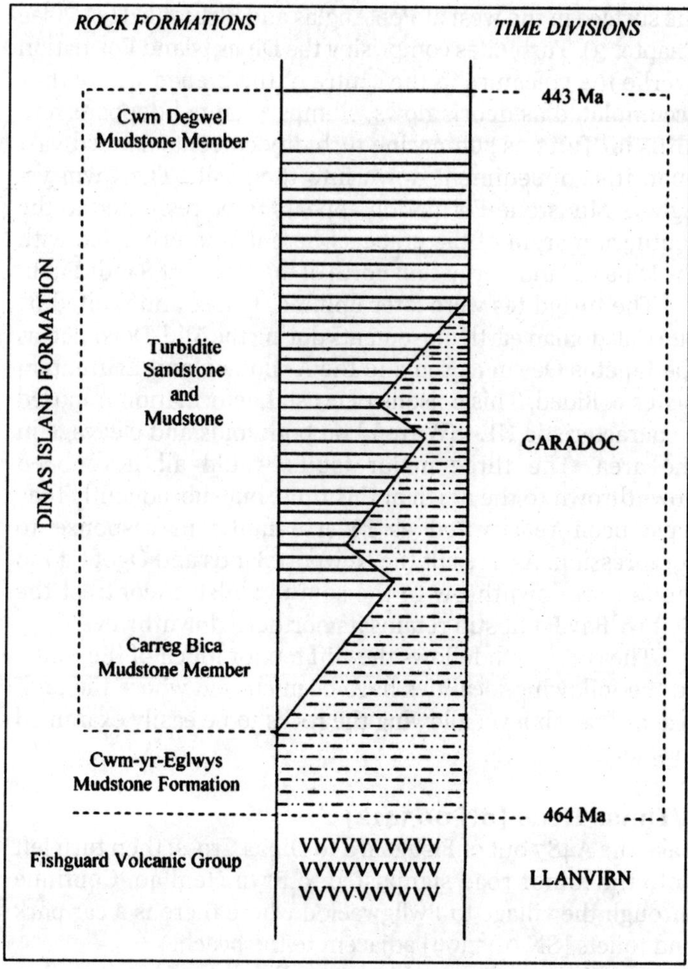

Fig. 5.2: Stratigraphical column for the Ordovician rocks on the coast between Fishguard and Cardigan (north of the Newport Sands fault)

the surface in the west at Pen Anglas and Strumble Head (see Chapter 3). Turbidites comprising the Dinas Island Formation overlie the volcanics in the centre of the graben where they accumulated as debris flows, slumps, channel deposits and **alluvial fans** as submarine turbidity currents carried vast quantities of sediment down into the basin. The Cwm-yr-Eglwys Mudstone Formation appears to be restricted to the southern margin of the graben where it is interbedded with the Dinas Island Formation north of the Newport Sands Fault.

The turbidites were later uplifted, folded and faulted by late Caledonian earth movements during the Mid-Devonian as the Iapetus Ocean closed and the Avalonian and Laurentian plates collided. This episode of crustal deformation imposed a characteristic NE–SW trend on both folds and cleavage in the area. The three major faults would all have been downthrown to the north at this time, but subsequently they have been reactivated as reverse faults in response to compression. As a result the Newport Sands and Ogof Cadno faults now downthrow to the south, whilst in contrast the Ceibwr Bay Fault still retains its northern downthrow.

The coast path follows the cliff top for much of the route, so the following localities have been chosen where the path reaches beach level allowing the rocks to be easily examined in safety.

1. Dinas Head [SN 005412]

Take the A487 out of Fishguard to Dinas Cross, then turn left onto the minor road signposted to Bryn Henllan. Continue through the village to Pwllgwaelod where there is a car park and toilets [SN 005399] adjacent to the beach.

The Cwm-yr-Eglwys Mudstone Formation is exposed in the cliffs on either side of bay at Pwllgwaeld. These turbidite mudstones contain the graptolite *Dicranograptus clingani* that is a characteristic **zone fossil** of the Caradoc Series.

Walk over to the north side of the bay where there is a small inlet accessible from the coast path. Here there are strongly cleaved and contorted mudstones cut by numerous quartz veins; the muds were originally deposited in relatively deep quiet waters off the continental shelf of the Welsh Basin. Subsequently during the Caledonian uplift lateral pressure imposed the slaty cleavage. As you are ascending the coast path there are several places where it is possible to measure the strike of this cleavage. It should be about 70/250° with a strong dip NNW.

The rock structure of the steep cliffed coastline is difficult to observe without using a boat. However, at Aber Pen Clawdd [SN 004410] there is an excellent south-facing cliff face that you can see from the coast path. This section in the Dinas Island Formation shows a thick turbidite sandstone resting on a sequence of interbedded sandstones and mudstones, all of which dip steeply NNW.

From the triangulation station (142 metres) on Dinas Head there is a marvellous view across Newport Bay to the cliffs that extends some 15 kms north-east to Cemaes Head. Westwards across Fishguard Bay, you will be able to see the Pen Caer peninsula projecting north to Pen Anglas and Strumble Head beyond. Looking south over Dinas Island look for the east-west aligned trough of low ground extending from Pwllgwaelod to Cwm-yr-Eglwys. This depression marks the line of the Newport Sands Fault which runs north-east towards Cardigan. It also forms part of the Gwaun-Jordanston meltwater system (see Chapter 11, Locality 3). With a little help from global warming, the sea level could rise sufficiently to submerge this trough and make Dinas Island into a real island!

2. Parrog [SN 049397]

Parrog was formerly a small port serving Newport until the Nyfer estuary became too shallow for shipping. You can reach this delightful seaside village from the A487 in Newport via a signposted minor road. There is a car park, toilets and a cafe near to quayside. Walk eastwards along the narrow seafront road to where the steps [SN 047398] provide access to a rocky foreshore section. Here the cleaved strata of the Cwm-yr-Eglwys Mudstone Formation are exposed. There is a prominent anticlinal fold in the centre of the section that admirably demonstrates **axial planar cleavage**. You can look along the E–W strike of the cleavage and see that it is parallel to the axis of the fold (see photo on page 54). The cleavage planes dip steeply north at about 80° whilst the gentle **plunge** of the fold axis is to the east. You will also notice that the cleavage is steeper than the bedding showing that the beds are the right way up unlike that in Abereiddi quarry where the limb of the fold was inverted (see Chapter 3, Locality 2).

The rocks often show cycles of alternate dark mudstone and light siltstone bands that were deposited in a turbidite sequence. These are sediments formed by the settling of grains from suspension in the quiet intervals between turbidity flows. The dark carbonaceous bands were laid down under anoxic conditions in the relatively deep bottom waters where organic sediment was preserved and **pyrite** developed. However, the light-coloured bands were exposed to the influence of oxygenated seawater that destroyed organic material and inhibited the growth of pyrite.

3. Newport Sands [SN 054405]

Take the minor road from Newport through Pen-y-Bont and cross the bridge over Afon Nyfer, then continue towards Molygrove. After about 2.5 kms turn left down the road signposted to the beach. Drive past the golf club and the road terminates in a large car park with toilets next to the coastguard station. Standing by the car park wall look due west for a good view of Dinas Island and the Cwm-yr-Eglwys valley.

The Newport Sands Fault crosses the coastline just north of the car park where the cliffs begin. At low tide it is possible to walk safely across the rocky foreshore to view the Cwm-yr-Eglwys Mudstone Formation. Here the rocks are composed of cleaved turbidite mudstones and sandstones that have been strongly folded by the Caledonian earth movements. At SN 054409 there is a first rate example of a chevron anticline with a NE–SW orientated axis that also demonstrates fan cleavage where the cleavage radiates outwards from the fold axis. Notice that the beds are thickened in the hinge line, evidence that ductile deformation occurred during folding. In the small cove near to Pen Pistyll waterfall there is a fold couplet (complementary anticline and syncline) where the turbidite mudstones show convolute bedding which suggests that they were in a fluidised condition when they were deposited.

4. Ceibwr Bay [SN 108458]

You can approach Ceibwr Bay from Newport by following the minor road to Moylgrove [SN 118447], then take the narrow lane down to the coast where roadside parking is available. I suggest that you bring a packed lunch and a drink since there are few facilities beyond Moylgrove. Ceibwr Bay is owned by the National Trust and preserved in its unspoilt condition. It would be well worth spending a full day around this locality for there is much to see apart from the rocks! In spring and early summer cliff tops are a bird watcher's paradise with nesting gulls, gannets, fulmars, cormorants and choughs, to mention but a few.

Ceibwr Bay is a steep-sided inlet cut into the Carreg Bica Mudstone Member at the base of the Dinas Island Formation. The strata consist mainly of dark mudstones interbedded with iron-stained sandstone bands (see photo on page 54). These sediments were laid down as turbidites in the Fishguard–

Cardigan graben when submarine channels carried large quantities of **siliciclastic** material down into the trough. At the end of the Caledonian orogeny, the rocks were deformed and folded as can be seen in the cliffs on the northern side of the inlet [Fig. 5.3]. The mudstones are characterised by a NE–SW trending slaty cleavage that is parallel to the axial planes of the folds. The Ceibwr Bay Fault is marked by a narrow gully at the north-western end of the inlet. It downthrows the strata in the headland by about 600 metres to the north. Thus whilst the basal Carreg Bica mudstones outcrop on the south side of the inlet, much younger beds form the northern headland.

After spending some time at sea level, you must then start to climb up the path to the top of the cliffs near Pen-castell and continue along the track for about 500 metres to Pen-y-

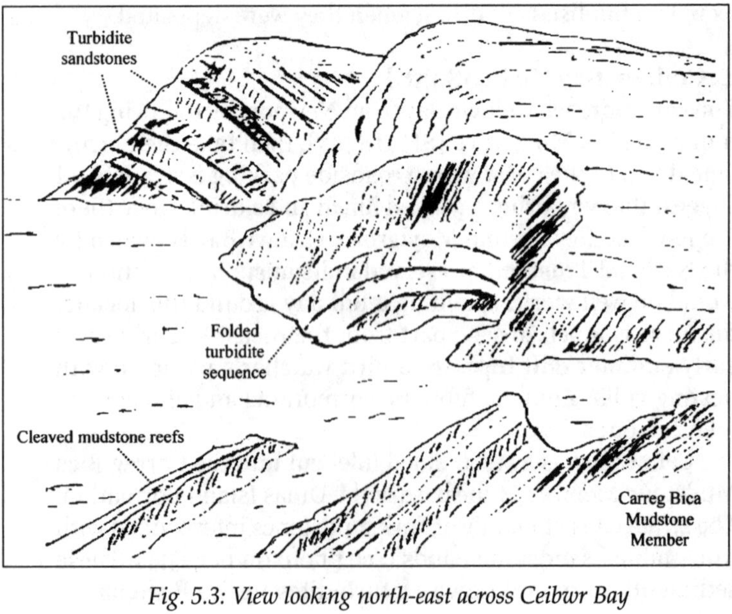

Fig. 5.3: View looking north-east across Ceibwr Bay

Graig [SN 112464]. Here there is a small headland that is formed of a turbidite sandstone unit some 3–5 metres in thickness that slopes steeply down to the sea. The base of the sandstone contains **flute casts** and is eroded into the underlying cleaved mudstones. A sequence of thinner fining upward turbidites rests on the sandstone body. The whole section represents an example of a turbidite channel fill that is typical of the sinuous channels that feed submarine fans.

Follow the coast path for a further 1 km to the promontory of Foel Hendre [SN 117474]. This locality provides an excellent viewpoint from which to study the structure of the cliffs extending from the headland of Pen yr Afr [SN 118486] to the waterfall at Pwllygranant [Fig. 5.4]. Here the sandstone-mudstone sequences of the Dinas Island Formation exhibit complex **harmonic folds** with associated faulting (see photo on page 55). Towards the headland of Pen yr Afr thick turbidite sandstones define the open, almost symmetrical folds near the cliff top, whereas nearer to Pwllygranant in the south-east there are tighter asymmetrical folds with steep limbs. Two faults cut the section: a normal dip slip fault occurs in the northern part of the bay whilst to the south there is a strong reverse fault upthrowing a thick mudstone unit. These fold and fault structures are the product of late Caledonian orogenic movements.

On returning to Ceibwr Bay it is worth examining the drift sequence that rests on the rock platform on the south side of the bay (see Chapter 11, Locality 2).

The second part of the expedition involves walking south-west for about 1.5 kms to Pwll y Wrach [SN 102450], which is also known as The Witch's Cauldron. However, for some obscure reason the Ordnance Survey does not refer to Pwll y Wrach by name, although it may be identified on OS maps by its proximity to the island of Carreg Yspar. The coastline in this area is deeply indented with NE–NW trending fissures

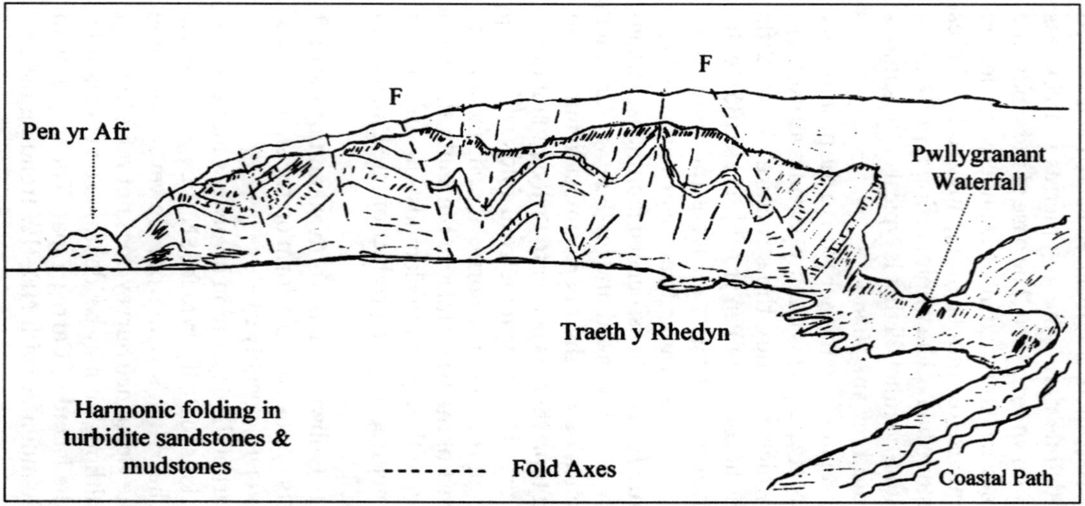

Fig. 5.4: View looking north to the cliffs of Pen-yr-Afr

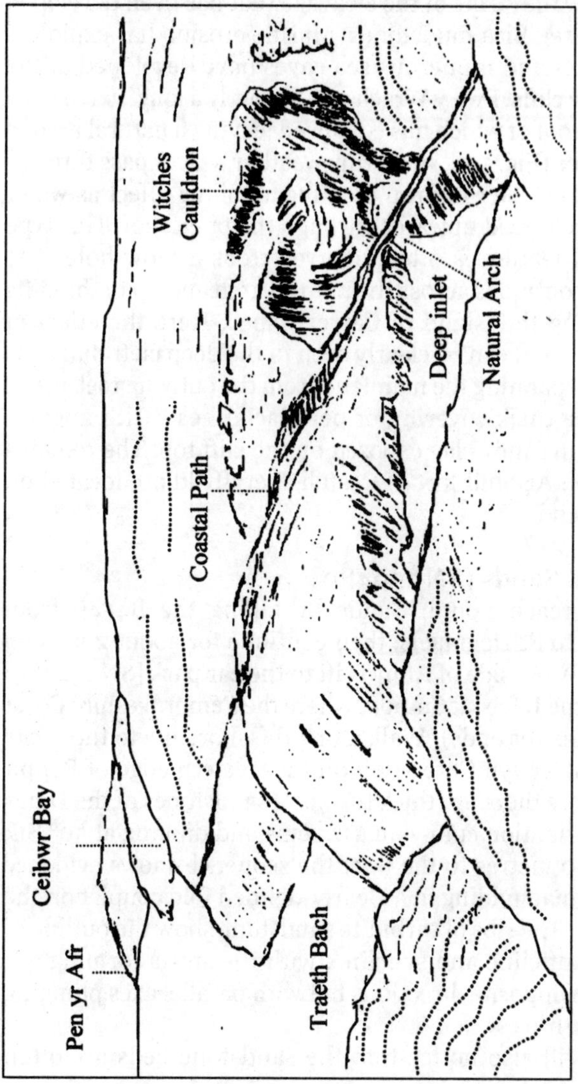

Fig. 5.5: View to the north-east across Pwll y Wrach

that follow the strike of the cleavage that has been developed in the Carreg Bica mudstones. Marine erosion has exploited the fissures and numerous sea caves have developed at the base of the cliffs. Pwll y Wrach was formerly a long, narrow sea cave, the roof of which has collapsed leaving a natural arch at its entrance [Fig. 5.5]. In stormy weather, waves pass through the arch into the cauldron creating a boiling effect as water and air are forced upwards through the open roof. This type of coastal feature is often referred to as a blow hole. The pathway continues across the natural arch and up to the cliffs overlooking the island of Carreg Yspar. Here the effect of marine erosion can be clearly seen in the deep cleft that runs NE–SW separating the mainland from the outlying rock mass. Notice the thick covering of periglacial head with angular clasts set in sandy clay exposed on the cliff top. The remains of the Iron Age hill fort of Castell Treryffydd are located on the headland.

5. Poppit Sands [SN 150489]

You can reach Poppit Sands by taking the B4546 from Cardigan to St Dogmaels, then continue for about 2 kms on the south-west side of Afon Teifi to the car park [SN 152485] opposite the Lifeboat Station, where the Pembrokeshire Coast Path begins (or ends). Walk along the shoreline to the rocky outcrop at Trwyn Careg-ddu on the western edge of Poppit Sands. Here there are thick turbidite sandstones of the Dinas Island Formation cut by quartz veins and dipping at 50° SE. About 200 metres to the west the sequence shows evidence of Caledonian folding in a clearly-defined fold couplet on the foreshore. The ribs of turbidite sandstone show the outline of both an anticline and syncline, with the strata forming a V pattern in opposite directions but with parallel axes plunging to the north-west.

You will also notice that the sandstone beds are often

interbedded with mudstones with alternating coarser light and finer dark bands (see Locality 2). These mudstones, deposited from suspension, are resting on the coarser-grained sandstones that represent turbidite flows. Each fining up cycle represents part of what geologists call a **Bouma sequence.** Some of the mudstones contain rip up mud clasts, volcaniclastic pebbles and slump features that suggest they were deposited by a debris flow.

Proceed along the foreshore towards Cei-bach [SN 145489] and you will see that the steeply dipping laminated mudstones and sandstones are extensively bevelled, on top of which is a raised beach (see Chapter 11, Locality 6).

6
Silurian rocks in the Marloes peninsula and adjoining areas

The Marloes peninsula lies in the south-west corner of Pembrokeshire and it extends westwards towards the islands of Skomer and Grassholm. The latter are famous for their large population of breeding seabirds including the puffin that has been adopted as the logo of the National Park. The seas around Skomer are a designated Marine Nature Reserve providing protection for marine creatures and conserving their environment. The National Trust owns the western half of the peninsula so the area is maintained as much as possible in its natural condition. In spring, when the thrift and sea campion are in bloom on the cliff tops, walking the coast path is a wonderful experience

Whilst rocks of Lower Silurian age form a broad outcrop extending W–E between Haverfordwest and Narberth on the north side of the Pembrokeshire coalfield, exposures are relatively scarce, so it much more rewarding to examine the coastal outcrops on the Marloes peninsula where both the volcanics and sediments of the Skomer Volcanic Group can be seen in juxtaposition [Fig. 6.1]. The island of Skomer is similar in structure and geology to the mainland, but it is a National Nature Reserve and SSSI and therefore access is limited.

The Silurian rocks on the Marloes peninsula can be traced eastwards to the northern shores of the Milford Haven around Lindsway Bay. It is also worth investigating the anticlinal

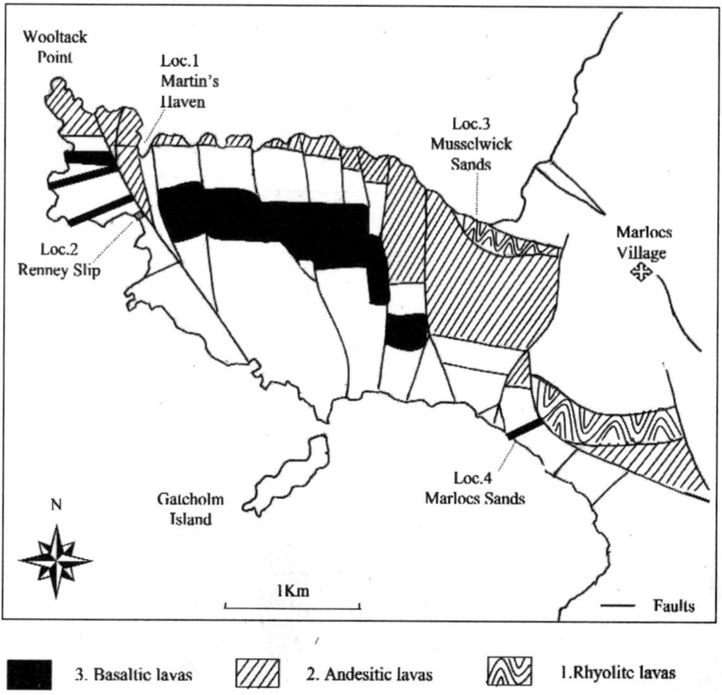

Fig. 6.1: Rocks of the Skomer Volcanic Group on the Marloes peninsula

structures in the Pembroke peninsula where Lower Palaeozoic inliers expose Upper Silurian strata, as for example at Freshwater East. The stratigraphical sequence within south Pembrokeshire is shown in Fig. 6.2.

Excursions are recommended to the following localities that show a range of sedimentary and igneous rocks of Silurian age.

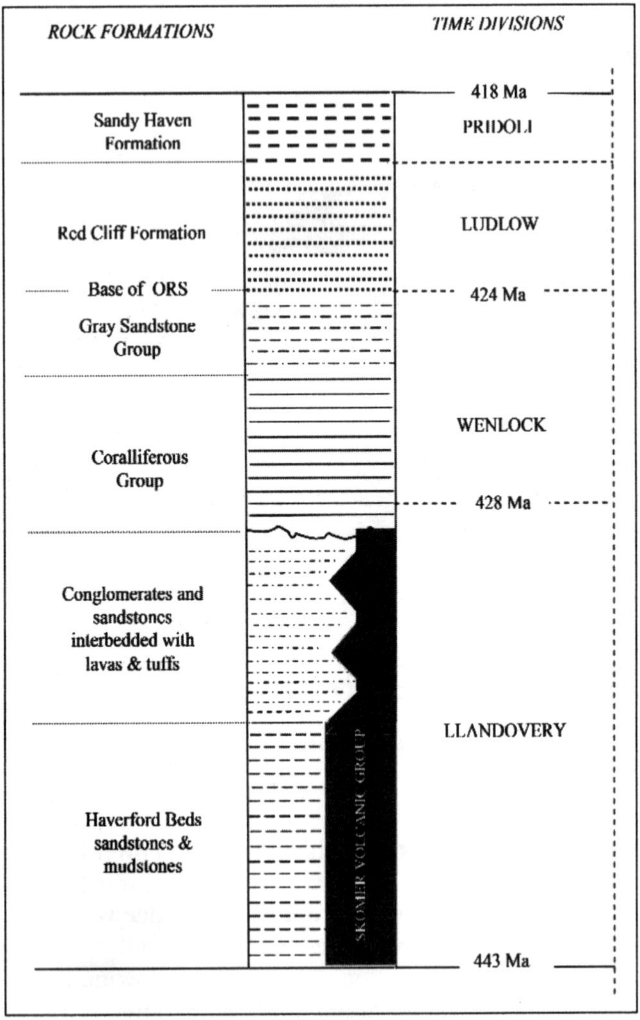

Fig. 6.2: Stratigraphical column for the Silurian rocks of south Pembrokeshire

1. Martin's Haven [SM 760091]

This tiny inlet lies at the north-western end of the Marloes peninsula. You should drive along the B4327 from Haverfordwest and take the minor road through Marloes village continuing onto the National Trust car park at Martin's Haven. When you walk down the road to the haven you will see, in the cutting below the car park, some exposures of quartzitic sandstone that occur within the Skomer Volcanic Group. On the eastern side of the shingle beach the low cliffs display several basaltic lava flows within the Skomer Volcanic Group that have a rough clinkery and blocky appearance that is sometimes known by the Hawaiian term áa [Fig. 6.3]. Some of these lavas have distinctively reddened top surfaces that suggests they have been exposed to **subaerial** weathering. At the head of the bay there is a bed of pyroclastic flow material sandwiched between the lavas. It contains several

Fig. 6.3: Martin's Haven, east side

blocks of basalt and smaller volcanic fragments or lapilli set in layered coarse ash. Much of the basalt here is vesicular, indicating that the lava was originally highly gaseous. There are patches where the basalt has been altered to the distinctive pistachio-green mineral epidote and later cut by calcite veins.

On the west side of the bay there is a small promontory leading to the landing stage that is used by the boats operating a summer service to the Skomer Island Nature Reserve. This outcrop is formed of rhyolitic conglomerate and tuff that is also present to the west of the N–S fault running down the access road. The conglomerate is composed of pebbles and cobbles of volcanic rocks up to 30 cm across. The fragments are angular to well-rounded and the unit is well-bedded implying that this is a deposit of volcanic material that was reworked and deposited in shallow water environment.

Whilst visiting Martin's Haven it is worth walking around the Wooltack peninsula that is also known as the Deer Park. Enter the park by the stone gateway and climb the path to the old coastguard lookout [SM 758092]. From here there are excellent views across to Skomer Island (Skomer Volcanic Group) in the west and to Skokholm Island (Old Red Sandstone) in the south. Wooltack Point and the north coast of the peninsula are composed almost entirely of basaltic/andesitic lava flows but on the south-west coast there are mudstones, sandstones and conglomerates interbedded with lava flows. The latter show well-developed pillow structures on the south side of Jeffry's Haven where a natural arch has been eroded in the basalt. The small bay to the south displays sediments that are folded into a tight-faulted syncline. About 200 metres further south is The Anvil where yet another basaltic flow forms the resistant headland.

2. Renney Slip [SM 760088]

This small bay lies on the south side of the narrow neck of

land that separates it from Martin's Haven. From the National Trust car park follow the track to the southern end of the Deer Park wall that overlooks Renney Slip. Here there is a steep narrow winding path down the cliffs to the beach and you must take great care in negotiating this path. In the interests of safety it is recommended that you do not attempt the descent alone. The highest basalt flow in the Skomer Volcanic Group is about 7 metres thick and has been traced from Limpet Rocks 200 metres off shore through the headland dividing Anvil Bay and Renney Slip [Fig. 6.4]. It is repeated by faulting and so can be seen outcropping near to the bottom of the path at beach level in Renney Slip. The basalt is vesicular and has a cindery upper surface. The mudstone immediately

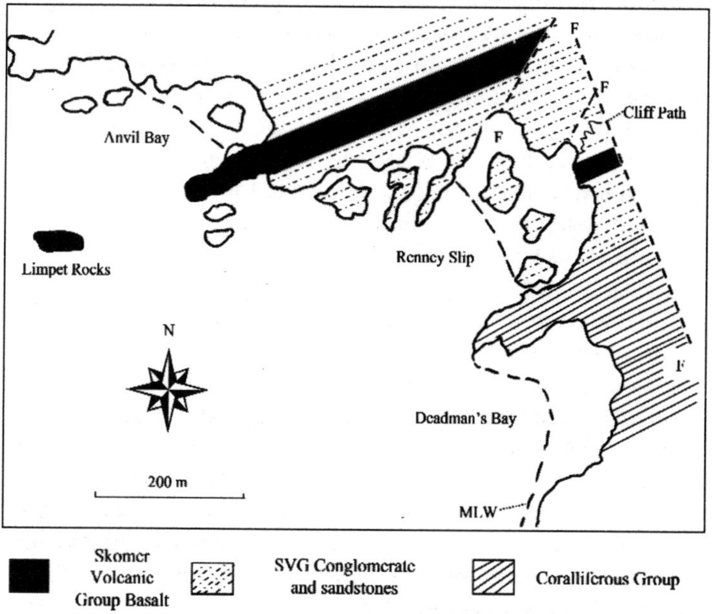

Fig. 6.4: Renney Slip and Deadman's Bay

above the basalt contains pebbles of igneous material. The succeeding conglomerates and sandstones that outcrop in the north side of Renney Slip display ripple marks and cross-stratification on the bedding planes that dip steeply to the south-east. The overlying micaceous mudstones, which can be seen in the sea stacks in the centre of the bay, contain a diverse brachiopod fauna. The brachiopods include *Eocoelia hemisphaerica*, which is an important **zone fossil** of the Upper Llandovery. Casts of *Eocoelia* can be seen in some of the blocks on the foreshore.

In the steep-sided promontory along the southern side of Renney Slip, there are siltstones overlaid unconformably by sandstones that belong to the lower part of the Coralliferous Group. The latter contrast markedly with the succeeding grey mudstones that outcrop at the top of the rock wall and dip south-east into Deadman's Bay. Unfortunately it is difficult to access Deadman's Bay even at low tide, but there are many large fallen blocks of the grey mudstone at the foot of the rock wall containing the casts of brachiopods such as *Costistricklandia lirata*. The latter is restricted to the Upper Llandovery and so gives an indication of the age of the base of the Coralliferous Group in this area.

3. Musselwick Sands [SM 785088]

Musselwick Sands are located on the north coast of the Marloes peninsula and can be reached from the Marloes to Martin's Haven road by a footpath that begins near to Marloes Beacon [SM 786085]. You will find parking space available alongside the road. Follow the footpath across the fields to Black Cliff [SM 785090]. This locality lies on the faulted junction between the Skomer Volcanic Group and dark grey Ordovician mudstones. The cliff face provides an excellent exposure of the mudstones that represent a turbidite sequence deposited in the deeper waters of the Welsh Basin during the

Upper Llanvirn stage. The mudstones contain several thin ash bands about 5 cm thick that would have been derived from pyroclastic airfall material. The bands dip at about 30° SSE, but the whole sequence is intensely deformed by strong cleavage with a NE–SW strike direction, resulting from the Caledonian earth movements. Above the high tide mark the mudstones weather to a rusty orange colour, which is indicative of the presence of iron sulphide and this mineral commonly forms in muds under anoxic conditions on the sea floor. About 200 metres north-east of Black Cliff the mudstone outcrop is terminated by the Musselwick Fault that thrust Ordovician strata northwards over younger Old Red Sandstone rocks. The fault can be traced across country reaching as far east as Sandy Haven Pill on the shores of Milford Haven.

On the south-west side of Musselwick Sands the mudstones are faulted against rhyolitic lavas of the Skomer Volcanic Group that extend for about 200 metres along the cliff face to Hopgang [SM 779089]. The exposure in these cliffs is a silicified type of rhyolitic lava that can be examined in the fallen boulders on the beach. The faulted junction between the mudstones and the rhyolites is difficult to see due to rock falls, but the volcanics appear to have been thrust northwards over the mudstones. Please be aware that there is a danger of being cut off by the incoming tide on this beach, as the only way out, via Black Cliff, becomes impassable after half tide.

4. Marloes Sands [SM 781077]

This is a popular beach for holidaymakers in the summer months, and at low tide there is a large area of sand and rocks exposed for people to explore. You can get to this locality from Marloes village by following the narrow road that is signposted at the turning near to the church. There is a

National Trust car park at the end of the road [SM 780082] near to Runwayskiln Farm. You will need to bring your own refreshments as there are no facilities on the beach. Walk back up the road and turn right onto Sandy Lane that leads down to the coast. Before you get onto the beach do take the opportunity of looking westwards towards Gateholm Island. This is a view beloved of local artists showing the upstanding jagged rocks on the foreshore with the eroded plateau surface of Gateholm in the background (see photo on page 55).

When you reach the beach, turn left and walk about 250

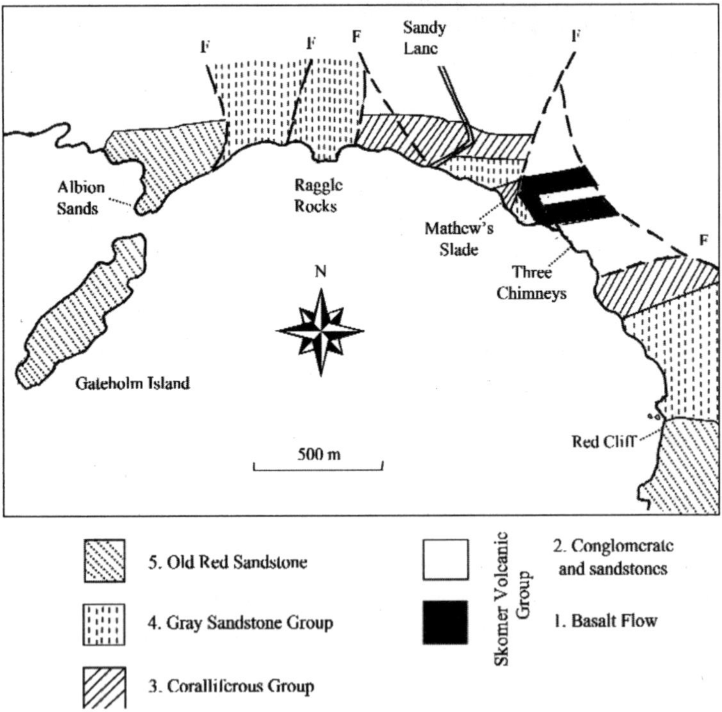

Fig. 6.5: The geology of Marloes Sands

metres to a large grass-covered hollow in the cliffs known as Mathew's Slade [Fig. 6.5]. This is a good point to start examining the succession of Silurian strata that extends upwards into the Old Red Sandstone at Red Cliff about 1 km to the east. The mudstones at Mathew's Slade [SM 784075] are a faulted slice of the Coralliferous Group where the brachiopod fauna includes *Costistricklandia*, *Eocoelia* and *Atrypa*. These fossiliferous beds are faulted on the east against a sequence of feldspathic sandstones belonging to the upper part of the Skomer Volcanic Group. The sandstones are succeeded by two basaltic lava flows that are exposed in a deep gully about 100 metres to the east of Mathew's Slade [SM 785074]. The lavas have a total thickness of about 25 metres, and they are vesicular, being full of gas bubbles when originally extruded. The brecciated and weathered **scoriaceous** tops of the flows suggest that they were produced by subaerial volcanic activity.

The lavas are succeeded by a sequence of about 90 metres of conglomerates and sandstones interbedded with tuffaceous mudstone bands containing the brachiopod *Lingula*. Cross-stratification, ripple marks and scour structures in the sandstones provide evidence of a shallow water coastal environment. Airfall deposits from nearby volcanoes would produce **volcaniclastic** sediments as the volcanic ash was deposited in the shallow seas.

Approximately 200 metres to the east of the basalt you will see a cliff feature known as The Three Chimneys (see photo on page 56). This rock face is formed of near vertical sandstone pillars that stand out in the cliff from the less resistant interbedded sandy mudstones. The succeeding flagstones at the top of the Skomer Volcanic Group contain brachiopods such as *Lingula* and *Leptaena*.

About 100 metres to the east of the Three Chimneys the beds are faulted and overlaid unconformably by the

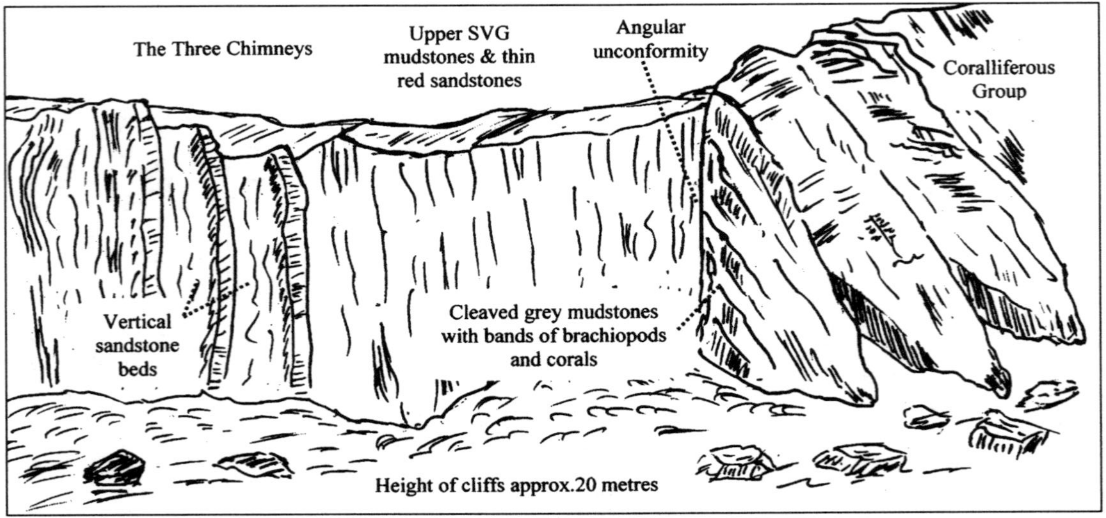

Fig. 6.6: Marloes Cliffs

Coralliferous Group [Fig. 6.6]. There is an angular discordance of about 10° between the two units that is best seen by standing several metres back from the cliffs. The lower beds of the Coralliferous Group consist of sandstones, cleaved mudstones and shelly calcareous lenses. The latter are exposed in the fallen blocks and cliff recesses around SM 787072 that yield the brachiopod *Eocoelia sulcata* and the coral *Palaeocyclus porpita* both of which determine the Upper Llandovery age of the rocks. A few metres higher in the succession the brachiopod *Costistricklandi lirata* becomes abundant along with the tabulate colonial coral *Favosites*.

In the 1960s Alfred M Ziegler demonstrated that brachiopod communities can be used as water depth indicators. *Lingula* communities generally occupy shallow littoral environments; *Eocoelia* communities are found in water about 20 metres deep and *Costistricklandia* communities inhabit depths of up to 50 metres off shore. Thus the changes in brachiopod species within the strata outcropping between the Three Chimneys and about the first 20 metres of the Coralliferous Group suggest marine transgression with deepening water conditions. However, further to the south-east towards the middle of the Coralliferous section, *Costistricklandia* disappears, indicating a return to shallow water conditions. Ziegler also argued that lava flows influenced the development of brachiopod communities. The lavas at Marloes Sands and Renney Slip flowed out onto sediments containing an *Eocoelia* community causing a shallowing of the sea. The *Eocoelia* were buried beneath the lavas and a *Lingula* community slowly became established in the shallow littoral zone above the flow, where sandy and tuffaceous sediments were being deposited.

The junction between the cleaved mudstones of the Coralliferous Group and the overlying Gray Sandstone Group is obscured by fallen blocks but the flaggy sandstones and mudstones which extend some 350 metres to the south-east are rather barren of fossils. However, the gradual increase in grain size up the sequence indicates stronger current activity and increased sand supply. This suggests that the environment was changing from shallow marine to low lying deltaic conditions.

The highest beds of the Gray Sandstone Group are exposed in the sea stacks just west of Red Cliff. Here they are interbedded with thin red-coloured sandstones that herald the approach of Old Red Sandstone sedimentation. At Red Cliff [SM 789067] the base of the Old Red Sandstone is indicated by a bench-mark cut into the rock in 1916 by officers of the Geological Survey. However, at that time it was considered that the major environmental change from marine Silurian to terrestrial Old Red Sandstone took place at the start of the Devonian period, but more recent research has shown that the change occurred much earlier, in the Upper Silurian around 424 million years ago.

5. Lindsway Bay [SM 843067]

This beautiful, quiet and little-known bay should not be missed, despite the fact that it lies within 2 kms of the LNG terminal at South Hook. It is best approached from St Ishmael's village where there is a small car park and toilets [SM 839072] adjacent to the sports field. You should follow the footpath that leads from the car park to the coast path, then turn left and take the coastal track for about 200 metres to the steep steps that lead down to the beach in Lindsway Bay. Care should be taken when descending the steps as there are no safety rails. Walk across the beach to Sprat's Point on the west side of the bay where the alternating sandstones and mudstones of the Gray Sandstone Group can be seen dipping at about 70° SW. These beds pass conformably upwards into the basal Old Red Sandstone marls (Red Cliff Formation) on the north-east side of Sprat's Point where the faulted junction is marked by a steep gully.

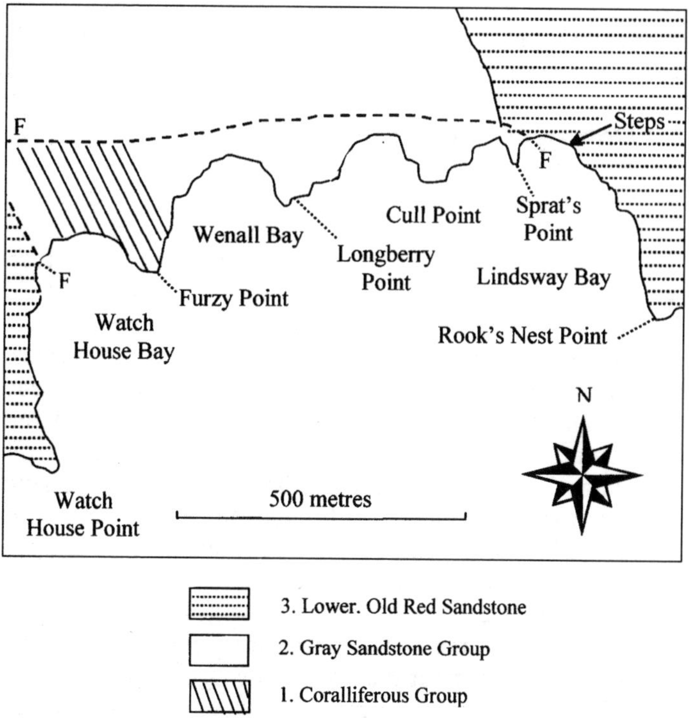

Fig. 6.7: The geology of the coast between Watch House Point and Lindsway Bay

The Silurian rocks in Lindsway Bay form the most easterly exposure of the fault-bounded Marloes inlier [Fig. 6.7]. They also form the cliffs along the coast to the west, as far as Watch House Bay, but it is difficult to access the foreshore without using a boat. Even so, it is well worth walking along the coast path to observe the cliff structures from above. Longberry Point can be easily recognised by its massive sandstone beds that dip inland at a high angle. Furzy Point and Watch House Bay are formed of calcareous mudstones belonging to the

Coralliferous Series that are folded into a major anticline, the axis of which runs roughly N–S through Furzy Point.

6. Freshwater East [SS 015980]

Drive along the A4139 Pembroke-Tenby road, then take the B4584 in Lamphey, and follow this road to the outskirts of Freshwater East village. Turn right down a steep minor road that leads to the shore where there is a large car park. Much of the solid geology is obscured by blown sand, beneath which is the Freshwater East anticline [Fig. 6.8]. This asymmetrical fold plunges gently WNW and its core has been eroded to expose Ordovician shales. These are flanked by the Gray Sandstone Group and the basal conglomerates of the Old Red Sandstone.

At low tide walk across the beach to the south-west corner of the bay [SS 016975] where the Silurian strata outcrop at the foot of the cliffs. They dip SSW at about 45° and you will find that the strike direction on this southern limb of the fold is around 112/292°. A sequence of about 30 metres of brown sandy siltstones, sandstones and 'rotten stones' is exposed on the foreshore. There are some fossils particularly in the decalcified 'rotten' bands that are honeycombed where shells have been dissolved out. Fragmented remains of some brachiopods, gastropods and trilobites have been found here. Large boulders of Old Red Sandstone conglomerates rest on the Silurian outcrops on the beach. These conglomerates belong to Freshwater East Formation that occurs at the base of the Old Red Sandstone. Conglomerates and sandstones form the cliffs that extend out to Trewent Point.

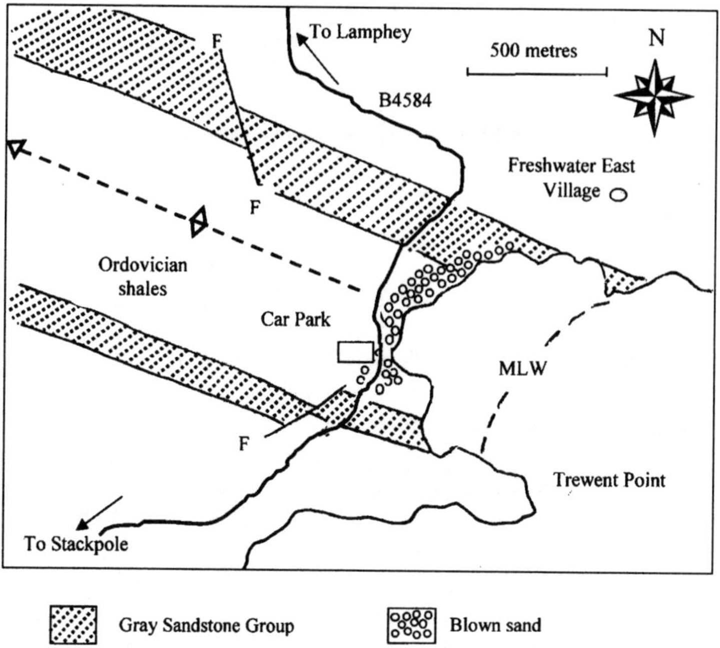

Fig. 6.8: The geology of Freshwater East

7
Old Red Sandstone in south Pembrokeshire

The magnificent red cliffs on the south coast of Caldey Island, in Manorbier Bay and at St Ann's Head are all formed of the Old Red Sandstone; a collective term for a succession of red mudstones, sandstones and conglomerates that have been folded, faulted and eroded to form the present day coastal scenery. How and when were these rocks produced? The story begins towards the end of Silurian times when the great upheaval of the Caledonian orogeny had created a vast mountainous zone that extended across much of Britain. Pembrokeshire lay on the southern margin of these highlands that were subject to intense erosion during the Devonian period. Torrential streams, heavily loaded with debris, flowed southwards off the mountains and deposited huge amounts of sediment on the coastal lowlands that occupied much of what is now south Pembrokeshire. Meandering **braided rivers** laid down thick sequences of silt, sand and pebbles that would later form the Old Red Sandstone. In a semi arid environment, the desiccated sediments often preserved mud cracks and the trails and burrows of organisms that were living on the muddy surface. Also under conditions of high evaporation, calcium salts were drawn up through the soils to form distinctive deposits known as calcretes that formed irregular white nodules in many of the red mudstones. However, the relative quiet conditions of Old Red Sandstone sedimentation were interrupted from time to time by violent volcanic outbursts across south Wales. Each **Plinian eruption** produced a huge gaseous ash cloud rising up to 20 km above the vent and the fall-out would spread over an area of several 1000 km^2. In Pembrokeshire, the occurrence of tuff bands formed of compressed ash in the Lower Old Red Sandstone shows that volcanic activity was relatively frequent and the sedimentary structures within the ash bands suggest that it was often laid down in shallow water. Despite the widespread occurrence of these layers of ash, there is no visible evidence of the presence of the volcanic centres that generated the airfall material.

As you will see from the Stratigraphical Column in Fig. 7.1, there is a different succession of rock formations on either side of the Ritec Fault that runs roughly east to west from Tenby to Milford Haven. Whilst it is possible to correlate most of the beds on either side of the fault, you should recognise that Old Red Sandstone sedimentation began earlier to the north of the fault, beginning with the deposition of the Red Cliff Formation. On the south side of the fault, the basal conglomerate of the Old Red Sandstone lies unconformably on the underlying strata and is several million years younger than the Red Cliff Formation to the north. The Ritec Fault must have played an active role in controlling sedimentation in south Pembrokeshire, since by the end of Lower Devonian times the uplifted northern block was increasingly subject to erosion, whilst to the south, deposition continued. The Ridgeway Conglomerate Formation was laid down on the southern downthrown side of the Ritec Fault. Later, during the Upper Devonian, this was covered unconformably by the Skrinkle Sandstone Group.

The Old Red Sandstone is a continental-type deposit and not a geological time period. It was laid down from around 424 Ma in the Upper Silurian to the end of Devonian times

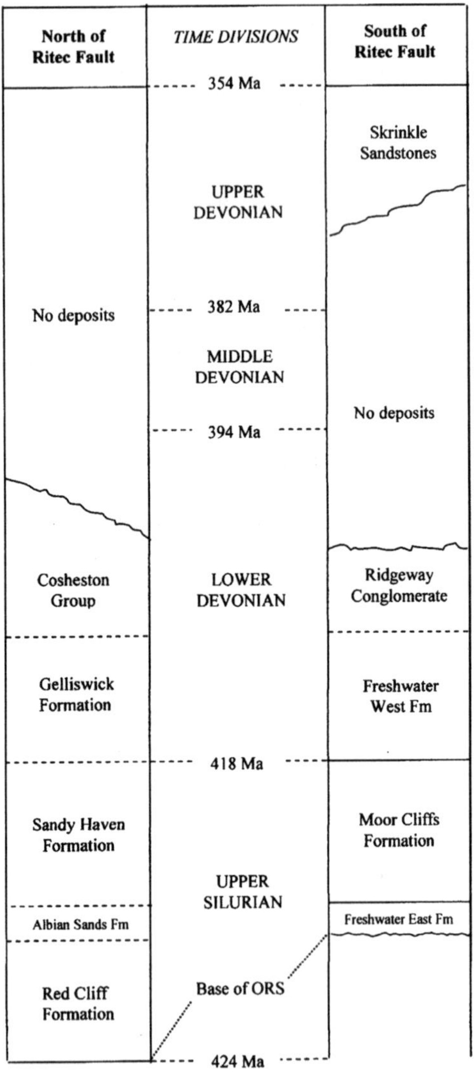

Fig. 7.1: Stratigraphical column for the Old Red Sandstone in Pembrokeshire

(354 Ma). Since 1972, the internationally-agreed boundary between the Silurian and Devonian periods has been set (using the base of a graptolite zone in the marine sediments of the Barrandian region of what is now the Czech Republic) at around 418 Ma. Thus, the base of the Devonian in south Pembrokeshire, north of the Retic Fault, is marked by the start of the Gelliswick Formation and to the south, by the Freshwater West Formation.

Much of the Old Red Sandstone has been affected by the Variscan orogeny that began in Upper Carboniferous times. The resulting tectonic structures can be seen across south Pembrokeshire, as for example in the Castlemartin Corse Anticline, the Ridgeway Anticline and the Pembroke Syncline, all of which display characteristic east-west trending fold axes. The Ritec Fault was reactivated at this time, and the Flimston Fault that cuts through the Old Red Sandstone on the foreshore at Freshwater West provides another example of Variscan tectonic movements.

The following localities have been selected to show you some of the geological highlights of the Old Red Sandstone where it is exposed along the shoreline and is accessible from the coastal path. Localities 1–6 lie to the south of the Ritec Fault and localities 7–9 are to the north of the fault [Fig. 7.2].

1. Skrinkle Haven [SS 080973]

When you travel along the A4139 road from Pembroke to Tenby, turn right onto the B4585 road signposted to Skrinkle Haven. Drive past the army married quarters and then take the military road leading to the firing ranges of Manorbier Camp and continue onto the Manorbier Youth Hostel where there is a car park and picnic area [SS 080976]. You can get into Skrinkle Haven by descending the steps into Church Doors Cove and scrambling through the rock tunnel in the limestone promontory that divides Church Doors Cove from

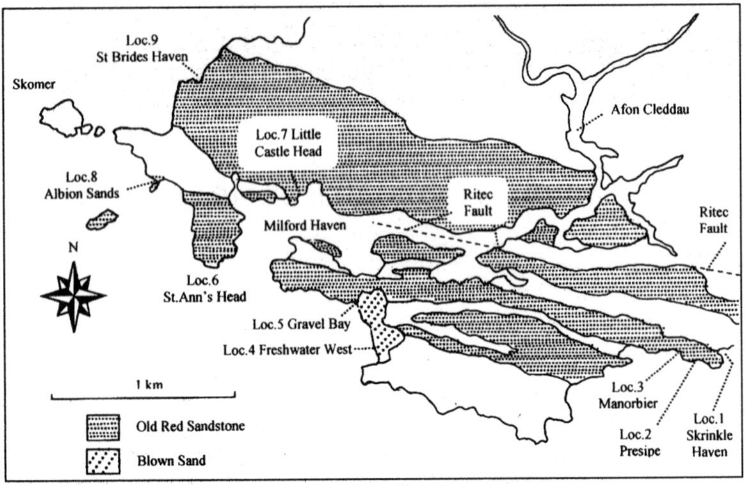

Fig. 7.2: Old Red Sandstone outcrops in South Pembrokeshire

Skrinkle Haven. For safety reasons this should only be attempted when the tide is ebbing; once you are on Skrinkle beach do keep an eye on the tidal situation from time to time so as not to be cut off on your return through the tunnel! There are steps up to the top of the cliff on the south side of Skrinkle Haven but unfortunately they have been closed to the public in recent years.

Walk across to the south side of the beach to where the Ridgeway Conglomerate forms a vertical outcrop striking WNW–ESE [Fig. 7.3]. There are several massive fallen blocks of the conglomerate at beach level that can be examined closely. The rounded pebbles can be up to 30 cm in diameter and are formed largely of sandstone and vein quartz. They often rest directly on each other with only a limited amount of sandy matrix and so they are described as being clast supported. This suggests that the conglomerate was the product of flash flood conditions where the finer sediment was still in suspension when the pebbles were laid down, as stream velocity rapidly diminished. This would happen as a braided stream deposited sediment into alluvial fans along the edge of an arid basin.

The age of the Ridgeway Conglomerate is an enigma, since the lack of definitive fossil evidence makes dating uncertain. Many researchers have placed it in the Middle Devonian whilst others have favoured late Lower Devonian on the basis of its stratigraphical position. However, on the headland [SS 080972] the base of the Ridgeway Conglomerate is marked by an erosion surface where it overlies the Freshwater West Formation. There is also an unconformity separating the Ridgeway Conglomerate from the overlying Skrinkle Sandstone Group of Upper Devonian age. This lies in the south-west corner of the bay about 10 metres above a distinctive 4-metre-thick bed of massive calcrete. Unfortunately, the unconformity is difficult to see at this locality as it is obscured by fallen blocks.

You should next make your way along the beach examining the vertical beds of the Skrinkle Sandstone Group and notice that the beds become younger towards the north as you walk up the sequence. This is the type locality for the Skrinkle Sandstone Group. The basal beds consist of about 30 metres of sandstones followed by red mudstones. They represent the deposits of an **alluvial fan** and river flood plain respectively. In the centre of the bay are a sequence of conglomerates and red and green sandstones, about 46 metres thick, that are mainly braided and meandering channel deposits. Lastly, in the north-west corner of the bay, a series of grey mudstones and fine grained sandstones record an increasing marine influence heralding the approach of the Lower Carboniferous sea, as the strata passes conformably up into the calcareous beds of the Avon Group (see Chapter 8, Locality 5).

2. Presipe [SS 069970]

This is the name of a small bay immediately to the west of Old Castle Head. You can reach this locality from the military road leading to Skrinkle Haven Youth Hostel. Parking is available on the roadside near to the main entrance gates of Manorbier Camp [SS 075974]. You should take the coastal path in a south-west direction around the boundary of the MOD firing range and walk across the fields to the cliff top where there is a steep flight of steps leading down to Presipe beach. These steps follow approximately the line of a major **dextral** wrench fault with a displacement of 250 metres. This brings the Moor Cliffs Formation on the west side of the bay into contact with the Freshwater West Formation that outcrops to the east of the fault [Fig. 7.3]. These rocks strike across the bay with a

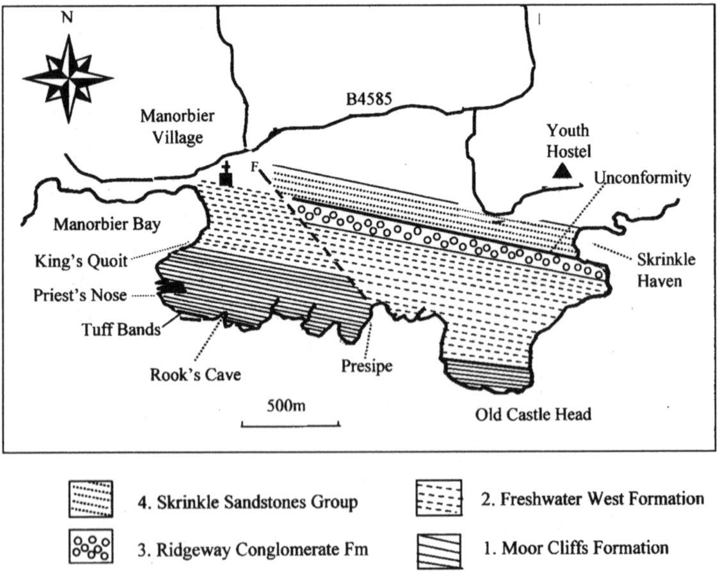

Fig. 7.3: The geology of the coast between Manorbier and Skrinkle Haven

dip of about 85° NNE. The steep bedding surfaces display a variety of sedimentary structures associated with an arid environment in which mud and sand are drying out. Near to the base of the steps there are sand-filled pipes up to 10 cm in diameter that stand proud of the sandstone bedding plane. These are the infilled vertical burrows of the **trace fossil** *Beaconites* where the sediment infill is harder than the surrounding sandstone (see Locality 4 for more details of this trace fossil).

You will find a large recess in the cliffs about 50 metres east of the steps where a massive slab exposes a magnificent rippled surface, evidence of shallow water currents. This ripple formation is preserved as a mould on the underside of the steeply inclined sandstone bed since the strata dip northwards, and so are getting younger in that direction. In the centre of the bay there are several large bedding planes representing desiccated surfaces with mud-filled polygons where the cracks have been infilled with carbonate material. You will also see an excellent cross-section through a sequence of fining upward units in the small valley known as Water Come On [SS 072968] through which a stream enters the bay. Each cycle consists of pebble-sized conglomerates, sandstones and mudstones with calcrete beds. The conglomerates rest on well-defined scoured surfaces. These repeated sequences are the successive deposits of a meandering river system bordered by a wide floodplain where **lag gravels** and coarse sands were laid down in the river channel and over bank silts were deposited on the flood plain.

3. Manorbier [SS 066978]

It is best to approach Manorbier from the A4139 Pembroke–Tenby road by turning onto the B4585 about 1 km to the east of Jameston village. There is a large car park near to Manorbier Castle, a well-preserved twelfth-century fortification that was the birthplace of the great medieval chronicler Giraldus Cambrensis. The nearby church has a conspicuous stone whitewashed tower that can be seen for miles around. Refreshments are available in the village at the Castle Inn or the local café and there are toilets in the car park.

Walk from the car park down to the beach, then follow the coast path on the east side of Manorbier Bay to the cromlech known as King's Quoit [SS 059973], formed of a massive capstone supported by three upright stones, one of which has now fallen over. At this locality there is a deep indentation in the cliffs marking the junction between the Moor Cliffs Formation and the overlying Freshwater West Formation. Looking across the bay from King's Quoit, you can clearly see the strike (285/105°) of the sandstone ribs crossing the foreshore. The beds dip steeply NNE towards the axis of the Pembroke Syncline. Now continue along the footpath towards Priest's Nose observing the deep recesses cut into the cliff line where volcanic ash bands have been eroded by the sea. These tuff bands are obviously much less resistant than the adjacent sandstones and they form deep gullies where the path crosses them.

Next make your way eastwards for about 400 metres to Rook's Cave [SS 062971]. This is a deep-faulted cleft crossed by another airfall tuff band that follows the strike of the rocks (see photo on page 56). You can easily scramble down to the foreshore across the red mudstones with well-developed calcrete horizons. You will see that the Rook's Cave tuff band is about 70 cms thick and is offset by several metres by a **sinistral** wrench fault. There are a variety of burrows and faecal pellet clusters on the surface of the red mudstone that underlies the base of the Rook's Cave tuff. These trace fossils have been preserved as a result of rapid burial by the ash fall.

4. Freshwater West [SR 885994]

Take B4319 road from Pembroke to Castlemartin and then continue for a further 3 kms to the car park at Gupton Burrows where the road runs alongside Freshwater West Bay. In this area there are several km^2 of windblown sand dunes that cover the underlying solid geology. However you will find plenty of excellent rock exposures on the foreshore to the south of Little Furznip headland. You can get a good view of the whole foreshore section from the roadside overlooking Little Furzenip, which is only about 100 metres from the car park [Fig. 7.4]. Here the beds dip steeply southwards on the south flank of the Castlemartin Corse anticline.

On the north side of the headland next to the sandy beach there are some poorly exposed siltstones and sandstones belonging to the Gray Sandstone Group. The basal Old Red Sandstone conglomerate known as the Freshwater East Formation, lies unconformably on the scoured surface of the Silurian sediments. However, these beds and much of the succeeding Moor Cliffs Formation are difficult to observe in detail due to the thick growth of seaweed and barnacles obscuring them. You will be able to see them much more clearly at Locality 5 where they are better exposed. It is therefore more productive to start your examination of the rocks on the south side of Little Furzenip headland where red mudstones contain well-developed calcrete horizons near the top of the Moor Cliffs Formation [Fig. 7.5]. The mudstones contain a variety of calcrete forms including nodules, vertical rods and fan-shaped calcretes (see photo on page 57). The latter are gentle upfolds known as **pseudoanticlines** where the calcite is often arranged perpendicular to the bedding. These structures were formed as a result of internal pressure building up during the formation of the calcretes that represent fossil soils or palaeosols produced in a hot savannah climate of alternating dry and rainy seasons. In the wet

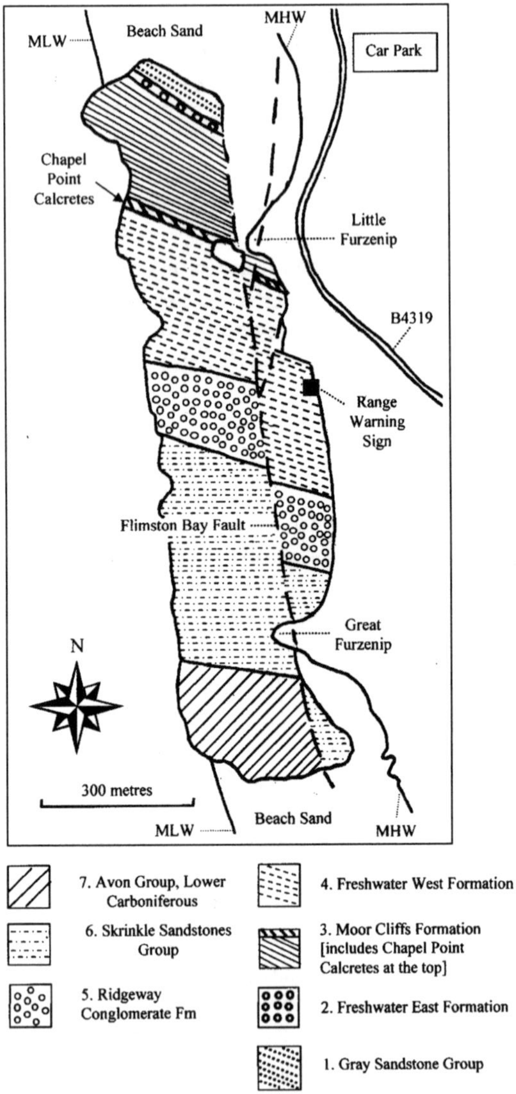

Fig. 7.4: The geology of Freshwater West foreshore

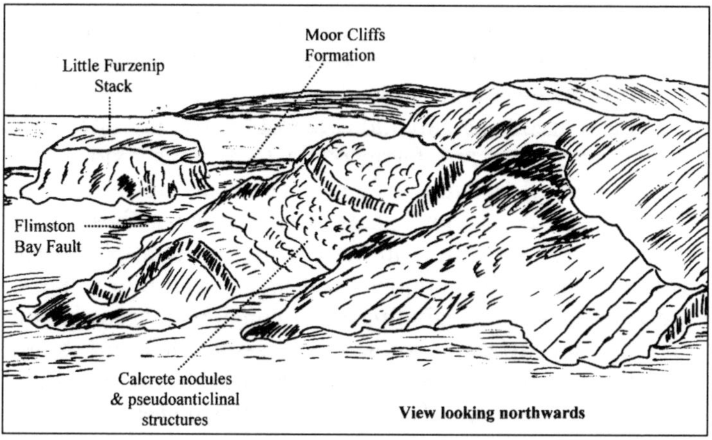

Fig. 7.5: Chapel Point calcretes at Little Furzenip

seasons, ground water percolated down through the mudstone and picked up calcium carbonate and other minerals. In the dry seasons, the waters were drawn up by capillary attraction and precipitated much of their mineral load, commonly replacing or filling rootlets or making irregular nodular masses within the soil. Calcrete beds occur in the Moor Cliffs Formation throughout south Pembrokeshire and are referred to as the Chapel Point Calcretes after the type section on the south coast of Caldey Island where there is a comparable sequence to that at Freshwater West.

The Flimston Bay Fault bisects the whole succession of beds on the foreshore at Freshwater West. It is a dextral wrench fault with a displacement of approximately 120 metres and is responsible for isolating Little Furzenip stack from the headland. The fault can be traced south-eastwards across the Castlemartin Ranges to Flimston Bay on the south coast.

The succeeding Freshwater West Formation is 345 metres thick and is well-exposed to the south of Little Furzenip and to the east of the wrench fault. The red mudstones and sandstones of this formation are rich in ferric oxide formed under oxidising conditions in the dry desert atmosphere. The green-coloured layers are indicative of the presence of water that reduces the red ferric oxide to ferrous oxide. The sequence consists mainly of a series of fining upward cycles that illustrate deposition in meandering streams. These cyclic units are best examined in the vicinity of the MOD Range Warning Sign. The complete unit is often no more than a metre in thickness, beginning with a conglomerate resting on an erosional surface, followed by cross-stratified sandstones that pass into fine-grained sandstones that often demonstrate ripple drift bedding. This is a type of small-scale cross-stratification is formed by the down current migration of ripples during the deposition of sediment. The ripple sets are usually only a few centimetres thick and in a rock section appear to be climbing over each other. Finally, at the top of the unit there are mudstones usually containing calcretes. In terms of **fluvial** deposition, the conglomerates represent the lag gravels that accumulate on the erosional base of the river channel on the inside of a meander bend. Here the cross-stratified sands gradually build up over the gravels as a bank of sediment called a **point bar**. The mudstones are laid down on the surrounding flood plain as overbank deposits and when this mud dries out, calcareous soil profiles may develop in which calcretes are formed.

The Range Warning Sign is an important reference point that you can use to locate the next feature of geological interest. I suggest that you pace out 15 metres to the south of the sign which should bring you to a distinctive **bioturbated** light grey sandstone approximately 1.5 metres thick which is known as the Beaconites Bed [Fig. 7.6]. Large burrows of *Beaconites barretti* occur perpendicular to the sedimentary layering. Some burrows are up to 30 cm deep and 10 cms in

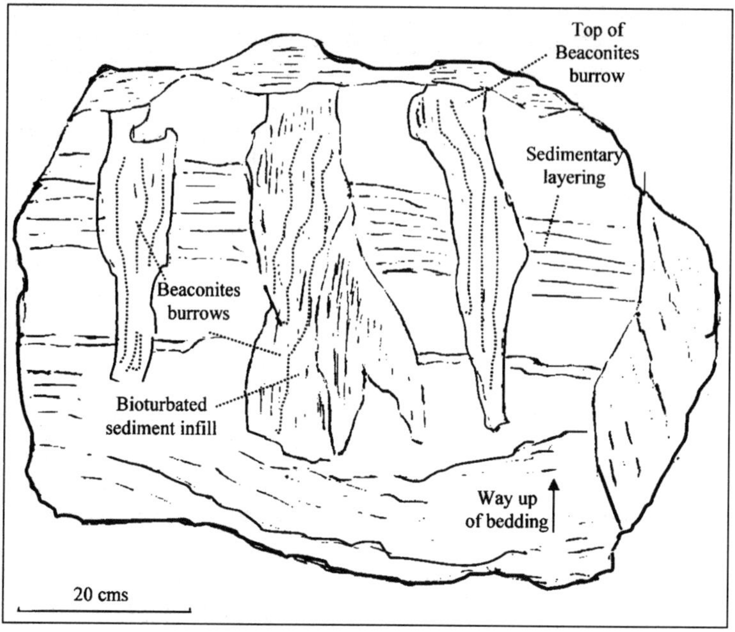

Fig. 7.6: Beaconites burrows in a sandstone block in the Freshwater West formation

diameter tapering downwards and filled with fine sand making a good 'way up' structure for the geologist. It is considered that the burrows were excavated by early Devonian terrestrial arthropods burrowing into soft overbank sediments of ephemeral streams in a semi-arid environment.

Beyond the Range Warning Sign the Freshwater West Formation is succeeded by the Ridgeway Conglomerate, which in turn is overlaid unconformably by the Skrinkle Sandstone Group. Unfortunately these outcrops lie well within the bounds of the Castlemartin Firing Range, and so if you do proceed further you do so entirely at your own risk since there is always the possibility of encountering unexploded ordnance on the beach.

5. Gravel Bay [SM 876006]

At low tide you can enjoy a pleasant walk across the sandy beach from Little Furznip to Gravel Bay on the northern margin of Freshwater West Bay, or you can reach it from the car park [SM 885004] at Broomhill Burrows alongside the B4319.

The Old Red Sandstone sequence that outcrops along the cliffs around Gravel Bay is on the northern flank of the Castlemartin Corse anticline. There is a 30 metre section on the foreshore between two wrench faults that exposes the Silurian Gray Sandstone Group [Fig. 7.7]. This is overlaid unconformably by a distinctive conglomerate belonging to the Freshwater East Formation at the base of the Old Red Sandstone, south of the Ritec Fault. The conglomerate forms upstanding resistant outcrops on the beach (see photo on page 57) and is dipping at 60° NE and striking parallel to the main anticlinal axis. You will see that this conglomerate contains clasts of Silurian sandstone together with quartz cobbles up to 10 cm across. The succeeding Moor Cliffs Formation is well-exposed in Gravel Bay itself where thick red mudstones form an excellent polished rock platform with well-developed calcretes. This formation outcrops along the south coast of the Angle peninsula for several kilometres and includes a good section through the Townsend Tuff Bed at East Pickard Bay. (See Locality 7 for details of this same tuff bed at Little Castle Head.)

6. St Ann's Head [SM 806028]

Drive along the B4327 road from Haverfordwest to Dale village and then follow the narrow lane to the National Trust car park [SM 803042] that is about 1 km north of the headland. You should then walk past the cottages at Kete, then turn right and take the footpath across the fields to the Frenchman's Bay. Here the Freshwater West Formation dips

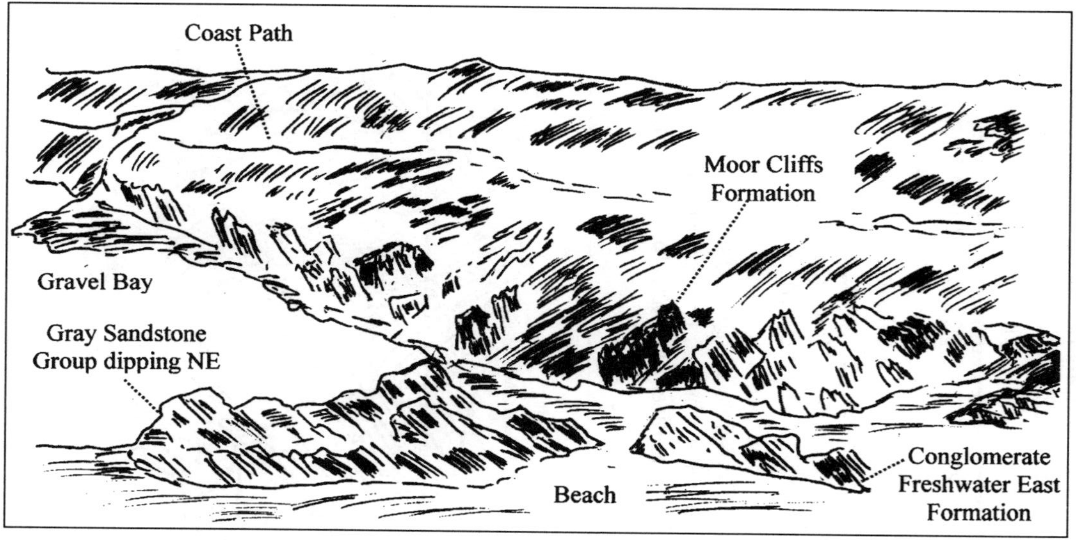

Fig. 7.7: View to the north-west across Gravel Bay

steeply north since the strata lies on the southern flank of the Pembroke Syncline. Follow the cliff path around the bay to the south side where the beds dip directly into the sea. During winter storms when these bedding planes are well lubricated, this area is subject to rock slides as huge boulders crash down onto the foreshore. Continue to the small cove with the delightful name of The Vomit where the path joins the road to St Ann's Head. Walk past the coastguard station to the steep-sided inlet called Cobbler's Hole. The warning sign says 'Do not proceed beyond this board' which is good advice considering that there is a sheer drop to the sea some 30 metres below. If possible I suggest that you visit this locality in the morning when the sun is in the south-east, so that it illuminates the magnificent Variscan fold structures displayed

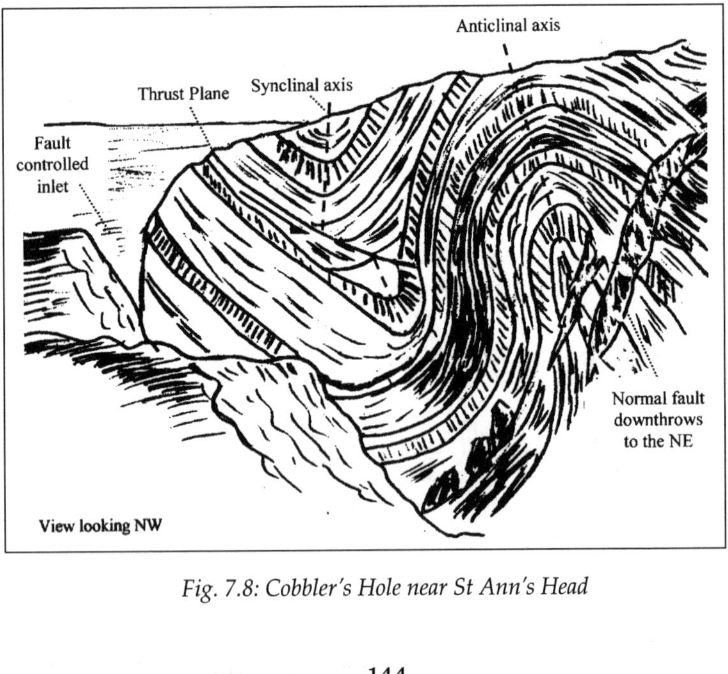

Fig. 7.8: Cobbler's Hole near St Ann's Head

on the north-west face of the inlet [Fig. 7.8]. Compression on the inner fold arcs and extension on the outer arcs has resulted in **flexural slip** between the beds. This is similar to what happens when a telephone directory is bent and the pages slide over each other. You should observe the prominent thrust fault that cuts across the nose of the syncline and offsets the fold axis. The beds below the fault have moved to the right in the opposite direction to those above. The sequence of mudstones and sandstone layers shows cleavage developed parallel to the axial plane of the folds. The eastern limb of the anticline is cut by a steep normal fault which downthrows the strata to the north-east by about 3 metres.

7. Little Castle Head [SM 855065]

This headland stands at the entrance to Sandy Haven on the north side of the Milford Haven. You can get to this locality by taking the minor road from Milford Haven through Herbrandston, around the head of Sandy Haven Pill and then turning left down a narrow road signposted to the hamlet of Sandy Haven where stepping stones cross the mouth of the pill (a local name for a small tidal inlet). Unfortunately there is no car park here, but there are several places where it is possible to leave vehicles alongside the road.

Take the coast path southwards along the western side of Sandy Haven for about 1.5 kms to Little Castle Head. Walk across the ditch and earthworks that protect the Iron Age Fort and make your way over to the east side of the headland, where there is a good overview of the small bay below the cliffs. Here the red mudstones of the Sandy Haven Formation are exposed on the foreshore and a distinctive greenish-coloured airfall tuff band known as the Townsend Tuff Bed can clearly be traced as a V-shaped outcrop pointing seawards. This band emphasises the outline of an anticlinal fold plunging to the south-east. Immediately below the cliff you should be able to see a complementary syncline in which the Pickard Bay Tuff Bed occurs. This tuff band is younger than the Townsend Tuff Bed since it lies about 20 metres higher in the Sandy Haven succession.

Take great care when you scramble down the rock slope leading to the foreshore in the south-east corner of the headland and carefully work your way round into the small bay which you have observed from above. This can only be achieved safely at low tide. It is well worth the effort to get to the shingle beach below the cliffs for here you will be able to have 'hands on' contact with the best exposure of the Townsend Tuff Bed in the whole of Pembrokeshire (see photo on page 57). The tuff is about 4 metres thick and it is made up of three fining up airfall units that were produced by Plinian type volcanic eruptions, each of which created a huge ash cloud that was dispersed by the wind and was eventually deposited in the surrounding shallow seas as a volcaniclastic sediment. Each unit begins with a relatively coarse crystal tuff and is overlaid by a fine-grained light-coloured tuff known as **porcellanite**. The Townsend Tuff Bed is named after the small settlement of Townsend near Dale where the bed cuts across the foreshore. However, the tuff outcrops consistently near the base of the Lower Old Red Sandstone in Wales and the Welsh Borders and so provides an important marker bed.

This tuff outcrop is remarkable in that it clearly shows all three separate airfall components [Fig. 7.9]. You will notice that all the beds are dipping at about 50° NE although the cleavage is at a high angle to the bedding. The basal airfall unit is strongly cleaved and can be seen on the west side of the outcrop, alongside the gully separating it from the underlying red mudstones. It is separated from the second airfall unit by a thin horizon of uncleaved ash that is formed mainly of faecal pellet debris. This suggests that there was a period of quiescence between eruptions in which organisms colonised

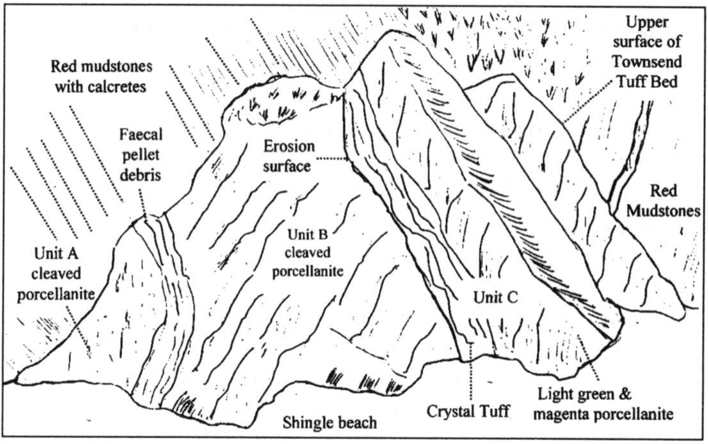

Fig. 7.9: The Townsend tuff bed at Little Castle Head

the muddy surface that covered the first airfall deposit. The overlying airfall unit is formed of highly cleaved porcellanite at the top of which is a distinctive wavy erosion surface, again marking an interval between eruptive outbursts. The third airfall unit begins with a coarse crystal tuff that passes upwards into another fine-grained porcellanite that has both light green and magenta coloured bands. Finally, on the eastern side of the outcrop, a gully separates the tuff bed from the overlying calcretised red mudstones.

8. Albion Sands [SM 772076]

You can reach this locality from the B4327 Haverfordwest to Dale road by turning right at Mullock Bridge [SM 810082] along the lane to Marloes. Before entering the village turn left along the single track road leading to the National Trust car park [SM 780081] near Runwayskiln Farm. Walk along the bridle track that runs south-west from the car park entrance; it is signposted to a youth hostel. Continue along the track past the Nature Reserve at Marloes Mere and then bear left along the footpath leading to the coast. You get an excellent view of Gateholm Island from the cliff top, from where you can look down to Albion Sands on the west side of the Gateholm promontory. The sands are named after the paddle streamer *Albion* that was beached here in April 1837 after striking a rock as it was negotiating Jack Sound, the dangerous tidal race between the Marloes peninsula and Skomer Island. The *Albion* was a two-masted, schooner-rigged, wooden vessel of 270 tons with her engines powered by coal-fired boilers. Unfortunately once the hull was holed, the engine room soon flooded and the crew were lucky to reach the relative safety of Albion Sands before the ship broke up. At low tide you can still see part of a cast iron beam standing out of the water. This is all that remains of the 170-year-old wreck.

There is a steep rugged path leading down to the foreshore at SM 772077 where the cliffs project towards Gateholm Island. This path can be slippery in wet weather so you should take great care on the descent. When tide is low you can walk around Gateholm stack and climb up onto the island if you wish, although the best rock exposures are in the cliffs around Albion Sands. However, Gateholm is a good example of what geographers call a tombola, which is an island separated from the mainland only at high tide.

The Red Cliff Formation at the base of the Old Red Sandstone succession in Pembrokeshire (north of the Ritec Fault) is exposed at the northern end of Albion Sands. These rocks rest directly on the Gray Sandstone Group of the Silurian inlier that forms the Marloes peninsula. The Red Cliff Formation consists of red mudstones and interbedded calcretes with cross-stratified fine sandstones, representative of a floodplain environment which from time to time dried out to produce mud cracks and calcrete deposits.

A metre-thick cleaved purple/red airfall tuff outcrops on

the foreshore at SM 772077 and this marks the junction with the succeeding Albion Sands Formation that contains red mudstones, yellow/buff coloured sandstones and conglomerate beds which can best be examined at the base of the cliffs around Horse Neck [SM 772075] on the north side of the gap between the mainland and Gateholm Island. The cross-stratified sandstone beds often rest on erosion surfaces and sometimes contain lenses of conglomerate in which there are large mudstone clasts. Some of the conglomerates contain sandstone clasts 40–50 cm across; such beds are characteristic of braided rivers which, when in spate, bring down large amounts of debris. Several darker-coloured igneous pebble conglomerates can be identified in the vicinity of Gateholm Stack, providing further evidence of volcanic activity in the area.

The most spectacular tectonic structures within the Albion Sands Formation are the sets of en échelon **tension gashes** that occur on the sandstone bedding planes around Horse Neck. These gashes or fractures are filled with quartz and lie parallel to each other at an angle of about 45° to the direction of the set. The staggered or en échelon arrangement of the mineral veins defines a shear zone within the rock in which the tension gashes were opened up as the rock mass moved in opposite directions in response to the compression created by the Variscan earth movements. You should be able to find examples where two sets of gash veins intersect on the rock face. These are referred to as conjugate sets of shear zones [Fig. 7.10].

9. St Brides Haven [SM 802110]

This is another of my favourite places on the south Pembrokeshire coast, being a quiet unspoilt bay that offers some fascinating structural geology. St Brides lies on the rugged west coast and can be reached by a narrow lane from

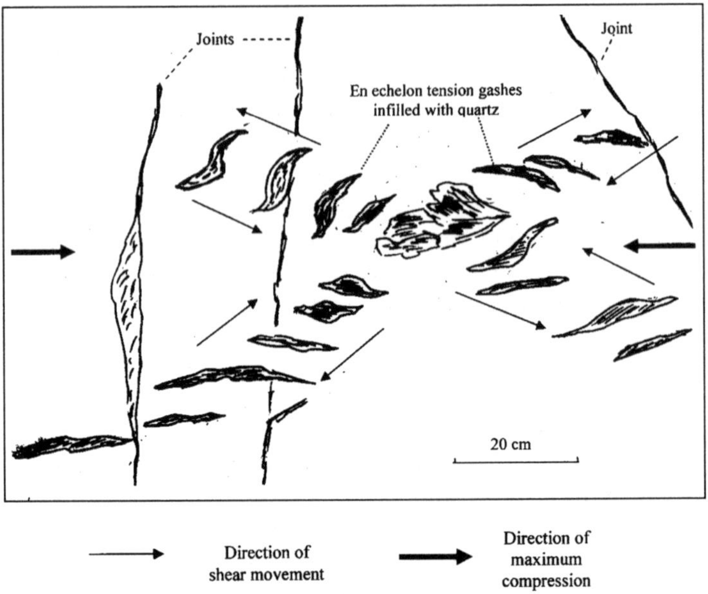

Fig. 7.10: Conjugate shear zones with gash veins in the Albian Sands formation

the crossroads at SN 833104 on the B4327 from Haverfordwest. There is a small car park next to the church overlooking the haven. You should visit this locality at low tide when most of the Variscan structural features are exposed on the foreshore [Fig. 7.11]. The mudstones and sandstones of the Sandy Haven Formation dip gently southwards at around 10° and they are cut by numerous dextral wrench faults running approximately N–S across the foreshore. Several smaller splay faults can also be seen. The positions of the main faults are marked by narrow gullies where the sea has eroded along the lines of weakness. The most obvious fault can be seen on the east side of the haven where a sandstone marker bed is offset dextrally by about 20 metres. Several sandstone beds can be traced across the foreshore although it is not always easy to identify them due to encrustation by barnacles.

You will notice Cliff Cottages standing above the east side of the bay. These provide ideal holiday accommodation for geologists wanting to be near to the rocks! About 50 metres north of the cottages there is a grey conglomerate unit about 2 metres thick, overlying cleaved red mudstones at the base of the cliff. You will see the calcretes in the mudstone have been flattened and elongated by the development of a near-vertical

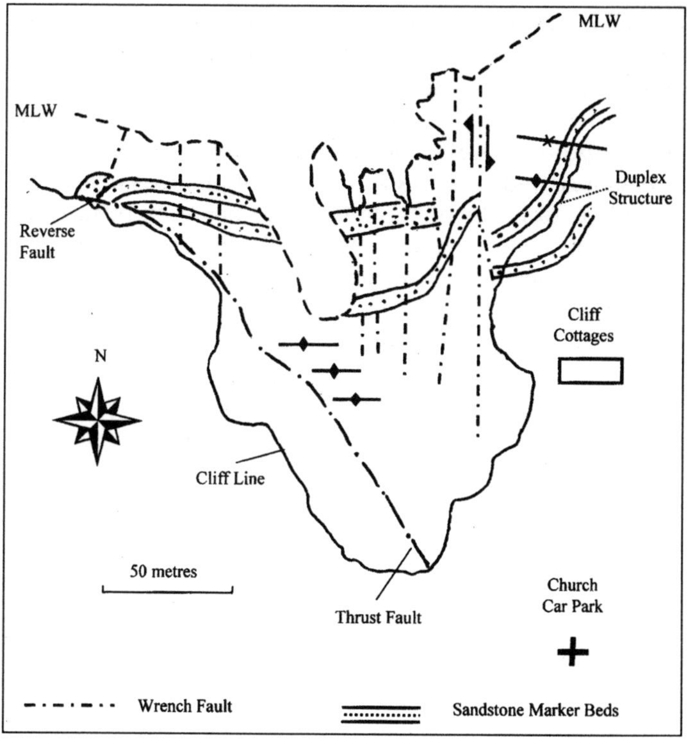

Fig. 7.11: The structural geology of St Brides Haven

cleavage. Now carefully examine the conglomerate and notice that it is cut by several sub-parallel thrust faults that separate the conglomerate into separate segments called 'horses' [Fig. 7.12]. The pressure has clearly come from the south since the **hanging walls** have been thrust to the north over the underlying footwalls. This displacement is up to 0.5 metre on each thrust and represents the amount of crustal shortening that has taken place. Look for slickenside striations on some of the thrust planes. There is a basal thrust plane below the conglomerate and a roof thrust above it. Here we have a marvellous example of what is known as a thrust **duplex** where successive segments from the **footwall** become incorporated into the hanging wall.

Finally, walk over to the north-west side of the haven where a prominent reverse fault runs along the base of the cliffs in a NW–SE direction. The sandstone beds above the fault plane form the hanging wall that has been pushed up and over the folded beds in the footwall. The thrust movement is again in a northerly direction.

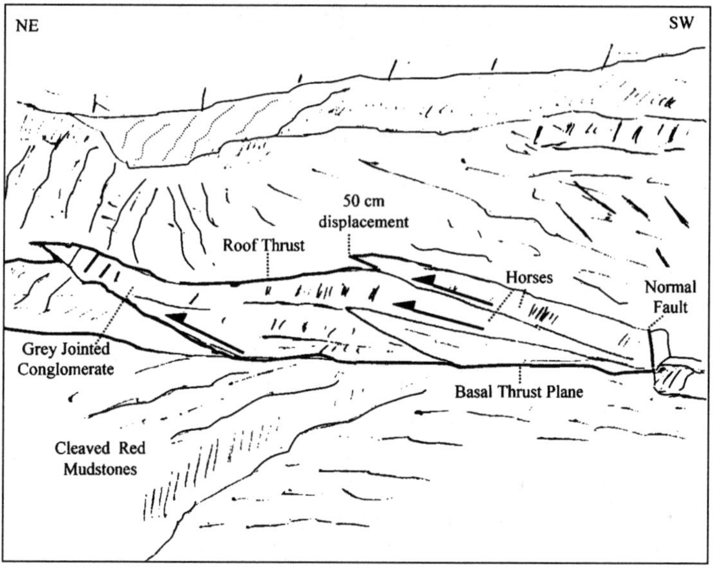

Fig. 7.12: A duplex thrust structure at St Brides Haven

8
Lower Carboniferous rocks on the Pembroke peninsula

The coast of south Pembrokeshire displays some spectacular cliff scenery developed in limestones that were formed during the Lower Carboniferous (or Dinantian) times between 354 and 327 million years ago. At this time shallow seas covered much of southern Britain, south of a landmass that stretched from Wales to Belgium. Pembrokeshire was located off the southern margin of this landmass in warm tropical coastal waters where coral, crinoids, sponges and brachiopods flourished. Initially as sea levels rose at the beginning of the Carboniferous, the seas advanced over the eroded Old Red Sandstone land surface and rivers brought sediments down from the neighbouring uplands. Thus the earliest Carboniferous rocks deposited offshore are thick carbonate mudstones that make up the Avon Group, formerly known as the Lower Limestone Shales [Fig. 8.1]. However, the main sequence of limestones that rest on these mudstones, were formed in much clearer waters on what geologists refer to as a carbonate ramp. This is essentially a platform that slopes gently seawards on which carbonate sediments are deposited. A barrier reef or a bank of **oolitic** sediment is usually established near the shoreline, often enclosing a lagoon. Seawards of the barrier, the deposition of **bioclastic** limestones occurs together with large mounds of carbonate mud. It is important to realise that throughout Lower

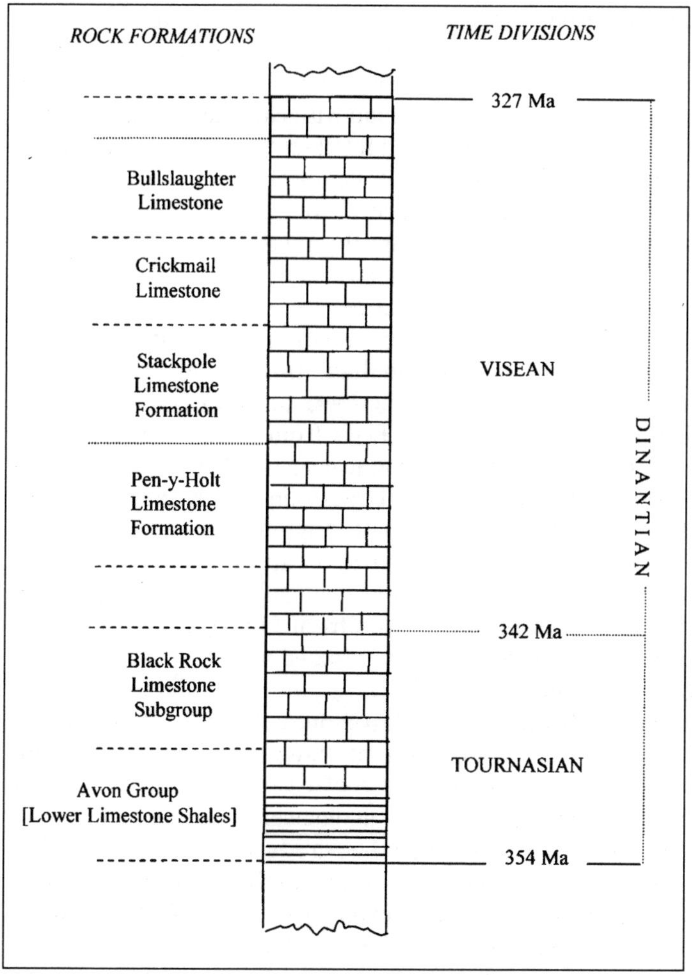

Fig. 8.1: Stratigraphical column for the Lower Carboniferous of south Pembrokeshire

Carboniferous times, over a period of some 27 million years, in south-west Wales the sea level fluctuated in a series of marine cycles of transgression and regression; hence a new carbonate ramp would develop with each new advance of the sea. Significantly, there is a north-south lateral variation in thickness of the limestone in Pembrokeshire with maximum sedimentation taking place in the south. The carbonate sequence is over 1000 metres thick near St Govan's Head but further north near Tenby the strata are reduced to around 500 metres in thickness [Fig. 8.2].

During the Variscan earth movements in Late Carboniferous (or Westphalian) times, powerful tectonic forces faulted and folded the rocks of south Pembrokeshire. The Ritec Fault that runs E–W from Tenby to the Milford Haven and the Flimston Fault near Castlemartin both slice through the Carboniferous Limestone, locally shattering and displacing the rocks. In Bullslaughter Bay there is a fine example of a synclinal fold that can be traced across the southern part of the Pembroke peninsula. Thus the limestones that are exposed in the cliffs from Linney Head to Caldey Island may be gently dipping, folded or faulted as a result of past earth movements. However, anyone walking along the coastal pathway above the limestone cliffs cannot fail to notice the level plateau surface that extends across much of the Pembroke peninsula. This surface was produced about 5 million years ago (recent by geological standards) during the early Pliocene period when the sea advanced over the existing landmass cutting indifferently across the Carboniferous rock structure and forming an extensive marine platform. More recently the sea has eroded the cliffs forming numerous inlets, caves, stacks, and arches including the well-known Green Bridge of Wales.

In terms of economic geology, the Carboniferous Limestone has been quarried for centuries to provide local

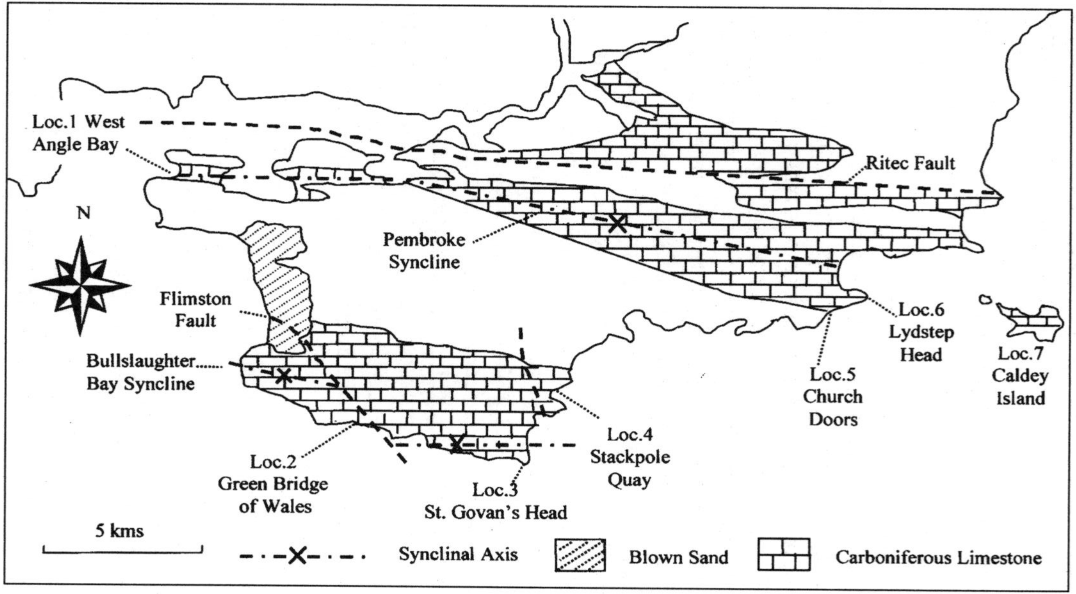

Fig. 8.2: The Lower Carboniferous outcrops in the Pembroke peninsula

building stone. It was also burnt in lime kilns to provide lime for agricultural fertilizer and mortar. The quarries at West Williamston [SN 025061] were worked in the late nineteenth century for their high quality stone that was shipped out by sailing barges on the Daugleddau (see Chapter 12, Locality 4). Aggregate for roadstone and concrete building blocks are now produced from large limestone quarries such as that at Carew.

The following localities, which are all easily accessible, should give you a real flavour of the geological highlights of the limestone coast of the Pembroke peninsula.

1. West Angle Bay [SM 855033]

You can get to this beautiful bay at the western end of the Angle peninsula by following the B4320 from Pembroke. Follow the road through Angle village and continue along the narrow road leading to the large car park adjacent to the beach. There is a café open during the tourist season and there are toilets next to the car park. The Hibernia pub in the village serves excellent refreshments.

At low tide, when the rocks are fully exposed, I suggest that you stand on the low sea wall near to the cafe and look out across the bay and the entrance to the Milford Haven. Large oil tankers and the new LNG vessels have to negotiate this relatively narrow stretch of water between West Angle and St Ann's Head and it was here that the ill fated 'Sea Empress' was grounded in 1996 with the loss of 72,000 tonnes of crude oil that polluted the coastline for miles around. This is part of the environmental price we have to pay for relying on imported oil and gas, but also from an aesthetic point of view, the existence of the three large oil refineries on the Haven is an ever present blot on the landscape, especially in a National Park!

From your viewpoint you will also be able to observe the line of the synclinal axis that trends WNW–ESE on the south side of West Angle Bay [Fig. 8.3]. You will see the dark grey limestones and shales of the Avon Group outcropping on either side of the bay with the younger Black Rock Limestone occupying much of the area beneath the sandy beach. Now walk along the foreshore to the first cove that lies below a ruined limekiln on the north side of the bay. Here you should be able to see the Avon Group strata dipping towards the south and resting discordantly upon the almost vertical beds of Black Rock Limestone. There has been a strong thrust movement pushing the Avon Group rocks northwards over Black Rock Limestone. The line of this thrust fault can be traced through Cove 2 and into the south side of Cove 3 [Fig 8.4] where a narrow zone of brecciated limestone marks the lower side or footwall of the thrust. These broken and

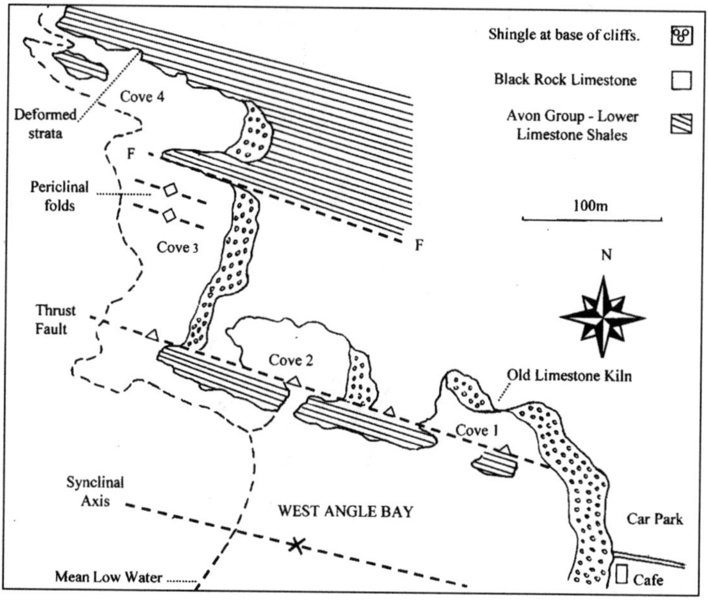

Fig. 8.3: The geology of West Angle Bay, northern shoreline

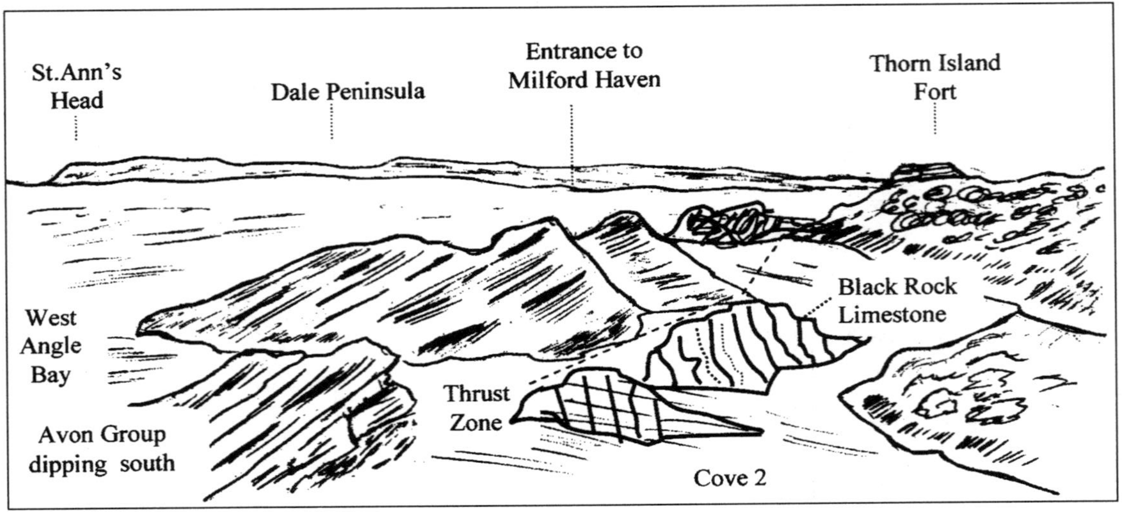

Fig. 8.4: View across the north shore of West Angle Bay

shattered rocks are the result of movement along the thrust fault during the Variscan earth movements.

Walk over the rocks into Cove 3 where you will see several other interesting geological structures on the foreshore including two periclinal folds that appear as shallow elongated domes rather like the upturned hull of a boat. The axes of the folds are orientated parallel to the main synclinal axis of West Angle Bay. The rocks are also cut by a series of en echelon veins that are where the rock has been sheared and the resulting tension gashes have later been filled with the mineral calcite. You may also notice some small circular holes with radiating fractures about 30 cms long. These are not natural features, rather they result from blasting operations during quarrying many years ago.

Some of the polished light grey limestone beds contain excellent examples of **stylolites** marked by an irregular suture-like contact that has been produced by pressure solution. This involves the removal of calcite grains in solution leaving a concentration of insoluble clay residues along the wavy stylolite surface. You will also find solitary corals such as *Zaphrentis*, crinoids and brachiopod shells preserved in the limestone. Some beds are much disturbed by burrows that cut across the bedding and are now infilled with slightly coarser sediment. These burrows are referred to as trace fossils since the original organism that produced them has long since been destroyed.

The northern wall of Cove 3 forms a faulted contact between the Black Rock Limestone and the deformed rocks of the Avon Group in Cove 4. You can get into this cove by scrambling through the gap in the steep dividing rock wall or alternatively it is possible to climb down the steep and narrow path that leads off the coastal track. It is well worth looking at the northern cliff face of the cove where there are some well-developed Variscan deformation structures. The dip here is approximately 70° SSW and a distinctive deformed sediment horizon occurs towards the western end of the cliff face at SM 851036.

Deformation features include a series of truncated minor folds and slump structures. These are found in the less resistant calcareous mudstone that is sandwiched between the harder limestone layers. The mudstone in the crumple zone is also strongly cleaved at an angle to the bedding due to the intense pressure exerted during earth movements.

2. The Green Bridge of Wales [SR 925944]

This well-known landmark is situated midway along the south coast of the Pembroke peninsula. You can approach from the B4319 Castlemartin-Pembroke road along a lane signposted to Stack Rocks that leads to the car park at this locality. Unfortunately it is not possible, without special permission, to examine the older limestone strata to the west of the Green Bridge because the cliffs lie within the MOD Castlemartin Artillery Range. The coast path to the east leading to St Govan's Head is usually open at the weekends but closed when firing takes place on weekdays. It is advisable to check accessibility with the MOD by telephoning 01646 662367 for a recorded message on the range opening times.

Brian John, now well-known as the author of the Angel Mountain/*Carn Ingli* novels, published an article in 1978 entitled 'The Valiant Cliffs of Pembrokeshire' in which he described this scenic coastline as being 'remarkably popular with both local people and visitors ... who flock to photograph the great natural arch called 'The Green Bridge of Wales' and to gaze across from the cliff tops to the spectacular Stack Rocks, locally called the Elegug Stacks'. Large numbers of guillemots, fulmars and gannets nest on these cliffs and stacks during the summer breeding season. Apart from its bird life, the Green Bridge is a spectacular natural arch formed by marine erosion (see photo on page 58). It is cut into the well-bedded Pen-y-Holt Limestone that dips gently northwards. However, eventually the main arch will collapse and leave two stacks similar to the nearby Elegug Stacks (see photo on page 58) which provide a superb example of sea stacks left standing as the cliff-line recedes under constant attack from the waves. 'Elegug' is the Welsh name for the guillemot.

Although the Green Bridge is visited by thousands of people every year, only a small proportion of them walk eastwards along the coast path to explore this superb cliffed coastline. About 750 metres beyond Stack Rocks is the promontory known as Flimston Castles [SR 930945] on which stand the ramparts of an Iron Age fort. This locality is riddled with caves and arches but is dominated by the deep shaft called the Devil's Cauldron. This may be described as a blow hole since the sea 'boils' and surges up through it in stormy weather. Take great care when exploring here as there are 50 metre cliffs on either side of the pathway in some places. It has been suggested that the Devil's Cauldron may be the remains of a former swallow hole or pothole in the limestone that has since been broken into by marine erosion. This is quite possible since you will see many other examples of **karstic** weathering as you walk along the cliff pathway including solution hollows and the remains of a limestone pavement where the rock is pitted and fluted. Essentially these features are produced by rainwater reacting with the calcium carbonate in the limestone and slowly removing it in solution.

Flimston Bay lies on the east side of Flimston Castle where the Flimston Fault reaches the coast. You must look for the fault shatter-zone that can easily be recognised by the orange-coloured gash breccias in the cliffs. This is a major wrench fault that runs NW–SE from Freshwater West (see Chapter 7, Locality 4). This type of fault involves the horizontal movement of the land on either side of the fault in opposite directions. (The San Andreas Fault in California is the best-known example of this type of fault.) The Flimston Fault has moved dextrally (to the right as you are looking across the fault) and offsets the Bullslaughter Bay synclinal axis by some 750 metres. As a result of this movement, the Stackpole Limestone is exposed on the coast to the west of the fault, whilst to the east the younger Crickmail and Bullslaughter Limestone outcrop in the cliffs.

Between Flimston Bay and Moody Nose the strata are dipping steeply southwards indicating that the E–W trending axis of the Bullslaughter syncline lies offshore, but in the cliffs to the east of Moody Nose, the beds dip steeply north showing that the synclinal axis now lies to the north crossing Longstone Down before emerging in Bullslaughter Bay. This is one of my favourite geological sites where it is almost possible to feel the strength of the earth movements that folded and shattered the rocks. It is also a magical and beautiful place where the sea crashes onto the rocks to demonstrate its awesome erosional power. Not many people venture down the steep pathway to the beach but it is well worth the effort to be able to view the rocks at close quarters.

You should follow the coast path around to the north-east side of Bullslaughter Bay where access to the beach is possible down a narrow gully. At the base of the gully the cliffs are stained red and contain a melange of large boulders and smaller clasts set in a sandy clay matrix; this is what is known as a **gash breccia** deposit. It may have been formed when limestone caverns collapsed and became filled with boulders and sandy sediment during flash floods in Triassic times. Alternatively, the brecciation may result from tectonic forces, since these deposits are often found in association with major faults (eg. Flimston fault) or near fold axes. Chemical weathering of the limestone could also have provided the residual clay matrix as surface waters percolated down through the shattered rocks forming infilled pockets and pipes.

When the tide is out you can walk over the beach to the cliffs on the west side of the bay where the beds are folded into the asymmetrical Bullslaughter Bay syncline [Fig. 8.5], the axis of which runs E–W across the bay. The Bullslaughter Limestone is thinly bedded with abundant chert and silicified corals and brachiopods. You will notice the contact with the underlying pale-grey-coloured Crickmail Limestone on the southern tip of the headland [SR 939943] on the west side of the bay. There are also further examples of gash breccias immediately to the north of the synclinal axis.

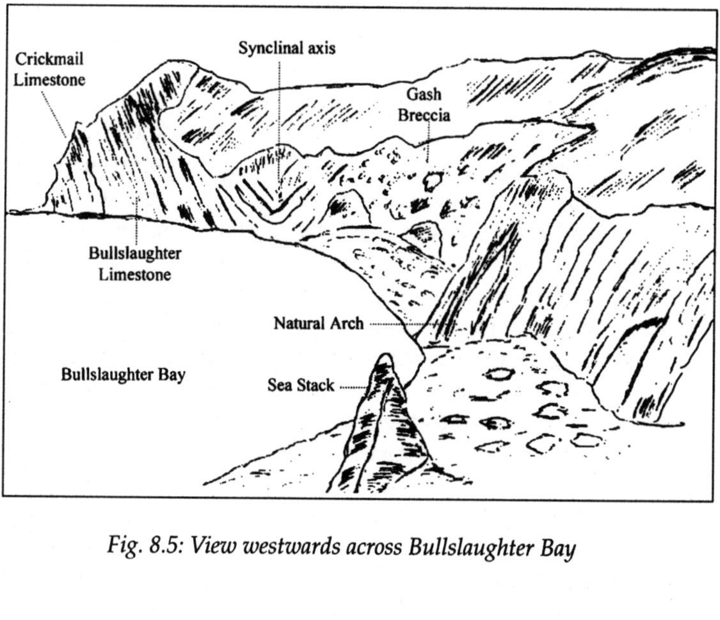

Fig. 8.5: View westwards across Bullslaughter Bay

3. St Govan's Head [SR 975927]

When you drive along the B4319 road from Pembroke, turn left at Sampson Cross on the signposted road to Bosherston village, then continue on the military road due south to the car park at St Govan's Chapel. Similar weekday access restrictions by the MOD apply as at Stack Rocks. The small eleventh-century stone-built chapel is worth a visit. It is built at the base of the cliffs and is reached by climbing down a set of about 70 stone steps. Nearby is the cleft in the cliff where St Govan is reputed to have taken refuge from marauding pirates! (See photo on page 59.)

Follow the footpath westwards to explore the indented coastline as far as Saddle Head [SR 958928]. The steep narrow inlets along this part of the coast are known as geos. They are formed by the sea eroding the limestone along faults that are aligned at right angles to the cliff line. The most famous of these geos is Huntsman's Leap (see photo on page 59), a deep vertical chasm that is only a few metres wide at its entrance; narrow enough to be jumped by a galloping horse! However, this is not a recommended practice since the drop to the sea below is over 40 metres. The next inlet to the west is the Devil's Barn that includes two blowholes and a natural arch; and as these features eventually collapse, a new geo will be formed.

Return to the car park and then walk eastwards to St Govan's Head where the well-bedded Stackpole Limestone dips gently seawards. You can see the large joints in the limestone that facilitate rock falls, producing enormous blocks which crash down onto the wave-cut platform at the foot of the cliffs. The headland forms an excellent viewpoint from which to look back along the coast towards Saddle Head and also to view Broad Haven and Stackpole Head to the north-east.

You can walk from St Govan's Head across Trevallen

Downs into the dry valley that leads down to the inlet of New Quay [SR 974931]. The development of this inlet is due to the existence of two parallel faults that have created a line of structural weakness in the rocks along which marine erosion has been actively removing rock material. The dog-leg shape of the inlet suggests that the main fault is offset by a transverse fault some 200 metres east of the entrance. You will be able to see that the beds strike N–S across the inlet and dip steeply seawards although there are several reverse faults that dip in the opposite direction so you will have to look carefully to distinguish between the true bedding and the fault planes. At the head of the inlet, the rocks are highly fractured or brecciated as a result of movement along the fault zone. The best time to visit this locality is at low tide when you can walk over the sandy floor of the inlet to examine the limestone walls at close range.

4. Stackpole Quay [SR 994958]

You can visit this delightful harbour from Stackpole village via a narrow lane leading to the National Trust car park just above the quay. This was originally built to facilitate the export of limestone from the quarries on the Stackpole estate, although it now serves as a base for inshore fishing boats. The quay is a popular venue for tourists in the summer when the Boathouse café does a brisk trade. There are also toilet facilities nearby.

There is much to see along the coast within range of Stackpole Quay so I recommend that you spend several hours at this location. Firstly I suggest that you walk down to the shingle beach in Quay Cove and examine the northern side of the cove. You will see the well-bedded Pen-y-Holt Limestone dipping at about 50° NE. Look for the dark **chert nodules** which tend to stand proud of the limestone surface due to the fact that they are formed of hard resistant silica. Chert is a form of silica that has been derived from the remains of silica secreting organisms such as sponges, diatoms and radiolarians that form a siliceous ooze on the sea bed. You will often see where the chert has infilled burrows and shell cavities within the limestone; and so there has been a secondary replacement of the original carbonate minerals. Look for some cross-sections of individual corals where the radiating internal structure can be seen, now preserved in chert.

Walk up to the north-eastern corner of the cove where calcareous mudstones to the west are faulted against shattered limestones to the east of the fault. This is the site of the Stackpole wrench fault that has horizontally displaced the nose of the Stackpole anticline by about 100 metres to the right. The fault plane dips steeply to the east and the fault line runs NNW–SSE through the harbour and truncates the mudstones on the south flank of the anticline that outcrop opposite the harbour wall to the west of the fault. You can see the fault again in the old quarry face on the south side of the harbour where the displaced nose of the anticline can be observed to the east of the fault. I think that you will appreciate the dextral movement of this fault better by referring to the map [Fig. 8.6], preferably in the field.

Climb up the path that runs over the ridge into Middle Cove where you can feast your eyes on some marvellous corals that are embedded in the rocks, but please don't damage these specimens in any way. The limestones on the south side of the cove belong to the Pen-y-Holt Limestone Formation and contain excellent well-preserved specimens of the colonial coral *Lithostrotion* and the single coral *Caninia gigantia*. Some of these single corals are up to 20 cm long and they are beautifully preserved both in cross-section and long section. They are clearly not in life position but have been transported by currents after death and buried in calcareous sediment.

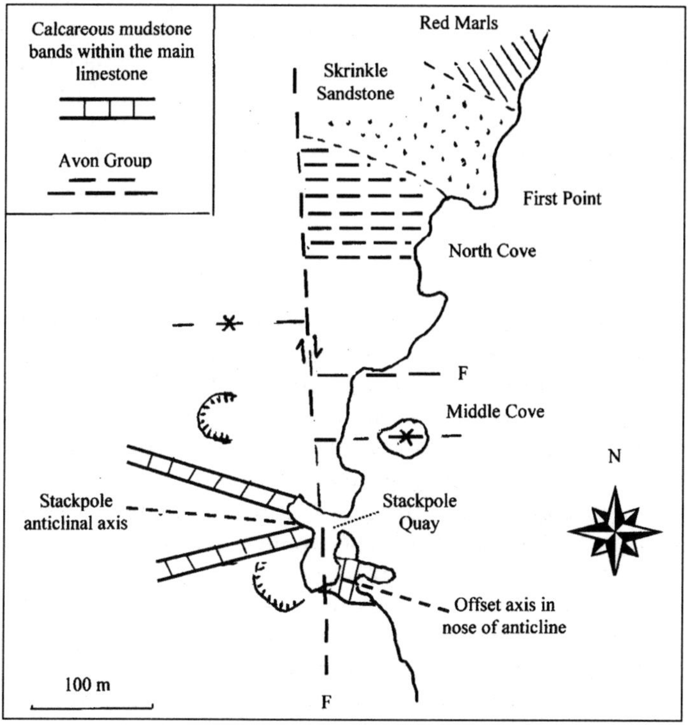

Fig. 8.6: The geology of Stackpole Quay

The other outstanding feature of Middle Cove is the synclinal fold axis that runs E–W through the small island in the centre of the cove where the structure is well-displayed at low tide. This axis is also dextrally offset to the south by the Stackpole wrench fault.

The next stop is on the headland overlooking North Cove where the junction between the Avon Group and the Upper Old Red Sandstone can be observed. Access to North Cove is difficult from the coast path; but the basal shales and thin limestones of the Avon Group can be seen to be thrust against the red mudstones and sandstones of the Skrinkle Sandstone Formation. When the sun is shining there is a wonderful view to the north-east towards Greenala Point and Trewent Point, which shows the red cliffs of the Lower Old Red Sandstone.

Return to Stackpole Quay for a drink and a snack in the café before walking south up the steps to the headland where there is a fine view overlooking the harbour. Now continue along the coast path for about 1 km to Barafundle Bay. This is one of the gems of the south Pembrokeshire coast. It is owned by the National Trust and although it is popular with visitors, it is nevertheless unspoiled. I suggest that you stop at the top of the pathway leading down to the sandy beach and admire the view across the bay southwards towards the majestic limestone cliffs of Stackpole Head.

A synclinal axis runs E–W through the centre of Barafundle Bay although it is concealed beneath the coastal sand dunes. This is complemented to the south by the Bosherston anticline that extends towards Stackpole Head. At low tide you can walk along the beach to examine the Crickmail Limestone that outcrops on the north side of the bay. Here you will see that the bedding planes dip steeply south on the northern flank of the syncline. There are numerous examples of **productid** brachiopods such as *Delepinea* in the limestone, and single corals of the genus *Dibunophyllum* are also relatively common. About 20 metres east of the base of the steps leading down to the beach, there is a good example of a gash breccia composed of a melange of haematite-stained limestone blocks set in a matrix of red clay.

If you have time and sufficient energy left, then walk across the golden sands of Barafundle Bay and climb up the coastal path leading to Stackpole Head [SR 995942] (see photo on page 60). From the headland look back towards the Barafundle syncline and the three natural arches known as the Lattice Windows. The massive limestone beds at Stackpole Head are almost horizontal and where the limestone is exposed on the plateau surface there is much evidence of the karstic weathering. However, if you look carefully at the bedding plane forming a prominent ledge about halfway up the cliff face you will see a pot-holed surface [Fig. 8.7]. This was subjected to karstic weathering in Lower Carboniferous times during a pause in the deposition of the limestone when the surface was exposed as a land area. This ancient solution-weathered limestone surface is called **palaeokarst**. Continue

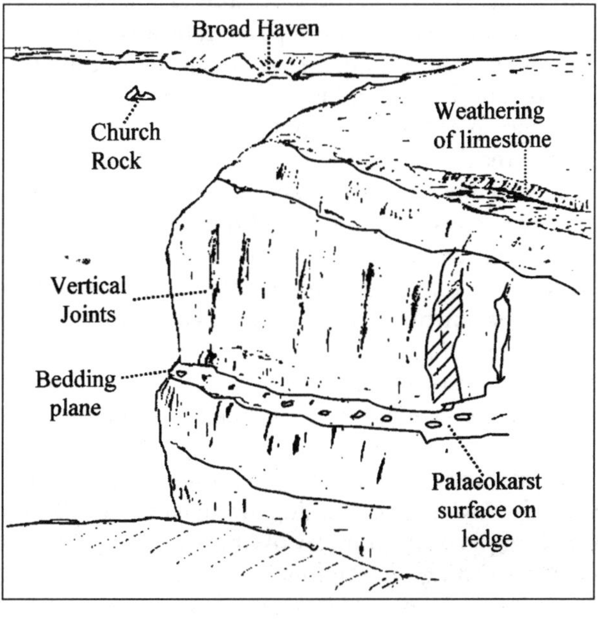

Fig. 8.7: View looking west from Stackpole Head

around the headland to Mowingword Bay where there is an impressive stack and a partially collapsed blowhole.

5. Church Doors Cove [SS 081974]

As you drive along the A4139 road from Pembroke to Tenby, turn right onto the B4585 road signposted to Skrinkle Haven. Drive past the married quarters of Manorbier army camp, then follow the military road to the army ranges and the Manorbier Youth Hostel where there is a picnic site and car park [SS 081976]. I think that it is best to first obtain an overview of Church Doors Cove and Skrinkle Haven from the cliff top where the magnificent natural arch known as the Horseback can be seen in the vertically-bedded Black Rock Limestone. The two coves are separated by a vertical wall of the Church Doors Limestone that lies in the middle of the Avon Group succession and is named after two caves in the rock wall known as Church Doors.

You can reach Church Doors Cove by descending the 160 steps that lead down to a small shingle beach. Here there is a series of calcareous mudstones and thin limestones that are almost vertically bedded with a strike direction approximately ESE–WNW. The mudstones contain numerous fossil burrows including the branching traces of *Thalassinoides* that can be seen on the base of individual beds. Sediments such as these, that have been disturbed by burrowing organisms soon after deposition, are generally described as having been bioturbated.

Providing that the tide is ebbing, it is safe for you to get into Skrinkle Haven by scrambling through the natural tunnel in the dividing rock promontory of Church Doors Limestone. Once you are through the tunnel, walk over the sands to the cliffs at the back of Skrinkle Haven to where a change of colour occurs from grey to red-brown rocks. This is the transitional boundary between the red desert sediments of the Upper Old

Red Sandstone and the grey calcareous marine sediments of the Avon Group. The latter also contain fragments of marine fossils including crinoids and brachiopods.

When you return to the car park you may wish to follow the coast path eastwards to the next locality at Lydstep Point. It is a pleasant walk along the cliff top, then down to sea level at Draught inlet before climbing up again to the headland at Lydstep.

6. Lydstep Point [SS 094975]

When approaching the village of Lydstep along the A4139 road from Pembroke take a right turn down the narrow lane leading to the National Trust car park on the headland [SS 088977]. From the car park you should follow the track on the north side of the headland to the disused Lydstep Quarry that overlooks Lydstep Haven. Here you will see that the strata is vertically bedded and strikes at approximately WNW–ESE. This rock is the Crickmail Limestone that was quarried and exported by sea in the nineteenth century. The south face of the quarry and much of the headland exposes the Stackpole Limestone. You will notice that the plateau surface is covered by a orange-coloured clay called *terra rossa*, which is an insoluble iron-rich residual deposit derived from the weathering of the limestone.

Next, walk across to Lydstep Point and spend a little time to admire the view looking eastwards. Try to line up the strike direction of the strata on the headland with the limestone cliffs of St Margaret Island and beyond to the north coast of Caldey Island. When visiting Caldey Island you can take a reciprocal bearing to Lydstep Point in order to reassure yourself that the upturned limestone beds were at one time continuous: that is, until the sea removed them by erosion!

You are now starting to follow the path around the headland and as you turn towards the west you will see the magnificent 'organ pipe' structure of the vertical limestone cliffs formed of Pen-y-Holt Limestone around Lydstep Hole. Take great care here because there is a sheer drop down to the sea at the bottom of the hole! At this point you should also be able to appreciate the saddle and ridge topography that is produced by the differential weathering of the vertical strata (see photo on page 60). The thicker beds of limestone form the ridges rising above the saddles that are formed of thinner less resistant beds.

Whitesheet Bay [SS 091976] is best approached from the western side where it is possible, with care, to clamber down to the rock platform in the centre of the bay [Fig. 8.8]. Here

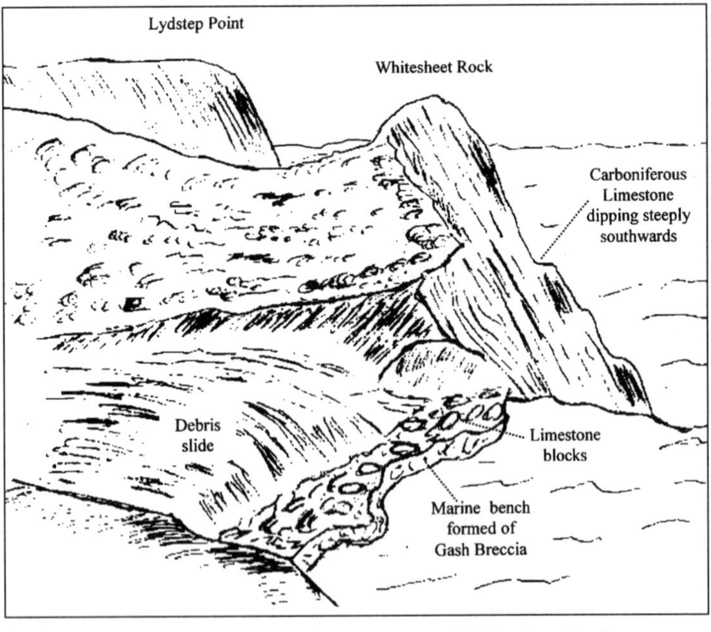

Fig. 8.8: View of Lydstep Point and Whitesheet Rock

there is a melange of boulders and cobbles cemented with finer sediment providing another example of a gash breccia deposit (see Locality 2).

Now you should continue to walk westwards along the coastal path before descending to Black Mixon [SS 088975], a low promontory where there is a 2 metre thick deposit of angular limestone set in clay matrix overlying steeply dipping limestones. This loose unstable debris has clearly slid down the coastal slope and may well be the result of frost shattering during a periglacial phase in late Devensian times (see Chapter 11, Fig.1). When the ground later thawed, meltwater would lubricate the debris and assist in its downslope movement.

Climb back up onto the plateau surface and look across to the west face of Draught inlet. Here again we have a chaotic jumble of boulders that form a typical gash breccia. There is a stunning view to the south-west towards The Horseback and Skrinkle Haven and beyond to the Old Red Sandstone cliffs around Old Castle Head.

7. High Cliff, Caldey Island (Ynys Byr) [SS 143971]

It is well worth spending the day on Caldey Island but do not forget that the last boat returns to the mainland at about 5 pm. The regular boat service from Tenby runs throughout the tourist season. The crossing takes about 20 minutes to Priory Bay [SS 135970] on the north side of the island. There is a public track across the island to the lighthouse at Chapel Point on the south coast and thence by a circular route back to the monastery and the village which has a café, tourist shop and toilet facilities. However, please note that Caldey is a private island owned by a reformed order of Cistercian monks and permission is required to visit coastal locations off the main tourist track.

You will find that the sea trip across to Caldey provides a good opportunity to do some geology from the boat. I suggest you try to sit on the starboard (right) side so that you can get a good view of the coast to the south of Tenby where extensive windblown dunes rise at the back of a long sandy beach that leads to the headland of Giltar Point [SS 125983]. On a fine day you will see the beds of limestone dipping steeply southwards along the cliffs around Giltar Point. These beds are dipping towards the axis of the Pembroke syncline that runs E–W below Caldey Sound. Now as the boat alters course towards Caldey take a good look at the cliffs on the north-west side of the island and you will see that the limestone beds are dipping steeply north since they are on the southern flank of the syncline.

One of the most accessible exposures of the Carboniferous Limestone is at High Cliff, a few minutes walk across the sands from the landing stage at Priory Bay. Here on the north-east tip of the island, the well-bedded Crickmail Limestone strikes approximately E–W and dips at 80° N [Fig. 8.9]. The grey fine-grained rock contains abundant remains of brachiopod shells, particularly *Linoproductus hemisphaericus*. Some beds appear broken and fractured but this is not actually the case since the limestone has been recrystallised in patches allowing differential weathering to create a nodular structure in the rock which has become a **pseudobreccia**. On the east side of the headland there are the remains of the old quarry buildings marking the site of an important nineteenth-century quarrying operation that supplied building stone to the rapidly expanding holiday town of Tenby. High Cliff also offers a good viewpoint from which to follow the line of limestone cliffs from Eel Point to St Margaret's Island and Lydstep Point, showing the steeply-dipping limestones on the south side of the Pembroke syncline.

Whilst on Caldey you should take the opportunity of

visiting the Old Red Sandstone cliffs on the south coast (see photo on page 61), which provide nesting sites for thousands of seabirds in spring and summer. Some of the inlets are also home to colonies of grey seals. The rocky foreshore below the lighthouse is the type section for the Chapel Point Calcretes (see Chapter 7, Locality 4), but it is difficult to reach from the clifftop.

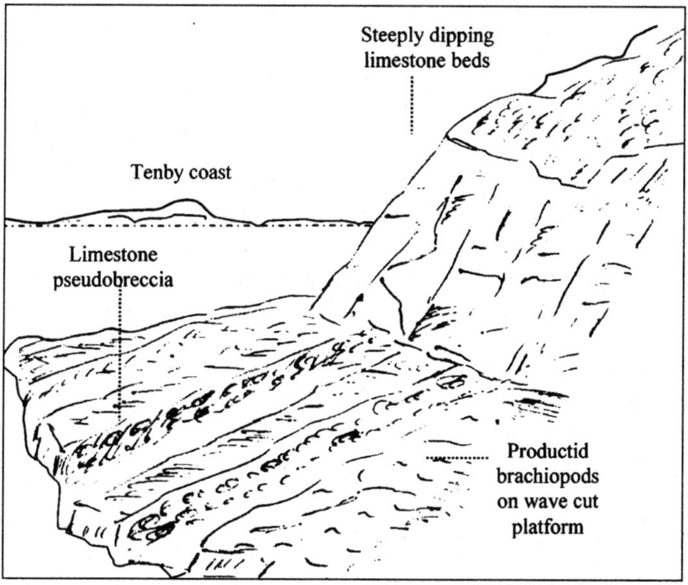

Fig. 8.9: High Cliff, Caldey island

9
Upper Carboniferous rocks on the west side of Carmarthen Bay

Today the rolling green countryside of central Pembrokeshire gives little hint of its nineteenth-century industrial past of coal mines, iron works and lime kilns. These economic activities were based on the local availability of coal, iron ore and limestone. High-quality anthracite was mined and shipped out from such ports as Landshipping on the Afon Daugleddau and Saundersfoot on Carmarthen Bay. Lower-quality coal known as 'culm' was in demand for firing lime kilns, brick ovens and domestic fires. The iron smelting works at Stepaside near Kilgetty utilised anthracite produced by neighbouring coal mines and bedded iron ore was also obtained from the coalfield. Interestingly, the site of the disused ironworks has now been restored and transformed into a heritage park and tourist attraction (see Chapter 12, Locality 8). Railways played an important role in transporting coal and ore, particularly the Saundersfoot mineral line which was opened in 1834. There were two branches, linking local collieries with the newly-constructed Saundersfoot harbour. Today the Pembrokeshire coast path utilises part of the old trackway between Saundersfoot, Coppet Hall and Wiseman's Bridge.

A glance at the Geological Survey map will show that the Upper Carboniferous rocks of the Pembrokeshire Coalfield extend in a narrow zone west–east across the county. They were deposited 327-311 million years ago during Namurian and Westphalian times [Fig. 9.1] in vast river deltas and low-lying coastal swamps under hot wet tropical conditions. The sea flooded the land from time to time, burying the swamp forests that would eventually produce the coal seams. Repeated fluctuations in sea level resulted in the formation of numerous units of sedimentation or **cyclothems** composed of mudstones, sandstones and coal seams.

During the Variscan orogeny, the strata were deformed into a compressed syncline with its axis trending WNW–ESE from St Brides Bay in the west across to Carmarthen Bay in the east. The southern limb of the syncline displays complex folding and faulting resulting from a major northward thrust

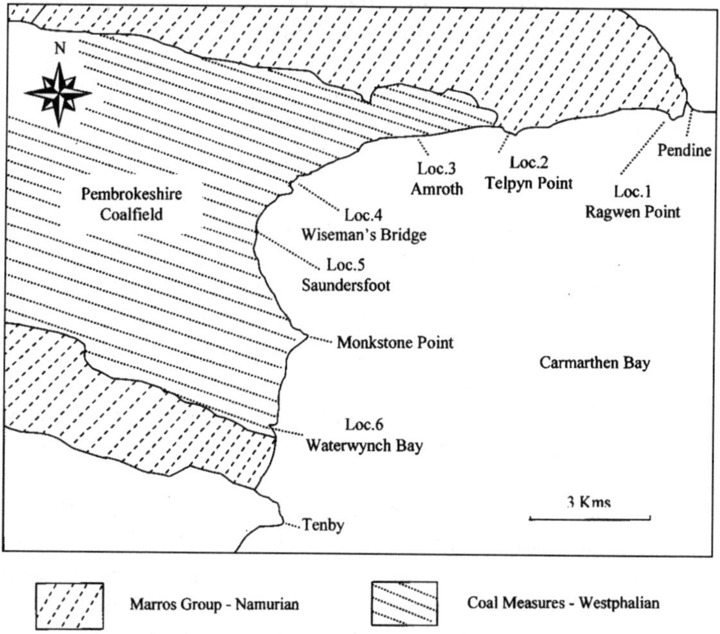

Fig. 9.1: Upper Carboniferous outcrops in Carmarthen Bay West

by the advancing front of the Variscan earth movements. Thus in the Tenby–Waterwynch section (see Locality 6) on the southern side of the coalfield, the strata is much more disturbed and the overall synclinal structure is difficult to recognise where folding and thrusting have considerably compressed the strata. Indeed, tectonic deformation along the southern margin of the Pembrokeshire coalfield has reduced its width to only one third of that of its counterpart in the main south Wales basin. By contrast on the northern edge of the coalfield around Amroth, the gently-dipping Namurian beds pass conformably into the Coal Measures and they are much less disturbed being farther removed from the Variscan Front.

The margins of the coalfield are occupied rocks of Namurian age, now called the Marros Group but formerly known as the Millstone Grit. These strata outcrop on the west coast of Carmarthen Bay immediately north of Tenby and between Amroth and Ragwen Point. There are three subdivisions of the Marros Group [Fig. 9.2]:

i) The oldest formation, called the Twrch Sandstone, rests unconformably on the underlying Carboniferous Limestone. It is formed of cross-stratified quartzitic sandstones interbedded with dark mudstones and is thought to represent the deposits of braided distributary channels meandering across a delta plain.
ii) The Bishopston Mudstone Formation contains several deltaic sequences but is dominated by thick mudstones which suggest a rise in sea level. There is also evidence of turbidity flows on the pro-delta slopes where silt and sand bodies have been deposited
iii) The youngest formation is the Telpyn Point Sandstone that is named after the headland immediately east of Amroth. Miners used to refer to this formation as the Farewell Rock' since they knew from experience that

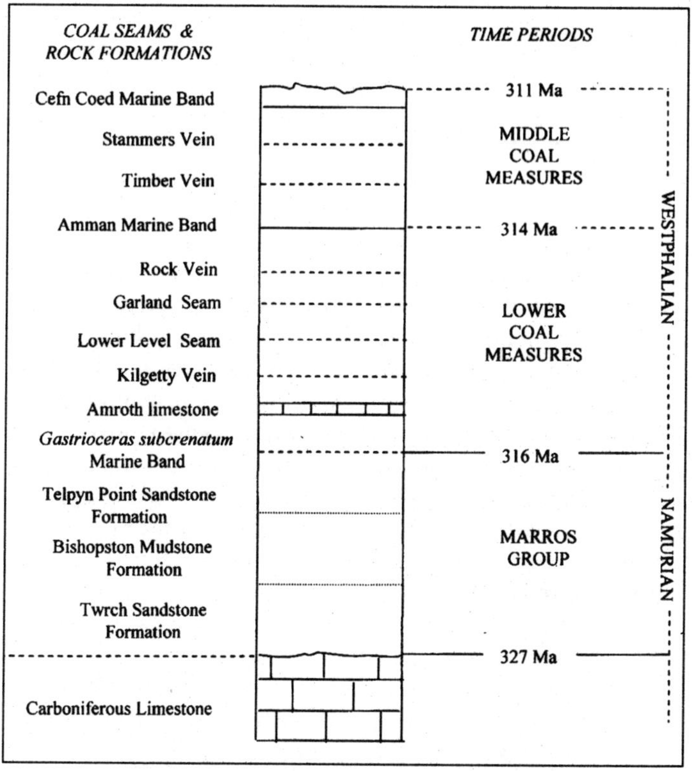

Fig. 9.2: Stratigraphical column for the Upper Carboniferous strata of Carmarthen Bay West

when they reached down to this level there would be no more workable coal seams available. The massive, cross-stratified sandstones often contain lag gravels at the base of the sequence and are typical of meandering river channel deposits.

The Coal Measures are rocks of Westphalian age that overlie the Marros Group and outcrop in the centre of the coalfield syncline. The base of the Coal Measures is marked by a **marine band** named after the goniatite, *Gastrioceras subcrenatum*. This thin layer of shale represents a time when sea level rose to flood the Namurian deltas before deltaic sedimentation was again established at the beginning of Westphalian times and the first coal seams were formed. Both the Lower and Middle Coal Measures are exposed on the coast between Amroth and Waterwynch Bay, near Tenby, where various anthracitic coal seams are accessible at beach level and it is possible to study the development of individual cyclothems. However, do not expect to see horizontal strata along this coast! The effects of the Variscan earth movements are very obvious with numerous thrust faults, complex folds and crumpled coal seams.

The following localities along the west coast of Carmarthen Bay have been chosen to give you a representative selection of the outcrops of Upper Carboniferous rocks.

1. Ragwen Point [SN 221071]

You can reach this locality from the A477 Pembroke to St Clears road by turning at Red Roses [SN 203118] onto the B4314 Pendine road. As you enter Pendine village there is a lay-by near to Great House Farm, about 200 metres south-east of Pendine Church. Park the vehicles in the lay-by and cross over the road to the farm from where a track leads down to the coast. About 100 m down the track bear left; then follow the path down to the bridleway leading south to Morfa Bychan, a storm beach at the head of the bay between Gilman Point and Ragwen Point. Alternatively, you may find it quicker to drive down the bridleway from the Green Bridge [SN 221091] on the minor road between Amroth and Pendine, and park behind the storm beach. However, be aware that this route is rough and narrow and is only really suitable for small 4x4 vehicles.

Walk across to the east side of Ragwen Point and look at the base of the cliffs where there is an erosional contact between the underlying Carboniferous Limestone and the Twrch Sandstone Formation. This is an unconformity that represents a time gap during which the top of the limestone was eroded before the deposition of the overlying beds. The grey blue limestones that are interbedded with dark mudstones belong to the Oystermouth Formation at the top of the Carboniferous Limestone succession. They display a rich brachiopod fauna and there are also large horizontal burrows occurring on some bedding planes. These are examples of the trace fossil *Thalassinoides*. The unconformity marks a major environmental change from the shallow shelf seas in which the Carboniferous Limestone was deposited, to the fluvial and deltaic conditions that produced the shales and sandstones of the Marros Group. A study of palaeocurrent directions has shown that the latter appear to have been derived from sediments brought down by rivers flowing south-west over uplifted Old Red Sandstone outcrops in the Brecon uplands.

Now look carefully at the cliff face towards the end of Ragwen Point and try to distinguish the following beds:

i) Dark-coloured quartz sandstones with cross-stratification and disseminated carbonaceous debris occur immediately above the unconformity. Remains of the roots (*Stigmaria*) of giant club mosses, are common on the surface of the sandstone bed that forms the wave-cut platform [Fig. 9.3]. These sediments have been interpreted as braided distributary channel deposits formed on a delta, building out into a shallow marine embayment.

ii) There is a distinctive undercut (cliff notch) immediately above the sandstone where carbonaceous mudstones and coal streaks have been eroded out by the sea. These represent **suspension deposits** laid down in a swampy channels on the delta plain.

iii) The overlying bed is a medium-grained quartz sandstone with small-scale trough cross-bedding that is considered to be a crevasse splay deposit produced when rivers in spate cut through their levees and laid down lobes of sediment on the flood plain. Iron-rich concretions occur in this horizon.

iv) At the top of the sequence there is a return to braided channel fill-deposits with a thick sandstones displaying

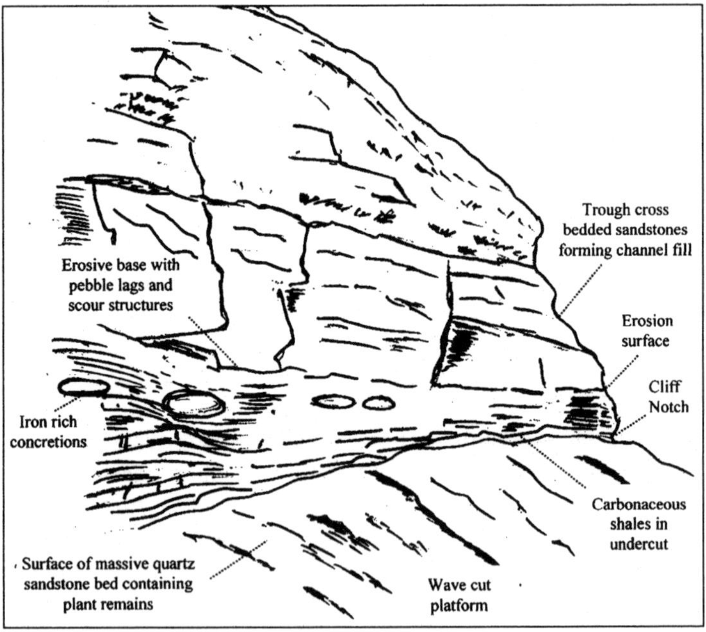

Fig. 9.3: The Twrch sandstone formation at Ragwen Point

trough cross-stratification. The sharp undulating contact at base of this bed shows lag gravels and scour structures. Where a steep-sided channel has been scoured out in the underlying sediment, the depression may become infilled with sand to form what is known as a **gutter cast**, several of which can be seen on the erosional base of the thick sandstones.

2. Telpyn Point [SN 186072]

It is about 6 kms from Pendine to Amroth [SN 171073] along the narrow coast road via Marros. You can park alongside the seafront in Amroth, opposite the New Inn, and then walk across the shingle beach to the cliffs. These cliffs display Lower Coal Measures that dip gently westwards. Continue to walk along the foreshore for about 1 km, but in the interest of safety, it is best to do this on a falling tide. Alternatively at high tide, you can use the coast path that leads down from the Pendine road through a narrow valley to a small inlet at SN 183073. The Telpyn Point Sandstone Formation is exposed from here to the eastern side of Telpyn Point. The inlet marks the location of a normal fault that downthrows the upper siltstones (to the east) against the underlying micaceous sandstones. Walk over the wave-cut platform to the face of Telpyn Point in order to examine the massive trough cross-bedded sandstones that form the lower part of the Telpyn Point Sandstone Formation, representing a large infilled **distributary channel**. A prominent undulating erosional surface with lag gravels marks the base of the sequence. However, above this base there are several other erosion surfaces marked by lag concentrates in addition to a melange of plant remains (including the tree fern *Calamites*), coal rafts and slumped beds.

Since the strata are dipping gently westwards, the older Bishopston Mudstone Formation will begin to appear at the base of the cliffs as you approach Telpyn Point. Here there is a thick sequence of dark siltstones that has been interpreted as the suspension deposits of turbidity currents flowing down a delta front slope. Below the cliff on the east side of Telpyn Point [Fig. 9.4] where several bands of **sinusoidal ripples** that form a distinctive feature. Each line of ripples is in phase with those directly above and appears to have been deposited from suspension by a series of turbidite flows.

3. Amroth Cliffs [SN 160069]

For this locality you should make for the western end of Amroth village where there is a large car park and toilets, and since this is a thriving holiday centre, there are also several cafes and pubs for refreshment.

The best rock exposures are seen in the cliffs immediately south-west of the promenade where the Lower Coal Measures are strongly folded and cut by several thrust faults. The

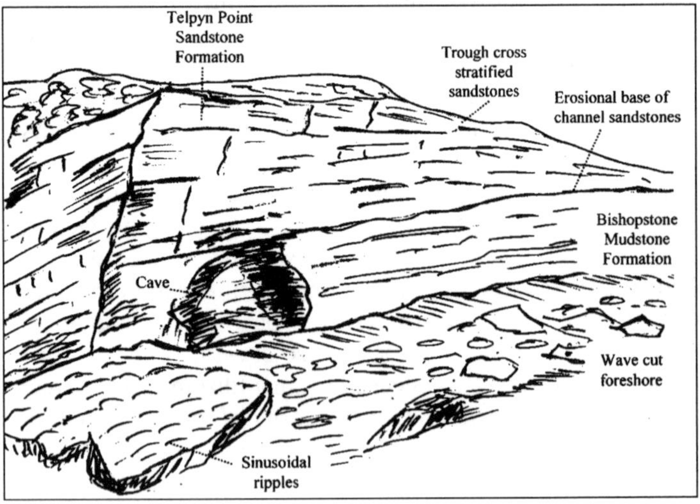

Fig. 9.4: The cliffs on the east side of Telpyn Point

Kilgetty Vein, which is the lowest seam in the coalfield, was worked in a small recess parallel to the cliff face, immediately to the left of a major thrust plane [Fig. 9.5]. The seam is overlaid by a mudstone and thick cross-stratified sandstones. South-west of this zone of disturbance there is a broad anticline (250 metres long) in which there are two distinctive marker horizons. First there is a light-coloured limestone with chert nodules that lies just below the Kilgetty Vein seam and can best be seen at the southern flank of the anticline. Secondly, about 6 metres below the cherty limestone is the distinctive Amroth Freshwater Limestone, which is a red-brown bed about 1 metre thick and composed of the carbonate mineral ankerite. It contains abundant remains of the freshwater bivalve *Anthracosia regularis* and there are many small solution cavities where the shells have been weathered out.

Fig. 9.5: Lower Coal Measures forming the cliffs to the west of Amroth

In the cliff sections extending south-west from the end of the anticline at SN 157068, you should be able to recognise the repeated coarsening upward sequences. Each cyclothem ideally consists of a seat earth and coal seam followed by mudstones and increasingly coarse sandstones. The succession of sediments was deposited as the delta was built up and extended seawards. The delta plain would have been covered by swamp forests and crossed by distributary channels in which cross-stratified sands accumulated.

You can visit the remaining cliff section either by continuing south-west along the foreshore, or by approaching from Wiseman's Bridge and walking north-east towards Amroth, as described in the next locality.

4. Wiseman's Bridge [SN 147062]

The coastal path provides the shortest route between Amroth to Wiseman's Bridge, otherwise you will have to drive inland to Summerhill before taking the narrow road down a steep hill to the coast where you can park on the seafront. This locality is first rate if you want to get hands-on experience at coal mining without the danger of going underground! Along this section of the coast there are several seams that crop out on the beach and are constantly being undermined by the sea so that the coal is washed clean by every high tide.

Walk past the Wiseman's Bridge Inn onto the foreshore beneath the cliffs and almost immediately you will see two high angle faults in a V-formation cutting the sandstone/siltstone sequence of the Middle Coal Measures that are gently dipping to the south-west. Some 20 metres to the north-east of the faults there are some excellent examples of minor distributary channels cross-cutting the bedding [Fig. 9.6]. The fill of each channel exhibits repeated fining up units with a lag deposit at the base. The lag material includes pebbles, small ironstone nodules, and siltstone fragments in a sandy matrix

Fig. 9.6: Cross-cutting channels in the Middle Coal Measures near Wiseman's Bridge

(see photo on page 61).

The Timber Vein coal can be seen high in the cliffs but where there is a gap in the cliffs marked by a rockslide, a thin coal seam crops out at beach level. Beyond this is a prominent sandstone reef [SN 151064] with two seams of the Timber Vein Group well-exposed in the centre of the reef. Abundant plant remains occur on the bedding plane below the lower coal seam, including branching root systems known as *Stigmaria*. On the north-east side of the reef there is a prominent sheared coal lying on a minor thrust plane.

The Amman Marine Band outcrops in the next embayment where it is partially obscured by a rockslide. It marks the division between the Middle and Lower Coal Measures and forms a 30 cm thick mudstone layer rich in brachiopods and **goniatites**. It indicates a period of marine transgression when the sea inundated the coastal plain. The next small headland [SN 153065] marks the outcrop of the Rock Vein seam capping a series of siltstones with large ironstone nodules.

Continue along the beach to the next reef where the Garland Vein can be identified at the base of the cliff immediately south-west of the thrust plane that cuts through the reef [SN 155067]. There are numerous deformation features in the cliff face including slumps and pseudo-nodules where rounded clasts have fallen into the underlying mud.

Beyond the thrust zone are the remains of an old mine building on the top of the cliff. The Lower Level Vein outcrops here; note also the large fallen blocks of siltstone with symmetrical ripple marks on their upper surfaces. These ripples would have formed in a shallow water environment where there was no tidal influence. The cliffs here also contain large **septarian nodules** and several thin coal seams. The next embayment is marked by another cliff slide, beyond which is the southern flank of the broad anticline described in Locality 3.

5. Saundersfoot [SN 138047]

In the nineteenth and early twentieth centuries Saundersfoot was a major centre of the coal trade. When the new purpose-built harbour was opened in 1834, some 11,500 tons of coal were exported during that year. Both anthracite and culm were transported on the Saundersfoot Railway which provided a direct link to the inland collieries. Bonville's Court [SM 125054], about 1.5 km north-west of Saundersfoot, was one of the largest collieries in the Pembrokeshire coalfield. It opened in the 1850s and continued production until 1930. Production reached a peak of 42,500 tons in 1913 which represented around 80 per cent of the total output for Pembrokeshire at that time.

Today Saundersfoot is a busy seaside resort that you can easily reach from the A478 Tenby road. During the tourist season you should plan to get to the harbour car park early otherwise it will be full and you may have a frustrating drive around the town looking for spaces to park. There is of course, a multitude of cafes, ice-cream parlours, fish and chip restaurants and pubs to provide refreshment!

The cliffs to the south of the town expose the Lower Coal Measures that have been strongly folded by powerful Variscan earth movements. The rockwall forming the south side of the harbour is the almost vertical northern limb of an asymmetric anticline with its gently-dipping southern limb reaching down to beach level. Beyond this there are several examples in the cliffs of overfolds cut by low-angle thrust faults where thin coals, including the Stammers Vein, have been crushed between the underlying fireclay and massive sandstones above. These anthracitic coals have been subjected to considerable heat and pressure during orogenesis and many seams are so crushed that the coal is fragmented into 'culm'. This was used as a fuel in limekilns where quick lime was produced by heating limestone and releasing carbon dioxide [$CaCO_3 = CaO + CO_2$]. Quick lime was in great demand in the nineteenth century for both agricultural fertiliser and building mortar.

One of the most spectacular structures in this locality is the Ladies Cave Anticline [Fig. 9.7] that is about 500m south of the harbour. The strata here have been steeply folded asymmetrically but the structure is much eroded on the seaward side. This anticline is an example of a **chevron fold** where the long straight limbs are joined by a narrow hinge line. The more competent sandstone bands stand out prominently whilst the softer shales are worn back. The fold axis runs approximately in a E–W direction which is perpendicular to the direction of pressure of the Variscan orogeny.

About 200 metres south of the Ladies Cave Anticline there is a major overfold in the massively bedded sandstones that are thrust over a sequence of coal-bearing units that are

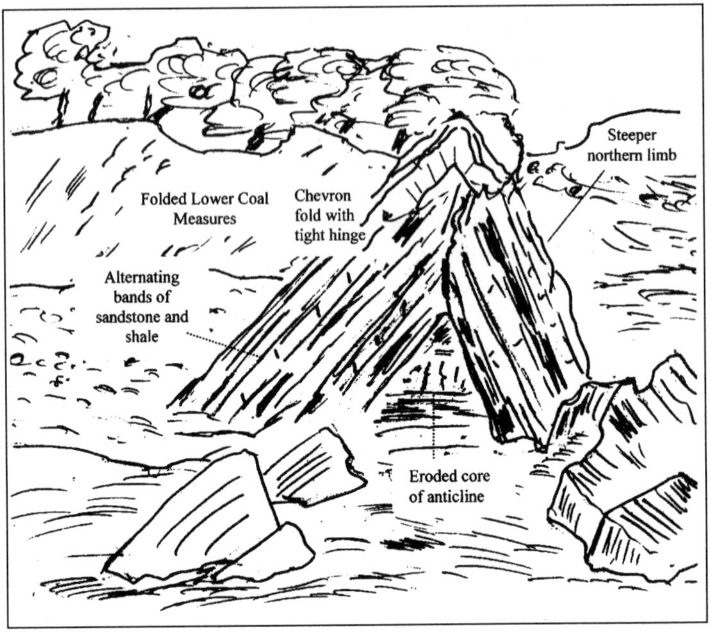

Fig. 9.7: The Ladies' Cave anticline, Saundersfoot

dipping southwards The erosive base of the sandstone is channelled into the underlying shales. There are ripple markings on the underside of the sandstone and evidence of lag gravels. Some of the shales are fossiliferous containing freshwater bivalves including the small dark mussel *Carbonicola communis*, which is a zone fossil of the Lower Coal Measures. You will see large red-brown concretions on the foreshore that are described as clay ironstones. These were much used in the early nineteenth century when iron smelting on the south Wales coalfield relied on local sources of ore.

Now, if you are feeling energetic it is a pleasant walk along the coast path through Rhode Wood and beyond to

Monkstone Point [SN 147033]. An alternative way is to drive from Saundersfoot to New Hedges and take the road to Trevayne Farm Caravan Park [SN 142032]. You should make for the south-eastern side of the headland where there are steps down to the sandy beach. Near the base of the steps you will notice that there are carbonaceous shales containing plant remains. These shales overlie a **seat earth** containing tiny rootlets. The seat earth is a layer of fireclay that represents an ancient soil or palaeosol.

You should next walk across the beach to the cave near the eastern end of the headland. Here you will see the base of the Monkstone Point Sandstone that forms a tightly-folded asymmetrical anticline with the southern limb dipping more steeply than the northern limb, and the axis trending approximately E–W. It may not immediately be obvious that this structure is an anticline since most of the sandstone is dipping to the south, but when you look around the corner of the headland you will see that the dip is clearly to the north. Look carefully at the erosive base of the sandstone that is formed of lag gravels containing a melange of quartz and ironstone pebbles mixed with fragments of coal and shale. These were obviously swirled around on the floor of a distributary channel. Now stand back and observe the core of the anticline. What do you see? Answer: a chaotic jumble of thin sandstones and shales. Why should this be? These beds have been caught between the jaws of a vice formed by the outer layers of the Monkton Point Sandstone as it was tightly folded by the Variscan earth movements. The rocks in the centre of the fold became compressed as the space available for them was progressively reduced. This caused the softer rocks such as shale to suffer ductile deformation as they were squeezed and stretched, whilst the harder and more resistant sandstone bands were broken under the intense pressure.

6. Waterwynch Bay [SN 137020]

You can get to this delightful little bay via a lane leading off the A478 about to 2 kms north of Tenby. It is best to park vehicles alongside the main road just south of the village of New Hedges [SN 129025]. Although the lane is private, there is a public right of way for walkers leading to a footpath that provides access to the beach. Alternatively you can walk along the coastal path from Tenby (1 km) and enjoy the fine views over Carmarthen Bay. However, please be aware that you can only walk safely along the foreshore from Waterwynch to North Beach, Tenby, at springs low tide when the tidal height is 1 metre or less. At neaps low tide it is usually possible to be able to reach Bowman's Point before turning back.

Waterwynch Bay lies wholly within the Lower Coal Measures and the cliffs on the north side of the bay demonstrate well-developed soft sediment deformation structures in a mudstone sequence. There are rafts of slumped sediment forming a melange of broken beds that must have moved down a depositional slope under the influence of gravity (see photo on page 62). Convolute bedding within the sediments suggests rapid deposition and liquefaction as quicksand under high water table conditions. Blocks of consolidated coarser material have clearly sunk down into the liquified sediment forming a chaotic jumble of rocks set in the deformed, contorted mudstone.

Next you should walk across the beach and negotiate the southern headland where the bedded Lower Coal Measure sandstones dip south at about 50° [Fig. 9.8]. As you enter North Cove you will notice a large rockslide which has occurred down a major bedding plane in the sandstones. Immediately to the south of this feature the ribs of several siltstone bands can be picked out on the beach striking E–W. These bands dip steeply south in the cliff face and pass into dark-coloured shales containing the *Gastrioceras subcrenatum* marine band that marks a major marine transgression. A few metres to the south there is a distinctive thin coal seam, thrust and contorted but containing abundant plant remains. This seam must lie near the top of the Telpyn Point Sandstone Formation since the *subcrenatum* band marks the division between the Lower Coal Measures and the underlying Marros Group.

The Telpyn Point Sandstone Formation is composed largely of repeated coarsening upward sequences of deltaic sediments and turbidite fan deposits. Walk over to the sea-cave at SN 137018 where there are several well-defined channel sandstone beds. These sandstones show extensive ripple-marking and if you stand back on the beach you will see that the beds are dipping steeply south. However, the ripples are on a north-facing bedding planes in the cave entrance, and given that the ripples must have formed originally on the horizontal top surface of the beds this means that the beds have subsequently been rotated through more than 90° and are now inverted. These sandstone beds form the northern limb of a major overturned anticlinal structure, the southern limb of which outcrops on the north side of First Point [Fig. 9.8].

Your next stop is only about 30 metres south of the cave, in Bowman's Cove [SN 136017] where there is a good exposure of a turbidite sequence. Look for the flute casts on the surface of one of the thicker turbidite sandstones that dip southwards. It has been suggested that these beds represent the deposits of a turbidite fan on the slopes of the delta front.

At Bowman's Point there are some spectacular chevron folds in a faulted crumple zone on the north-east face; however, most of the headland is composed of southward-dipping siltstones and fine sandstones which extend into Second Bay. Here the core of the main anticline is formed of siltstones and fine-grained sandstones of the Bishopston

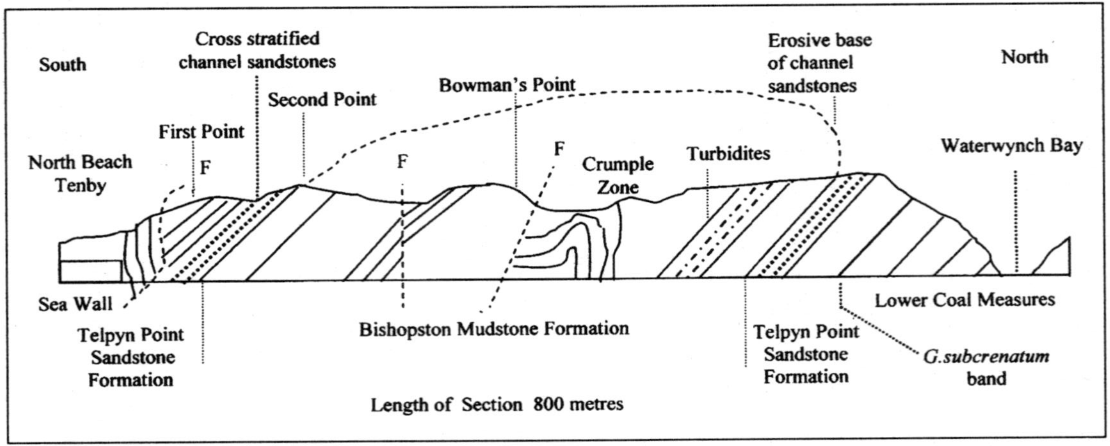

Fig. 9.8: Geological section from First Point to Waterwynch Bay

Mudstone Formation, which is the oldest unit in this coastal section. Unfortunately, the eastern limb of the anticline has been removed by a strong reverse fault on the south side of Bowman's Point.

Now you should walk around Second Point and into First Bay to examine the sandstones that form strong ribs cutting across the beach. These represent several channel deposits with strong erosional surfaces at the base of each cross-stratified bed. These are separated by thin interchannel siltstones. Finally, as you reach First Point you will recognise that the Telpyn Point Sandstone has reappeared; last seen in the cave to the north of Bowman's Point, and removed by erosion from the central part of the section! Here at First Point it is over 22 metres thick and is folded into a tight, overturned syncline cut by several thrusts. The vertical cliff against the sea wall shows a distinctive channel lag deposit made up of well-rounded ironstone pebbles and mudstone clasts which marks the erosive base of the sandstone. On the north side of the headland there are well-developed tabular cross-stratified channel sandstones. The individual beds are about 1 metre thick with well-defined erosional planes dipping 40° S. These sandstones represent the deposits of a fluvial distributary system at the mouth of a delta.

10
Upper Carboniferous rocks on the coast of St Bride's Bay

The western margin of the Pembrokeshire coalfield on the coast of St Brides Bay is even more contorted and deformed by the Variscan orogeny than the eastern side. It is difficult to recognise the overall synclinal structure since only the northern limb of the fold appears to be exposed and so most of the strata dip towards the south. The Lower Coal Measures along the southern boundary of the coalfield are mostly crumpled beneath Precambrian diorites and Lower Silurian sediments that have been thrust northwards by the Johnston Thrust [Fig. 10.1]. The folded and faulted rocks in the cliffs around Little Haven and Broad Haven clearly demonstrate the power of the Variscan earth movements. Further north at Druidston Haven, Ordovician strata has been faulted and uplifted against the Marros Group as a result of earlier Caledonian earth movements.

The only outcrop of Upper Coal Measures in Pembrokeshire occurs in the detached section of the coalfield between Nolton Haven and Newgale. Here the rock sequence is usually referred to as the Pennant Sandstone Formation and it contains far more thick sandstone units than the Lower Coal Measures in the main coalfield. These sandstones represent the deposits of meandering rivers flowing through heavily braided channels. The sandstones are interbedded with mudstones and several valuable anthracite seams including

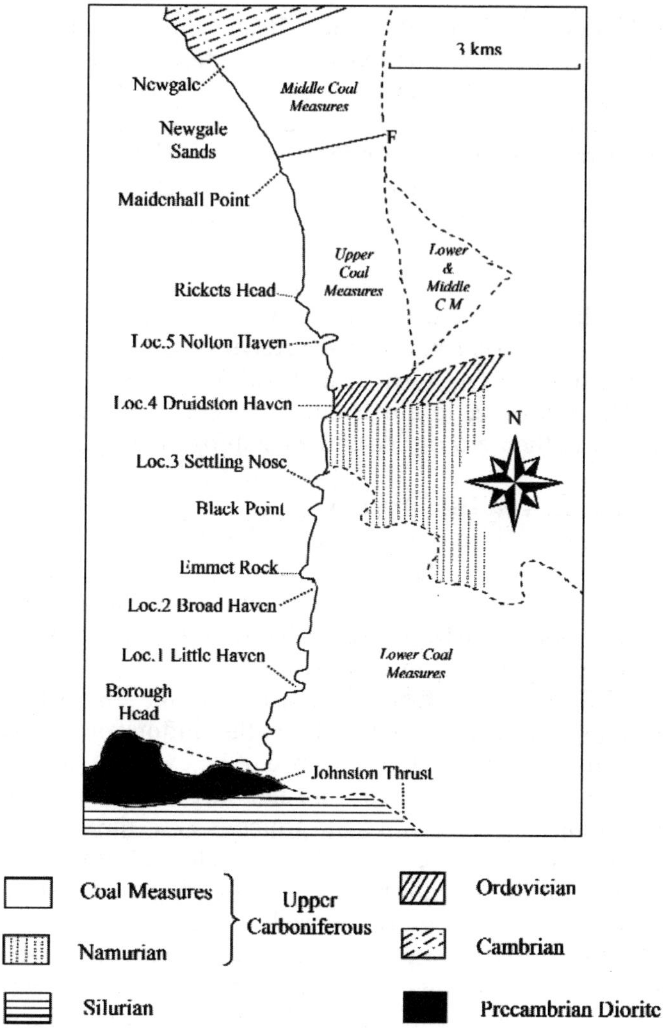

Fig. 10.1: The geology of St Brides Bay coast

the Black Cliff Vein and the Rickets Head Vein [Fig. 10.2]. The latter were mined extensively in the nineteenth century and exported from Nolton Haven. At Trefrane Cliff colliery seams were worked under the sea where there are probably considerable reserves still waiting to be extracted. However, the primitive mining technology at the time limited exploitation and accidents were frequent. One of the worst disasters occurred in February 1844, a few miles inland at Landshipping when forty miners were drowned as the tidal waters of the Daugleddau entered the mine workings. A monument to the victims of this accident can be seen today on the old quayside at Landshipping (see Chapter 12, Locality 3).

The following localities illustrate some of the main features of the western side of the Pembrokeshire coalfield.

1. Little Haven [SM 857129]

This pretty little harbour on the south side of St Brides Bay can be reached from Haverfordwest by taking the B4327 road. At Rosepool [SM 862115] turn right onto the narrow lane that leads down to Little Haven where there is a small car park and toilets opposite the St Brides Inn.

Walk south-west along the coast path from the harbour and make for Musselwick Bay. From the clifftop you can see Borough Head [SM 840127] formed of Precambrian diorite. The Johnston Thrust runs from the base of the headland across Goultrop Roads to a small promontory on the west side of Musselwick Bay where it appears about halfway up the cliff face separating the underlying crushed Carboniferous strata from the overthrust diorite intrusion. Walk about halfway down the steep narrow path that leads into the north-east side of Musselwick Bay, then stop to get an overview of the beach structures at low tide [Fig. 10.3]. The sandstone reefs outline the pattern of the overturned Musselwick syncline. You will notice that the E–W axis of the fold plunges seawards and the

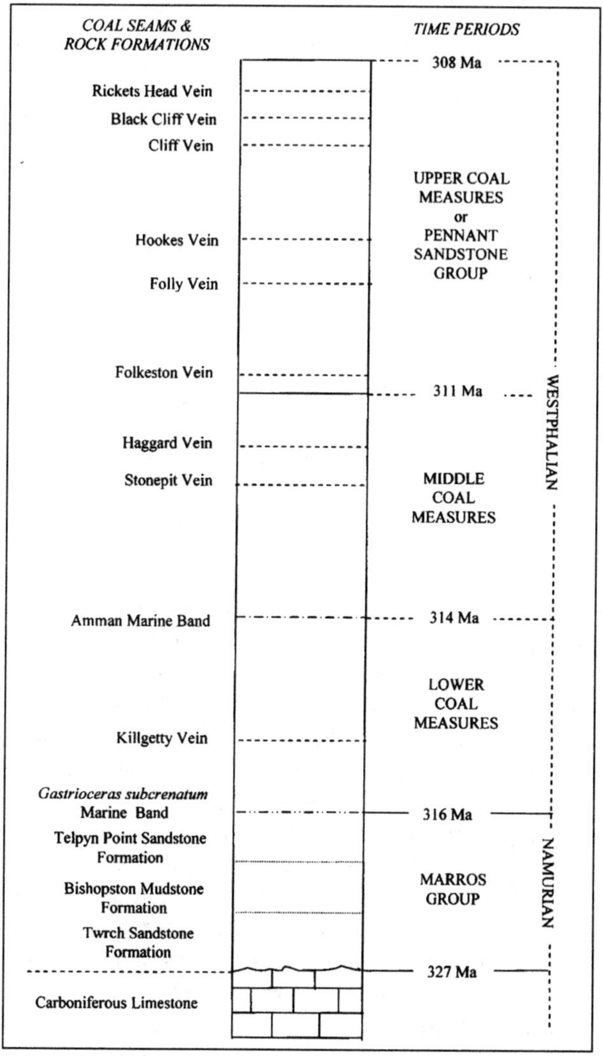

Fig. 10.2: Stratigraphical column for the Upper Carboniferous rocks of St Brides Bay

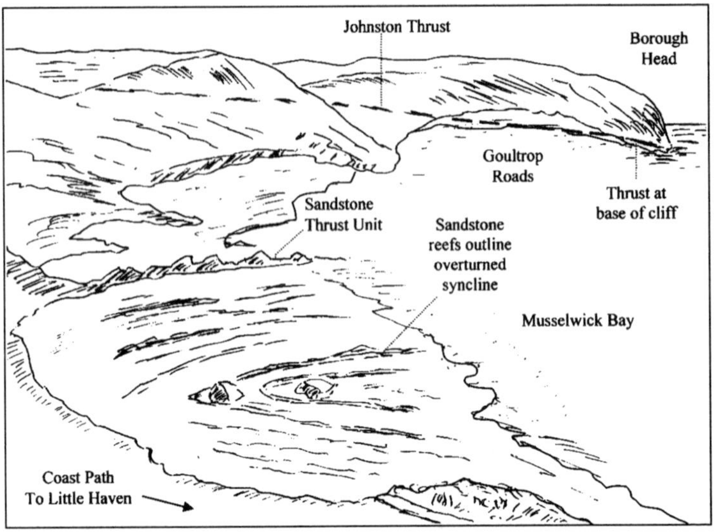

Fig. 10.3: View westwards across Musselwick Bay

nose points as a V shape in the opposite direction. The main ribs all appear to be dipping north-eastwards although those beds to the south-west of the synclinal axis are actually inverted. On the west side of the bay there are several secondary thrust units aligned parallel to the Johnston Thrust; they are marked by highly-inclined sandstone reefs striking NW–SE across the foreshore.

Return to Little Haven for refreshment, then walk across to the north side of the harbour which is cut by a strong reverse fault that dips at about 50° to the south and displays clear slickenside structures. The headland is formed of a thick sandstone unit of the Lower Coal Measures that is folded into a large asymmetrical anticline. The fold is orientated along an axis plunging to the west with its core having been partially removed by mining in the cave known as Fox Hole. A coal seam and the overlying shales in the cave are now being actively eroded by the sea. An adit on the north side of the anticline about 3 metres above beach level was probably a drainage and ventilation shaft for the workings behind the cliff.

Make your way into the bay known as The Settlands between Little Haven and Broad Haven. Here there are several cyclothem units that are folded asymmetrically and overturned by thrusting. The Amman marine band outcrops on the north side of the bay. It marks the top of the Lower Coal Measures but it is repeated by thrusting several times to the south.

2. Broad Haven [SM 862136]

This is a popular holiday resort with a wide sandy beach about 1 km north of Little Haven and there is a large car park and toilets at the northern end of the seafront. The best cliff sections are reached from the north side of the beach. Between Emmet Rock [SM 860141] and Settling Nose 1.5 kms to the north, the Lower Coal Measures dip southwards, hence the beds become older to the north and can be traced down to the *Gastrioceras subcrenatum* marine band at the base of the sequence.

The main cliffs immediately north of Emmets Rock display several thrust-displaced anticlinal overfolds showing evidence of the intense pressure from the south. Adjacent to the isolated stack and natural arch known as Dens Door, there is a much photographed classic thrust tip fold [SM 860142] [Fig. 10.4]. Initially an overturned asymmetrical anticlinal fold developed, followed by the propagation of a thrust as the folded limb in the hanging wall was carried forward along the thrust plane for several metres beyond the underlying base of the fold.

The Sleek Stone [SM 860144] is immediately north of Dens Door. I suggest that if possible you visit this feature at spring low tide, when you can walk safely around the base of

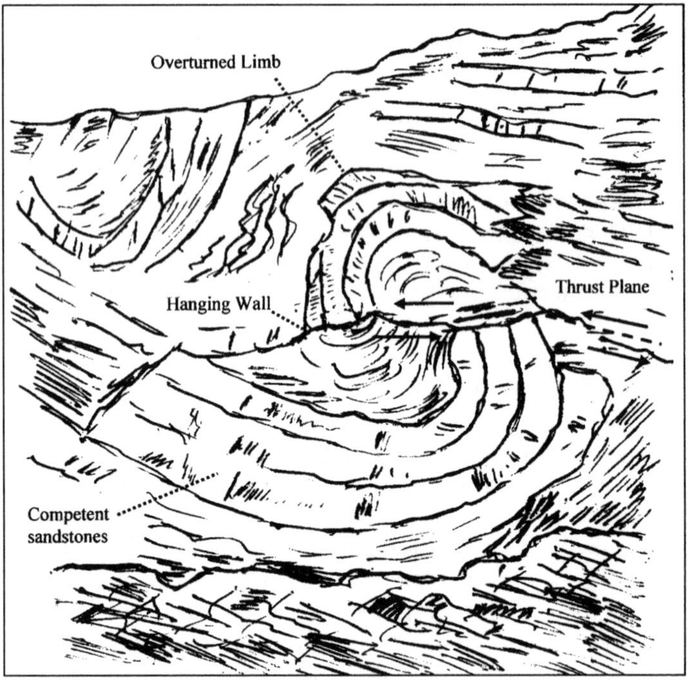

Fig. 10.4: Thrust tip fold in Lower Coal Measures near Dens Door

the structure. Superficially, when viewed from the sea-shore, the Sleek Stone appears to be a long gently-sloping rock platform dipping at about 30° SW with its long axis orientated approximately NW-SE. However, walk to the northern end of the outcrop and you will see that marine erosion has uncovered a magnificent monoclinal fold with a vertical wall forming its north-eastern limb [Fig. 10.5]. Excellent ripple-bedding has been preserved on the vertical sandstone wall.

The axis of the fold is plunging seawards at about 10° NW. A major thrust at the base of the Sleekstone overlies several coarsening up-cycles that include a distinctive 2-metre buff-coloured limestone containing non-marine bivalves (cf

Amroth Limestone). The Kilgetty Vein seam occurs a few metres above the limestone but its outcrop is much obscured by downwash in the soft shales. Several coarsening upward cyclothem units occur along the coast towards Black Point. Each unit is capped by a thin coal seam that is often undercut by marine erosion. The sediments were probably deposited in a lagoonal coastal plain environment that was subject to marine transgression from time to time.

3. Settling Nose [SM 858157]

You will be able to reach this locality either by walking along the coast path from Broad Haven or by driving along the narrow coastal road. There is a small car park at Haroldston Chins [SM 863163]. It is very difficut to access the foreshore from the coast path at Settling Nose. However, you can get a good view from the top of the cliffs looking down on the inclined wave-cut platform formed by the Telpyn Point

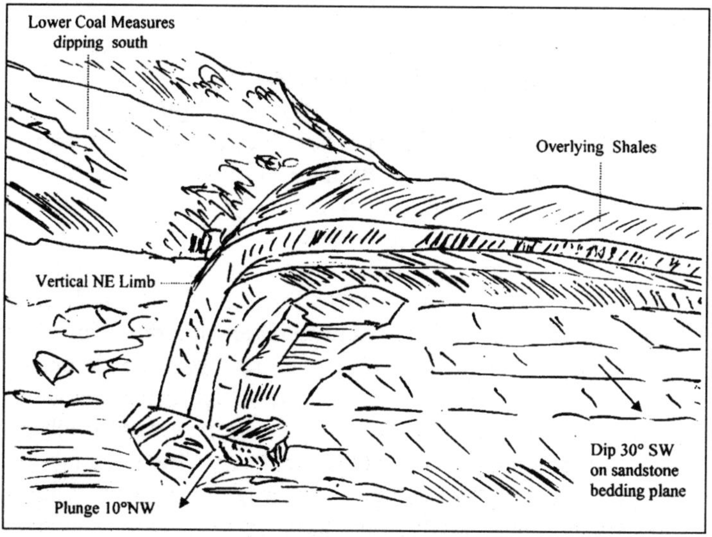

Fig. 10.5: The Sleekstone monoclinal fold

Sandstone Formation at the top of the Namurian sequence [Fig. 10.6]. The highest sandstone bed is known as the Farewell Rock and the *Gastrioceras subcrenatum* marine band lies immediately above this, marking the beginning of the Lower Coal Measures that dip southwards towards Broad Haven (see Locality 2).

Walk about 500 metres further north to the spectacular landslipped area of Haroldston Chins [Fig. 10.7]. Here the Telpyn Point Sandstone Formation overlies the Bishopston Mudstone Formation in cliffs up to 80 metres high. Since the beds are dipping seawards at about 30° SW, the sandstones are slowly sliding over the underlying impervious shales as percolating surface water lubricates the interface between the strata. Fissures opening up, close to the coast path, bear witness to this process of **mass movement** along this stretch of the clifftop. Please do not get too near to the cliff edge, which can be unstable, particularly after winter rains! (See photo on page 62.)

4. Druidston Haven [SM 862170]

Druidston Haven is another favourite place of mine, somewhat off the beaten track, but you can get to it along the coast path or via the narrow lane linking Broad Haven to Nolton Haven (see photo on page 63). Geologically it is significant in that the haven is eroded into Mydrim Shales of Upper Ordovician age, that are bounded on either side by parallel normal faults downthrowing to the north and south respectively [Fig. 10.8]. The central block of Ordovician rocks is upthrust to form a **horst**, which separates the main Pembrokeshire coalfield to the south, from the detached portion to the north. Furthermore, the horst is structurally an asymmetric anticline with its steeper limb to the south. It was formed during the Caledonian orogeny and was later subjected to Variscan deformation.

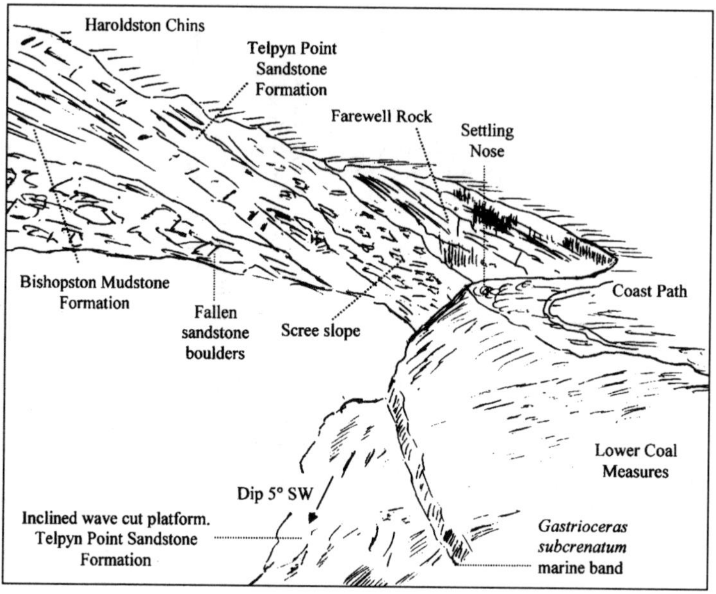

Fig. 10.6: View looking north over the cliffs at Settling Nose

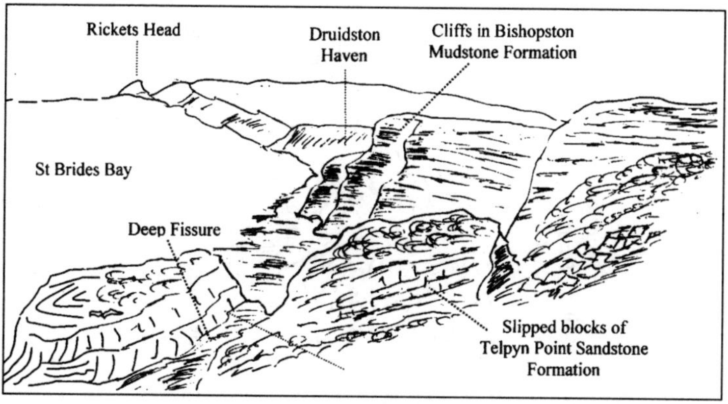

Fig. 10.7: View northwards over the Haroldston Chins landslip

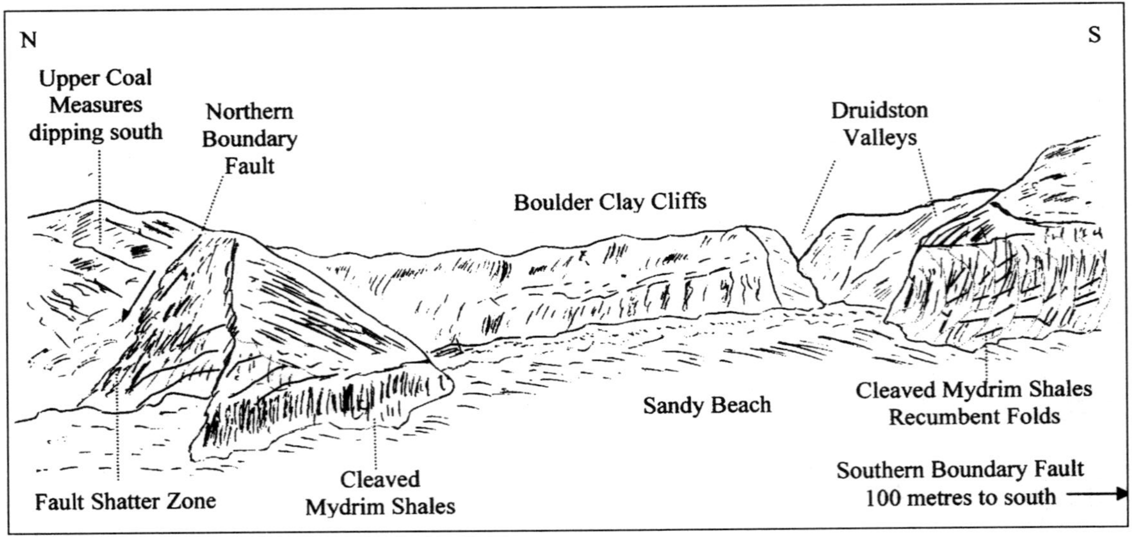

Fig. 10.8: View looking east towards Druidston Haven

You can park on the roadside near to the sharp bend at SM 864170 and walk down to the foreshore on the north side of Druidston Haven to examine the strata around the northern boundary fault. The Upper Coal Measure sandstones can be seen dipping south on the downthrow side of the fault whereas the Mydrim shales are dipping gently north on the upthrow side of the fault. The steeply-inclined slaty cleavage within the Ordovician rocks was produced by the Caledonian earth movements. Pleistocene deposits now occupy much of the two Druidston valleys and mask the underlying Ordovician rocks that form the horst (see Chapter 11, Locality 7).

Next walk to the south side of the haven where the steep southern limb of the Caledonian anticline is exposed in a 200-metre cliff section. South-facing **recumbent folds** have been produced by the refolding of earlier structures during the Variscan orogeny and the Caledonian cleavage that originally dipped north is now seen to be dipping in the opposite direction! Several south-dipping normal faults cut the folds, beyond which the strata are vertical and much deformed. The slates become brecciated where they are in faulted contact with the Bishopston Mudstone Formation. The southern boundary fault can be traced inland up the steep valley that leads to Druidston Villas.

Walk southwards along the beach to the first promontory known as Druidston Chins [SM 860165]. The stepped cliff cross-profile reflects the differential resistance to weathering of the massively-bedded sandstones and the softer shales that are dipping gently seawards (about 5° SW). The sandstones have a vertical profile in contrast to the shales that have a debris slope of approximately 45°. Furthermore, the cliff top sandstones are well-bedded and strongly fissured which allows water to pass through to lubricate the shales below, thus providing suitable conditions for gravity sliding and rock falls. The sandstones exhibit cross-stratification and channelling; evidence of their deltaic origin.

5. Nolton Haven [SM 859186]

This small inlet is located at the south end of the detached northern section of the Pembrokeshire coalfield. During the nineteenth century coastal sailing vessels, mostly sloops up to 40 feet long, would be moored to posts in Nolton Haven to be loaded with anthracite and culm. However, there was no deep, sheltered port near to the coalmines on St Brides Bay and this restrained the development of the coal trade. Even so Trefrane colliery was in production from 1854 onwards and in the 1890s the neighbouring Trefrane Cliff mine had considerable workings extending under the sea.

There is a small car park and toilets adjacent to The Mariner's Inn at the head of Nolton Haven. You should walk across to the north-west side of the inlet to examine the cliffs that display strata of the Upper Coal Measures that is also known as the Pennant Sandstone Formation. The beds consist of alternating siltstones and fine-grained **ferruginous** sandstones that produce fining-upwards sequences on either side of the Black Cliff Vein which is exposed near to the headland. This seam has been shattered and reduced to culm where it has been overthrust and thickened near the base of the cliffs. Several cross-cutting channels and well-developed cross-stratification reflect the delta plain environment in which these beds were deposited.

You will notice that since the beds dip gently to the south-west they are also getting younger in this direction. Hence the Folkeston Vein is the lowest seam of the Upper Coal Measures and this crops out in the north-east of the field, whereas the younger Black Cliff Vein can be seen in Nolton Haven, and the Rickets Head Vein, which is near the top of the sequence, forms part of the western headland.

Now climb up the coast path onto the clifftop to the north of Nolton Haven. Take time to admire the spectacular undercutting in Davy Williams Haven [SM 856185] and view the prominent promontory of Rickets Head [Fig.10.9]. Here we are at the very top of the Upper Coal Measures where a series of four or five cyclothem units can be identified on the south-east face of the headland (see photo on page 63). Each unit contains a shale bed followed by sandstone, and finally a thin coal seam. The Rickets Head Vein dips seawards below the headland and was worked commercially at Black Cliff colliery, the site of which is marked by a spoil heap at SM 857191. Continue your walk along the path to the highest point above Black Cliff where there is an excellent view northwards towards Maidenhall Point and the long sweep of Newgale Sands. About 400 metres further north near Trefrane Cliff, the path descends to beach level in a steep-sided valley below Cliff Cottages [Fig. 10.10]. Here the Cliff Vein outcrops on the

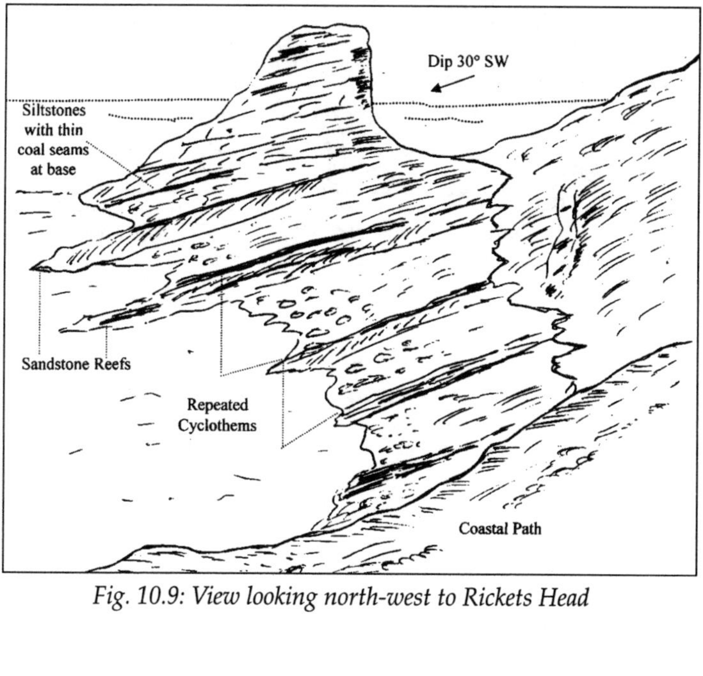

Fig. 10.9: View looking north-west to Rickets Head

valley sides (though now much obscured by vegetation) forming a V pattern in the direction of dip towards the sea. This valley was the site of Trefrane Cliff Colliery [SM 857197] that is still marked by the engine-house chimney standing close to a large spoil heap extending down to the foreshore.

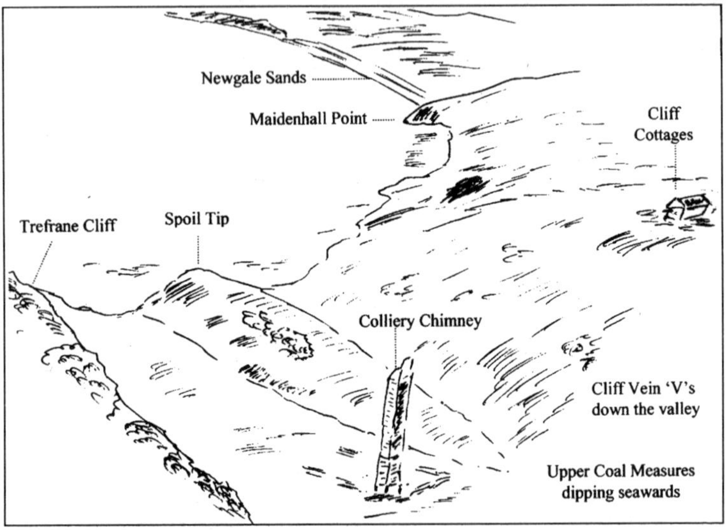

Fig. 10.10: View northwards from Trefrane Cliff

11
Quaternary coastal landforms in Pembrokeshire

The Quaternary Period is divided into the Pleistocene and Holocene epochs that may be further divided into stages relating to glacial and interglacial periods [Fig. 11.1]. However, in recent years, a more detailed succession has been recorded from deep oceanic sediment cores using isotope studies. They suggest that the major warm and cold stages are controlled by variations in solar radiation due to slight deviations in the earth's orbit known as Milankovitch cycles.

The Pleistocene began some 2.5 Ma ago and lasted until 10,000 years BP during which time there were repeated cycles of global climatic change marked by glacial episodes when sea level was low, and interglacials when sea level rose in response to global warming. The Holocene represents a temperate climatic stage that so far has lasted for some 10,000 years since the end of the last glaciation of Britain.

The earliest known glaciation of south-west Wales occurred at some time prior to the Ipswichian Stage (128–122,000 BP), possibly starting around 140,000 BP when Irish Sea ice advanced south-eastwards towards Pembrokeshire, overriding Mynydd Preseli and sweeping over the lowlands of the south coast. Local Welsh ice moving south-west down the Teifi and Tywi valleys would also have contributed to the overall depth of ice cover. Unfortunately, there are very few coherent deposits of till that can be confidently assigned to

CHRONOSTRATIGRAPHIC STAGES	CLIMATIC EVENTS	DRIFT DEPOSITS/LANDFORMS
Flandrian	Temperate phase	Blown sand/alluvium/peat Drowned river valleys, Milford Haven Submerged forest, Marros Sands
10,000 BP		
Late Devensian	Periglacial Irish Sea Glaciation [2]	Upper Head, Abermawr & Druidston Fluvioglacial sand & gravels, Mullock Bridge & Grugiau Cemmaes Irish Sea Till, Abermawr, Poppit Sands & Druidston Gwaun Meltwater Channels
26,000 BP		
Middle Devensian		
60,000 BP		
Early Devensian	Periglacial	Lower Blocky Head Abermawr
122,000 BP		
Ipswichian	Temperate Interglacial	Raised Beach deposits Poppit Sands & Broad Haven [Bosherston]
128,000 BP		
	Irish Sea Glaciation [1]	Erratic pebbles and boulders West Angle Bay Till

Fig. 11.1: Quaternary Stratigraphy in south-west Wales

this early glacial stage since much of older drift has been removed by later glaciation. However, at West Angle Bay a grey blue clay containing clasts of igneous rock was examined in an excavation at the base of the Quaternary sequence by Dixon in 1921 and later by Bowen in 1977. This glacial deposit is a **boulder clay** or **till** and is overlaid by **raised beach** materials that are thought to have been formed during the Ipswichian interglacial stage. Further evidence for the advance of the ice at this time comes from the occurrence of **erratic** boulders and pebbles that have been carried by the Irish Sea ice sheet from as far afield as north Wales and southern Scotland. You can look at a collection of erratics in the graveyard of Flimston Chapel [SR 924956] on the Castlemartin peninsula. They were found scattered over the surrounding limestone plateau surface and include a gabbro from St David's Head and a dolerite from Mynydd Preseli. At Whitesand Bay there are igneous erratic boulders sealed beneath the raised beach, hence using the **Law of Superposition**, these erratics must predate the Ipswichian beach deposits and have been transported during the earlier glaciation

Sea level may have risen by some 6 metres during this warmer Ipswichian interglacial stage. The term raised beach implies an **isostatic** uplift as is the case on the west coast of Scotland, but in Pembrokeshire the beach platforms are thought to have been produced simply by a eustatic rise in sea level; so they could be more appropriately referred to as relic beaches. The best example of a raised beach in Pembrokeshire is seen at Poppit Sands on the Teifi estuary where it rests on an eroded rock platform about 3 metres above present mean high water. Other raised beach localities include Broad Haven (Bosherston) and Ogof Golchfa (Porth Glais).

At all these localities the cemented beach material is overlaid by a deposit of the Lower Blocky Head. This is well-developed at Aber Mawr, although no raised beach deposits are present at this site. However, the blocky **head** consists of unsorted angular rock debris that has been produced by **solifluction**, a process involving the downslope movement of the water-saturated regolith under periglacial conditions. This frozen tundra-type environment existed during the Lower Devensian Stage (122,000–60,000 BP) that followed the Ipswichian interglacial.

The next major event in south-west Wales appears to be the Late Devensian (26,000–10,000 BP) glaciation, when the area was affected both by the Irish Sea ice sheet and local Welsh ice streams. The Irish Sea ice front probably did not reach the south Pembrokeshire coast where there is a conspicuous absence of glacial till in the exposed sections. In 1929 Charlesworth proposed that an elongated mass of glacial debris that he called the 'South Wales End **Moraine**' extended along the north Pembrokeshire coast. Indeed it has been argued that the upland landscape around Carn Ingli, 3 kms south of Newport, shows no sign of being glaciated and so supports the idea that the ice margin generally followed the north coast of the county [Fig. 11.2]. However, other researchers have suggested that the ice sheet reached as far south as the Cleddau estuary (Milford Haven) and in coastal localities such as Poppit Sands, Abermawr, Whitesand Bay and Druidston Haven, the characteristic blue-grey clay Irish Sea till is well-exposed. It contains a suite of erratics with a matrix of calcareous marine silt and clay together with marine mollusc fragments that suggest the ice sheet was moving from the northwest across Cardigan Bay southeast towards the Welsh coastline. There is a raised beach platform near the lifeboat station at Parrog in Newport Bay that has been polished and striated by the advancing Irish Sea ice sheet.

During the initial advance of the ice, the existing river drainage systems were disrupted as ice dammed proglacial lakes became established. The most extensive of these was Llyn Teifi that occupied the estuary of Afon Teifi and was blocked by the ice front to the west. Borehole logs show that silts and clays over 75 metres thick were deposited within this lake basin. There are also mounds and esker ridges of stratified fluvioglacial sands and gravels that were deposited as meltwater sediment when the ice front receded. These topographical features can now be seen on either side of the Teifi valley at Trefigin Quarry, Monington [SN 139435] and Banc-y-Warren [SN 204475]. Another well-preserved section through a fluvioglacial deposit was exposed in the 1970s in a gravel pit cut into the surface of the kame terrace at Mullock

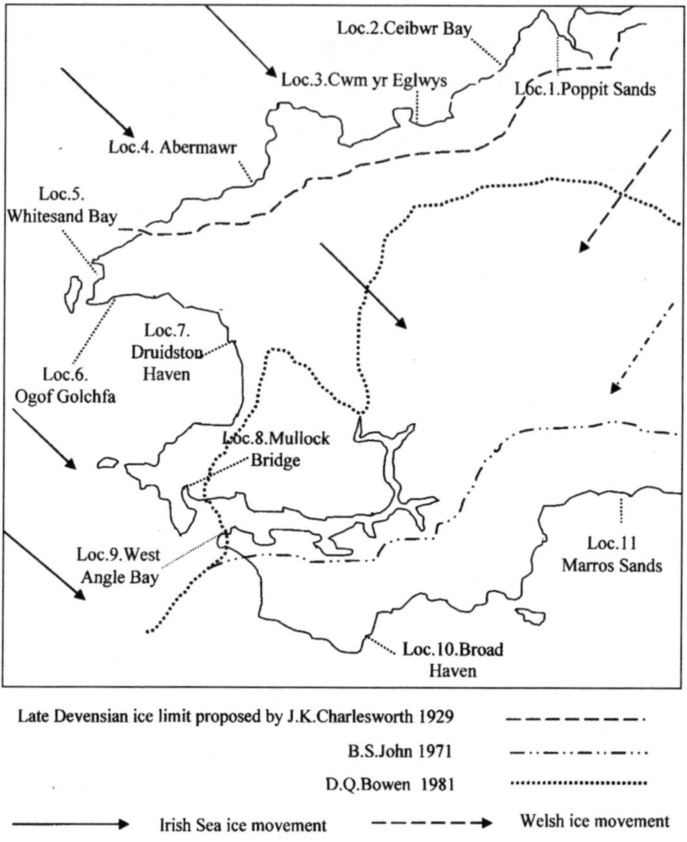

Fig. 11.2: Quaternary localities and late Devensian ice sheet movements in Pembrokeshire

Bridge [SM 811080] near Dale. A line of hummocks formed of stratified pebbly sand at Grugiau Cemmaes [SN 126415] has been interpreted as an esker deposited in a sinuous channel by a subglacial stream.

The spectacular Gwaun–Jordanston meltwater channel system in the Fishguard area was formerly thought to have been cut by the overflow waters from the proglacial lakes associated with the Irish Sea ice front during the Late Devensian, but it is now considered more likely that the system was eroded by subglacial meltwater flowing beneath and marginal to the ice sheet. The waters escaped westwards along the Gwaun valley into Fishguard Bay and southwards through the Scleddau overflow channel [Fig. 11.3].

Towards the end of the Devensian Stage, periglacial conditions returned to south-west Wales with the formation of the Upper Head deposits which may also include a rubble drift, or clay containing various-sized boulders of glacial origin.

The last stage in the Quaternary story is dominated by the Flandrian marine transgression of the Holocene period.

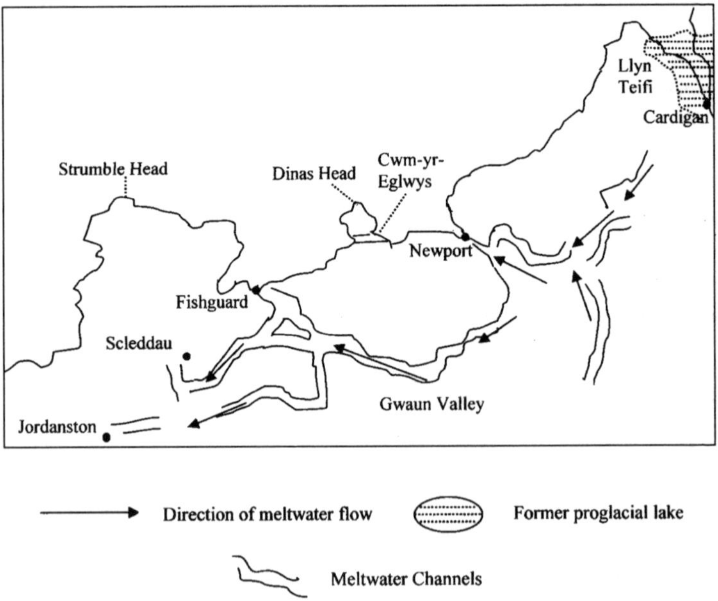

Fig. 11.3: The Gwaun-Jordanston meltwater channel system

Although the rate of eustatic sea level rise was greatest during the early Holocene, at that time sea level was considerably lower than at present and it was not until around 6000 BP that the present coastline of the Irish Sea Basin took shape. Submerged forests and peat bogs below mean low water bear witness to a former lower sea level (see Locality 11). Eventually the rising sea level caused the drowning of the lower reaches of pre-existing rivers and produced rias such as are seen at Milford Haven and Solva. Coastal features produced by recent marine erosion include wave-cut platforms, cliff lines, natural arches, stacks, geos (faulted inlets) and caves. These geomorphological phenomena are particularly well-developed along the limestone coast of south Pembrokeshire and in the turbidite sandstones of the north Pembrokeshire coast. The Green Bridge of Wales is probably the best-known example of a natural arch in south-west Wales. Deposition occurs in sheltered bays and estuaries where mud, sand and shingle accumulate to form mudflats, sandy beaches, stormbeaches and windblown dunes. Broomhill Burrows at Freshwater West provides an excellent example of a windblown dune complex. At Newgale on St Brides Bay, there is a well-developed stormbeach formed of shingle, pebbles and cobbles that have been driven onshore by the prevailing south-westerly winds and longshore drift.

The following Quaternary localities around the Pembrokeshire coast are well worth visiting. Some of these localities have been mentioned earlier with reference to their outcrops of bedrock, but here the emphasis is on the drift deposits that overlie the solid geology.

1. Poppit Sands [SN 145490]

Poppit Sands are located on the south-west side of the Teifi estuary about 3 kms north of St Dogmaels. The Quaternary sequence at Poppit Sands is exposed for several hundred metres between Cei-bach and Trwyn Careg-ddu, where the steeply-dipping turbidite mudstones and sandstones of the Dinas Island Formation are extensively bevelled to form a rock platform (see photo on page 64). This feature is about 3 metres above the present high-water mark and is thought to have been eroded during the Ipswichian interglacial. Cemented pebbles and cobbles, much stained by iron and manganese, form a raised beach resting directly on the bevelled surface [Fig. 11.4]. These sediments are up to 1.7 metres thick and are considered to be of Ipswichian age on the basis of **foraminifera** obtained from the cemented beach material. Overlying the raised beach is about 6 metres of Lower Blocky Head, a periglacial deposit of poorly-sorted subangular clasts of local rock. Finally, there is the Irish Sea till, 2 metres of boulder clay containing erratics and shell fragments deposited during the Late Devensian glaciation when Irish Sea ice extended across the coastal areas of the north Pembrokeshire coast.

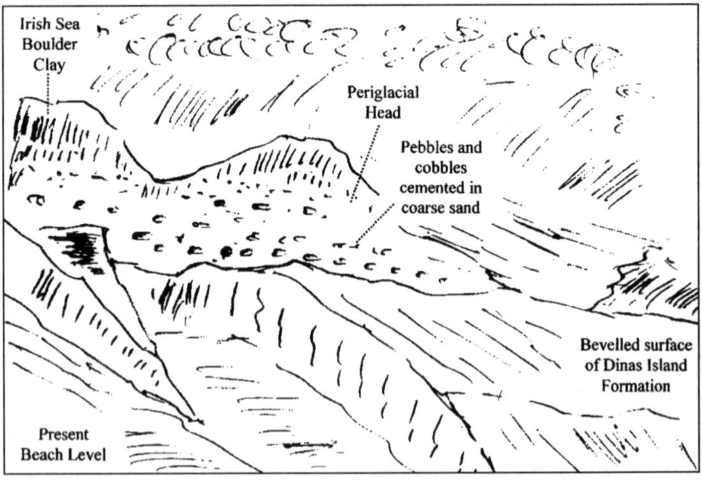

Fig. 11.4: The raised beach at Poppit Sands

2. Ceibwr Bay [SN 108458]

This bay lies about 7 kms south-west of Cemaes Head and can be accessed from the village of Moylgrove. On the south side of the bay there are several metres of cemented gravel and sands resting on a bedrock platform. The ill-sorted pebbles, angular clasts and cobbles are mainly vein quartz, sandstone and mudstone derived from local bedrock but there are also some exotic volcanic and granitic fragments. The clasts are partly consolidated by a red ferruginous cement. These drift deposits are thought to have been formed prior to the Late Devensian glaciation as local **regolith**, scree and alluvial sediment. The valley that is followed by the road from Moylgrove to Ceibwr Bay is probably a meltwater channel that drained the ice sheet occupying the higher ground to the north.

3. Cwm-yr-Eglwys [SN 010399]

The village is situated on the south-east corner of Dinas Island and can be reached by a narrow lane from the A487 Fishguard to Newport road. From the car park follow the coastal path westwards towards Pwllgwaelod through a steep-sided flat-bottomed marshy valley. This is part of the Gwaun–Jordanston meltwater system cut by sub-glacial streams during the advance of Irish Sea ice across north Pembrokeshire in Late Devensian times. The meltwater channel is floored by sediments deposited by sub-glacial streams. Overlying peat beds have yielded pollen grains that have provided evidence for reconstructing climatic change since the last ice age.

4. Aber Mawr [SM 883346]

Aber Mawr can be approached from the A487 Fishguard to St David's road. Leave the main road near Mathry and follow the narrow lane northwards for 2 kms bearing left just beyond Parc-y-nole farm. Park near to the where the lane takes a sharp bend, next to the National Trust sign at the entrance to Pen-yr-alt wood [SM 885337]. Walk along the woodland path that leads to the south side of Aber Mawr beach. You can see the Quaternary section above the northern end of the present stormbeach where there is a drift-cliff about 13 metres high [Fig. 11.5]. The latter rests on the eroded surface of vertically-cleaved Lower Ordovician mudstones. The lower part of the drift-cliff is composed of Lower Blocky Head with angular erratic blocks and rock fragments, above which there is a wedge up to 2.5 metres thick, of Irish Sea boulder clay known as the Aber Mawr Till (see photo on page 64). This is a blue-grey plastic clay that is highly calcareous. It contains abundant fragments of marine molluscs and carbonised wood, plus a variety of rounded igneous erratics from southern Scotland and the Lake District providing strong evidence for the

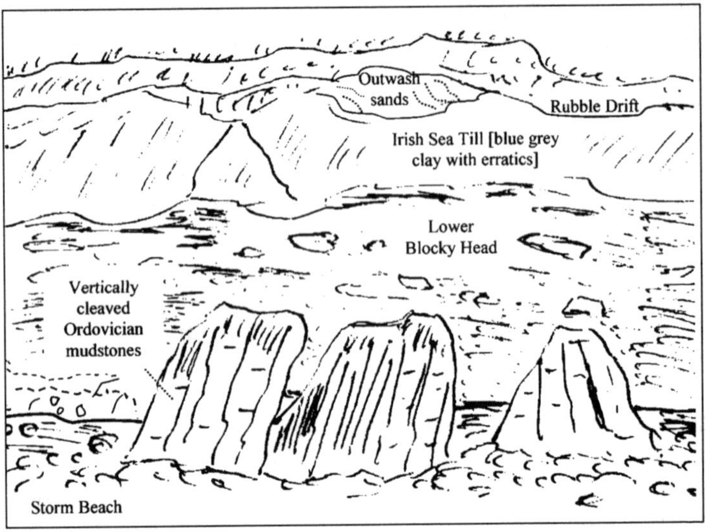

Fig. 11.5: Quaternary deposits in the Aber Mawr cliffs

movement of Irish Sea ice sheet southwards towards Pembrokeshire. The till is overlaid by a bed of outwash sands and gravels laid down by the retreating ice sheet. Above this lies a rubble drift topped by a sandy loam and blown sand. The rubble drift was described by T. J. Jehu in 1904 as 'a rubbly clay, full of boulders of all sizes, most of which are angular and subangular, and derived from rocks in the locality'. Today this drift material is recognised as the Upper Head that is a periglacial solifluction deposit incorporating both glacial and fluvioglacial rock fragments.

5. Whitesands Bay [SM 733272]

The bay is reached via the B4583 from St David's. Walk from the car park southwards along the beach for about 100 metres to where the vertical beds of the Menevian Group are planed off and overlaid by drift deposits. These consist of about 2 metres of a raised beach deposit containing well-rounded pebbles and cobbles some of which are igneous erratics that must be of pre-Ipswichian age. Resting on the raised beach is the Lower Blocky Head followed by the Irish Sea Till that in turn is overlaid by a rubble drift containing local rock fragments and lenses of sand and gravel. Sandy loam and sand dunes form a recent surface deposit.

6. Ogof Golchfa [SM 742237]

This is located about 200 metres west of the mouth of Porth Clais harbour. The drift deposits rest on several remnants of a rock platform bevelling steeply inclined Solva beds that are themselves cut by a wide microtonalite sill [Fig. 2.9]. A raised beach shingle including some local erratic boulders and pebbles rests on the undulating eroded rock surface. Overlying the beach deposit is a layer of Lower Head followed by a 2 metre thick red-brown till laid down by Irish Sea ice advancing south-east across north Pembrokeshire during the

Late Devensian. At Ogof Golchfa there is a variety of local pebbles and rock fragments within the till, including quartz porphyry pebbles from Ramsey Island. Interestingly, a large erratic boulder of Scottish picrite [porphyritic basalt] rested on the clifftop near Carreg Fran, about 1 km west of Ogof Golchfa, until it fell into the sea some years ago. The position of this erratic is marked on the 1:25,000 Ordnance Survey map.

7. Druidston Haven [SM 862170]

Druidston Haven lies on the west coast of St Brides Bay where there is a thick drift sequence plugging a deep meltwater channel. The present storm beach covers the iron-stained and cemented raised beach shingle that is occasionally revealed after high spring tides. The first clearly exposed unit is the Blocky Head, about 2 metres thick and containing iron-stained quartzite clasts [Fig. 11.6]. This is overlaid by 15 metres of Irish Sea till that is calcareous and contains igneous erratics, broken mollusc shells and fragments of carbonised wood. The blue grey boulder clay is being actively eroded by gullying during periods of heavy precipitation. The upper layers of the till contain a high proportion of sand and gravel, which then grades upward into rubble drift capped by a sandy loam.

8. Mullock Bridge [SM 811080]

This locality, located on the B4327 about 3 kms north of Dale village, is of considerable geomorphological interest since it provides a magnificent example of a kame terrace on the western side of the Gann estuary. This feature is a flat-topped mound of fluvioglacial sand and gravel that was deposited by meltwater at the junction of the wasting Irish Sea ice front and the valley side. The drift sequence, which was exposed in a large gravel pit about 400 metres south of Mullock Bridge,

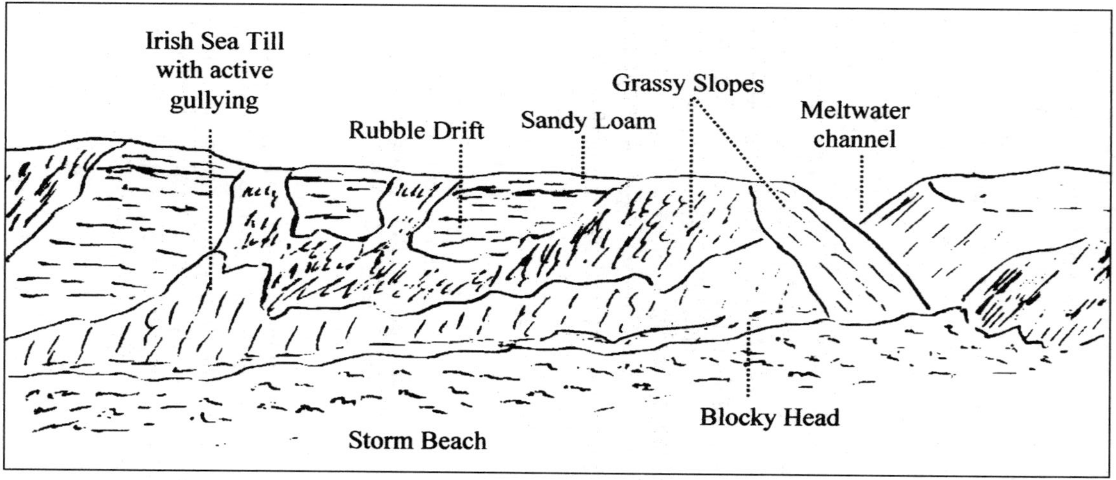

Fig. 11.6: The Druidstone Haven drift barrier viewed from the beach

was recorded in detail in the early 1970s. Unfortunately the pit has since been infilled and landscaped and is now entirely overgrown. However the topography of the kame terrace can be appreciated by viewing it from the south in the vicinity of Pickleridge, where there is a car park [SM 809067].

Walk along the shingle ridge past the flooded pits that are now lagoons supporting a variety of wild life. In the banks of the lagoons there are exposures of fluvioglacial outwash sands and gravel. Pickleridge is a shingle ridge that has developed in a north-westerly direction along the high water mark across the Gann estuary. This shingle barrier impedes the drainage on the marshy flood plain of Afon Gann that is inundated by the sea when there are spring tides. You will notice that there is a strong contrast in the natural vegetation between the dense colonies of reed mace (bullrushes) on the wet flood-plain of Afon Gann and the abundance of gorse and Scots pine that cover the dry sandy slopes of the kame terrace [Fig. 11.7].

9. West Angle Bay [SM 853031]

This bay is located close to Angle village in the north-west corner of the Pembroke peninsula. The main drift section extends for about 100 metres and lies immediately south of the car park. The exposed faces are strongly weathered so that downwash often obscures much of the stratification. Above the present storm beach there is a red sandy deposit containing pebbles from a raised beach that is now largely covered by shingle. Sub-rounded boulders up to 30 cm across also occur in this layer. A distinctive orange unit with large sub angular clasts forming the Blocky Head can be seen at the northern end of the section adjacent to the sea wall. This is succeeded by a sequence of sands, silts and dark grey clays containing shell fragments that may be related to a marine transgression. The dark clays have been washed down to beach level in the centre of the section. A red sand and pebble bed, about 3 metres thick, occurs near the top of the cliff and

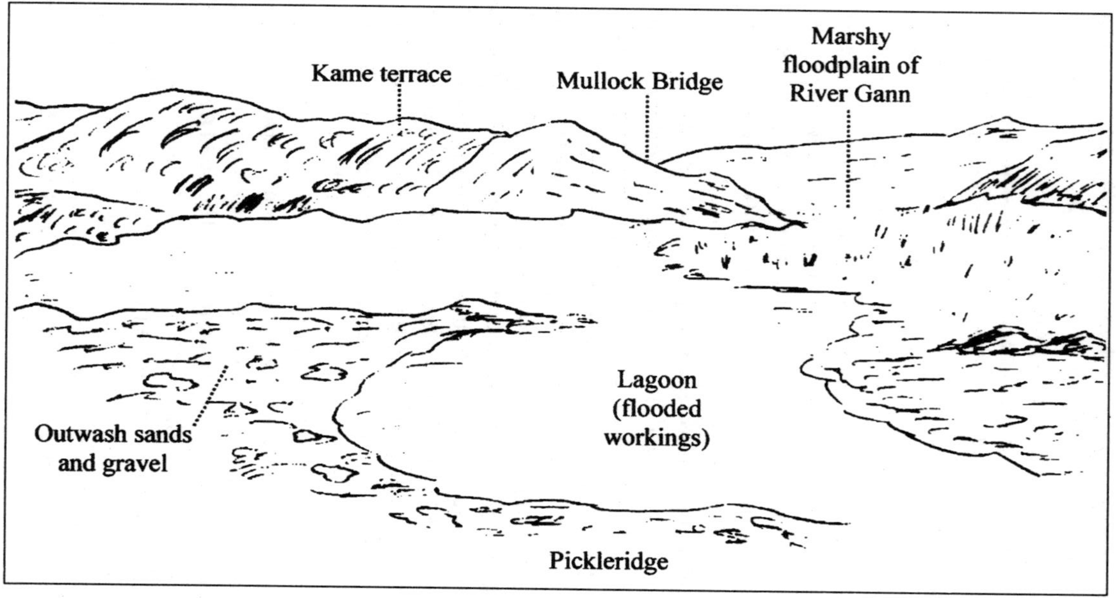

Fig. 11.7: View looking north towards the Mullock Bridge kame terrace

this could be the product of fluvioglacial outwash from the Irish Sea ice sheet. A layer of sandy loam caps the drift deposits around much of West Angle Bay.

The most significant aspect of this site is the existence of a stiff purple-coloured clay containing igneous erratics that was found in excavations made by both Dixon and Bowen. This till lies below the raised beach deposits and therefore must have been laid down by an earlier pre-Ipswichian glaciation. Thus West Angle Bay contains one of the longest sequences of Late Pleistocene deposition in south-west Wales, including glacial, interglacial and periglacial sediments ranging in age from around 140,000 to 10,000 BP.

10. Broad Haven [SR 980941]

Broad Haven is situated near to the village of Bosherston on the south side of the Pembroke peninsula. (This locality should not be confused with Broad Haven on St Brides Bay.) From the National Trust car park, walk across the beach to the limestone outcrop on the north-east side of the bay. At SR980941 the limestone beds that are dipping southwards have been planed off about 3 metres above the high water mark. [Fig. 11.8] This platform is covered by the remnants of a raised beach deposit of rounded pebbles and cobbles set in a sandy matrix with patches of cemented shelly deposits in places. However, the raised beach platform is much dissected and eroded by gullies, but it grades upwards into a layer of cemented Blocky Head composed of limestone clasts up to 20 cms across. There are also patches of sand rock up to 2 metres thick that appear to be incorporated into the head deposit. At the top of the section there are exposures of sandy loam and blown sand that form extensive dunes around Broad Haven. The lack of till at this locality and the presence of Blocky Head suggest that the area experienced periglacial conditions since it was located to the south of the ice front during the Late Devensian.

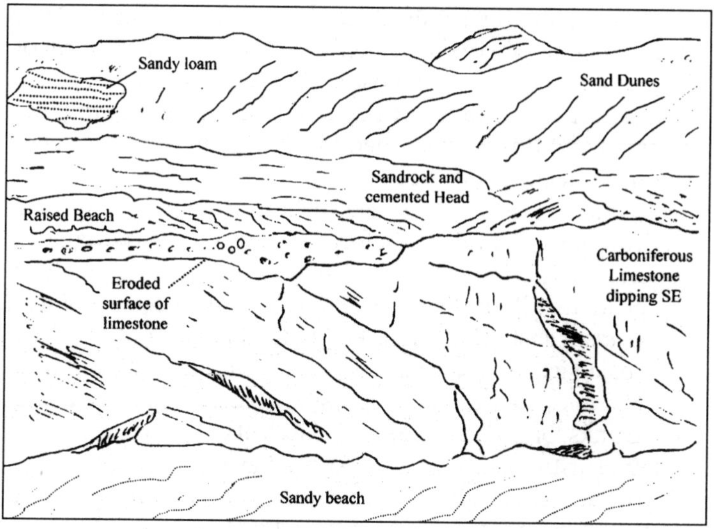

Fig. 11.8: The raised beach at Broad Haven (Bosherston)

11. Marros Sands [SN 206075-SN 219072]

Marros Sands provide an excellent Quaternary section extending from Marros Mill to Raglan Point. The site is best approached via the track leading south from Marros Church where cars can be parked. Follow the track to Marros Beacon where the route zig-zags down to the coast at Marros Mill. Here there is a low drift cliff behind the storm beach that exposes about 3 metres of dark brown head containing angular shale fragments and blocks. This is succeeded by a buff-coloured clay that may represent loess deposited by wind as the frozen land surface dried out at the end of Devensian times. On the eastern side of the cliff several examples of fossil ice wedges [Fig. 11.9] can be seen where fine sediment now fills the deep cracks that were formerly occupied by ice.

Walk along the sands at low tide to the western side of Ragwen Point where the drift cliff rests on a rock platform of Namurian sandstone that dips gently west. Immediately above the platform is a layer of black silt that contains organic remains and this is succeeded by several metres of orange-coloured head. It has been suggested that this silt deposit accumulated in dune slacks when a more temperate environment prevailed before the onset of periglacial conditions. It is important to note that the rock fragments in the head are all locally derived and thus the absence of any erratics suggests that the area lay to the south of the Late Devensian ice margin where periglacial conditions prevailed.

The fossilized remains of a submerged forest, including tree trunks, branches, roots and leaves of oak, hazel and alder together with peat beds, are exposed at low spring tides on Marros Sands. Around 7,500 BP sea level was approximately 20 metres below Ordnance Datum when forest growth would have spread well beyond the present coastline. Sea level rose as a result of the Flandrian transgression during the early Holocene leading to the submergence of coastal forests.

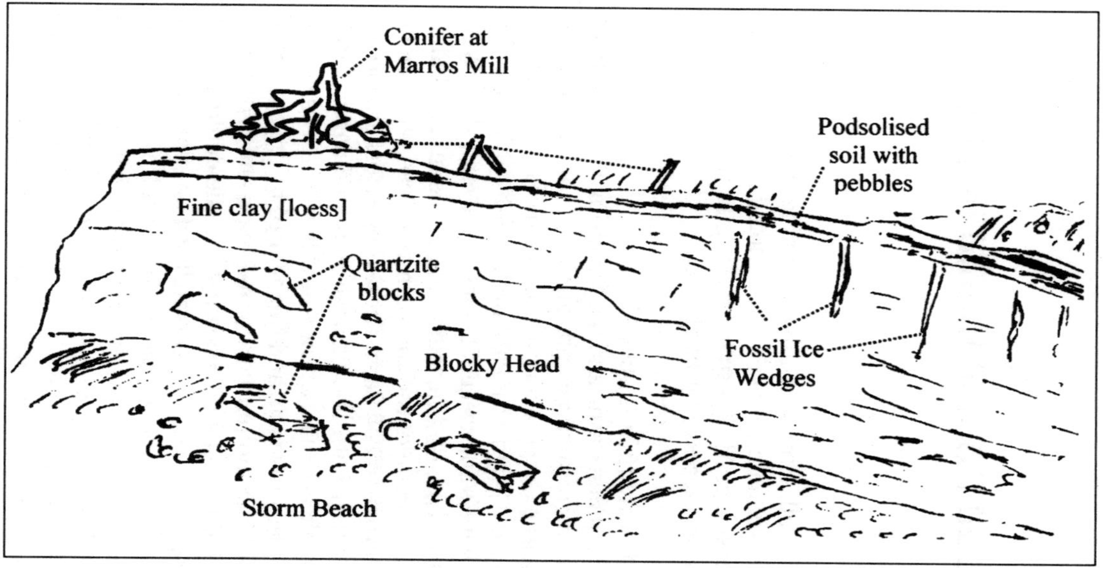

Fig. 11.9: The drift section at Marros mill

12
Some additional inland localities

There are a small number of inland localities in the Cleddau valley and surrounding area that you should find interesting and worth visiting. All the sites are open to the public and relatively easy to access [Fig.12.1].

1. Maiden Castle [SM 955248]

The crags of Maiden Castle and neighbouring Poll Carn form a prominent outcrop of Precambrian rhyolite on the west side of the Treffgarne Gorge, about 9 kms north of Haverfordwest on the A 40 road [Fig.12.2]. Park in the lay-by at Nant-y-Coy Mill where there is an excellent tea room and craft shop. Walk up the narrow lane on the south side of the mill and after about 100 metres take the footpath that leads to Maiden Castle and beyond to Poll Carn. These rugged tors are formed of flow-banded rhyolitic lavas, that are also nodular in places. The viscous, silica-rich lava flow would have had a congealed crust which was broken up and fragmented by the continued movement of the molten lava underneath the crust. This autobrecciated lava can be recognized in the outcrop by its fractured appearance that is recrystallised on some surfaces. The rocks at this locality belong to the Roch Rhyolite Group (Pebidian Volcanic Complex) that extend south westwards for about 8 kms to Roch Castle. Just to the east of Maiden Castle, the outcrop crosses the Western Cleddau valley where the Treffgarne Gorge has been cut through the resistant rhyolite.

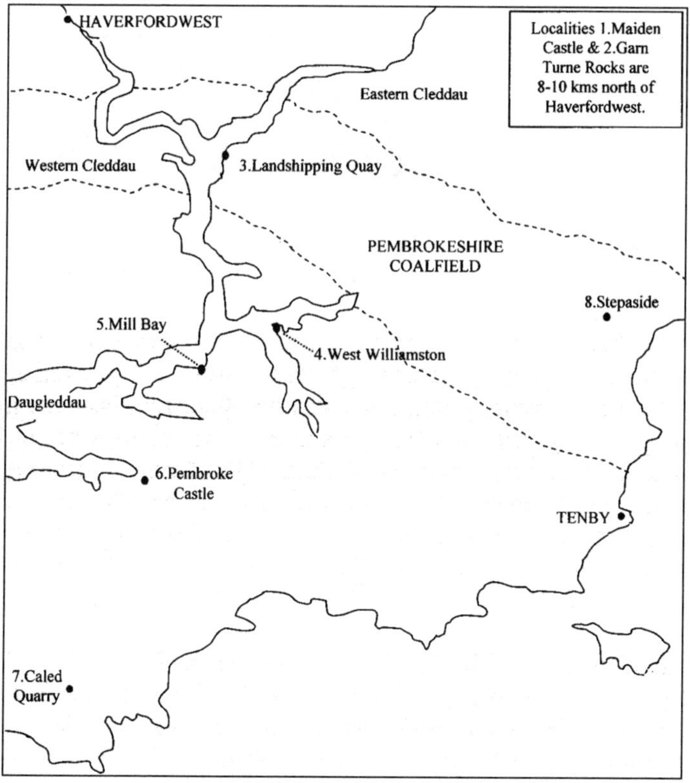

Fig. 12.1: The Cleddau valley and surrounding area

2. Garn Turne Rocks [SM 979272]

This craggy outcrop of Lower Ordovician volcanic rocks is located about 3 kms north east of Maiden Castle. Drive northwards along the A 40 road through Wolf's Castle; turn right on to the narrow lane leading to Sealyham, then turn right again, cross the bridge over Afon Anghol, pass St Dogwells Farm and Garn Turne Rocks occupy a slight rise about 1 km ESE of the farm. The rocks are not easily seen from

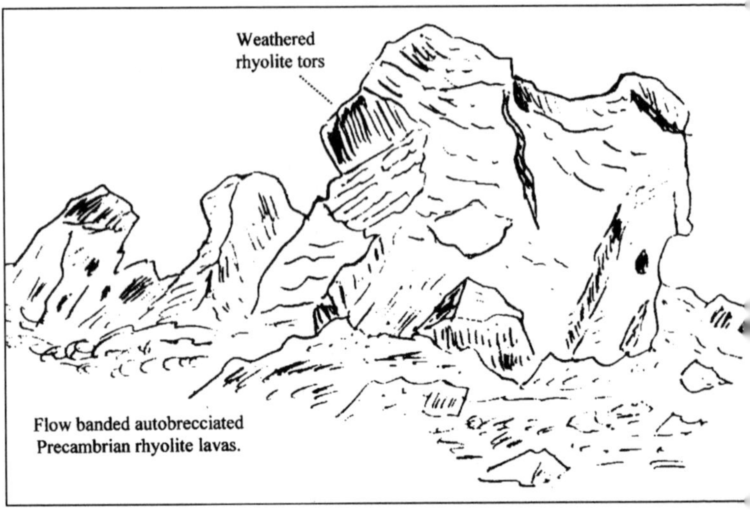

Fig. 12.2: Maiden Castle viewed from the west

the road due to the high hedges and you need to look carefully for the narrow overgrown entrance with a metal gate that stands alongside a small layby. There is no sign to mark the entrance despite the fact that it is a recognized archaeological site and contains the remains of a Neolithic chambered tomb. Cross the field to the rocky tors that outcrop beyond the standing stones. This is an important geological locality since it provides one of the few accessible exposures of the Sealyham Volcanics. The outcrop consists of a much weathered and fragmented rhyolitic rock. The fragments are mostly less than 10 cms across although there are a few larger-sized clasts. This rock can be described as an agglomerate containing fragments of lava that were blasted from a volcano in early Ordovician times. Pyroclastic material including volcanic ash, pumice and vesicular lava can be identified in the outcrop.

3. Landshipping Quay [SN 008108]

This was one of the most important nineteenth-century coal exporting ports on Afon Cleddau. The remains of the stone quay can be seen on the south side of Landshipping Pill, a small inlet about 1.5 kms beyond Landshipping village. You can reach the village via a lane from Cross Hands on the A4075 Canaston Bridge to Carew road. There is a small car park on the bridge near to the quay and nearby is a memorial to the forty miners who lost their lives in the infamous Garden Pit disaster in 1844 when the mine workings were flooded by river water.

At low tide walk along the foreshore below the low river cliffs on the north side of the pill where you will see the Middle Coal Measures exposed. Thin coal seams and seat earths containing plant remains within the Timber Vein Group crop out at the western end of the section but they are much contorted by Variscan folding and thrusting. There are examples of sandstone-filled channels, wedging-out structures and numerous bedded ironstone nodules. At the far end of the section there is a distinctive 2-metre-thick bed of orange coloured ironstone concretions. A large shallow anticline on the foreshore shows rectilinear jointing, ripple bedding and evidence of polygonal mudcracks.

About 300 metres south of the ruined quay, the foreshore exposes cyclothem units of the Lower Coal Measures dipping at about 50° SE. However, there is considerable evidence of northward propagating Variscan thrust movements in the folded strata. One example at SN 105005 shows a thrust fault where the upper half of a fold has been carried northwards along the thrust plane. There are several folds showing spaced cleavage in the siltstones between the more competent sandstone layers. The fold axes generally trend NW–SE as in the synclinal structure outlined by sandstone ribs on the foreshore near to the southern end of the section. The foreshore rock exposures are cut off by a major E–W fault at

SN 003101 and south of this point there are no further coal measure outcrops.

4. West Williamston Quarries [SN 025061]

These quarries were major producers of limestone in the early nineteenth century when their tidewater location enabled the stone to be transported around the Welsh coast. Barges of 15-20 tons were loaded in the tidal channels that joined the quarries to the river and then moved to Lawrenny quay to be transhipped on to coastal vessels. The limestone was in great demand at the time for use in limekilns to produce agricultural lime, mortar and whitewash for houses. Records show that in 1839, a 40-ton sloop called *Ranger* carried 10 cargoes of limestone from Lawrenny to Abercastle on the north coast of Pembrokeshire. Since the time of the Napoleonic wars there has been a great demand for stone to build the complex of fortifications that protected the Milford Haven. West Williamston quarries were ideally located to supply limestone blocks via the Daugleddau waterway. Some of the Admiralty buildings in Pembroke Dock were also constructed of limestone from the quarries.

You can get to the old quarries from the A4075 road at Carew by following the narrow lane past Carew mill pond to West Williamston. There is a small car park at SN 033059. Follow the driveway to Williamston Park from where a public footpath leads down to the salt marsh alongside the Carew River. The site is on a promontory at the confluence of the Carew and Cresswell rivers. About 200 metres before reaching the north west end of the site, there is a footpath leading through the trees to Point Quarry where the limestone is exposed. Today the quarries are largely overgrown but they provide a haven for wildlife and natural vegetation protected as a designated SSSI and managed by the Wildlife Trust of South and West Wales.

The Lower Carboniferous succession at West Williamston is about 300 metres thick and the strata lie on the flank of the Carew Anticline dipping at about 25° NE. The fine grained grey oolite at Point Quarry belongs to the Black Rock Limestone and its homogeneous texture make it an excellent building stone [Fig.12.3]. On the top of the ridges between the tidal creeks there are several metres of 'rotten beds' that are deeply weathered. This is a palaeokarst horizon where the limestone is pitted by chemical weathering and some faces show solution hollows up to 30 cm in diameter. There are also numerous infilled fissures. The reddish clay infill appears to represent a weathering residue of insoluble clay minerals in which there are rounded fragments of unweathered limestone. The deeply weathered beds were probably formed as ground water percolated through bedding planes and joints resulting in solution of the limestone at depth. During Lower Carboniferous times, the hot wet tropical conditions would have been ideal for the development of these palaeokarst features.

5. Mill Bay [SN 002049]

This beautiful bay is well off the tourist track in a relatively quiet stretch of Afon Daugleddau near to the village of Cosheston. Drive along the A477 from Pembroke Dock, turn left on to the road leading to Cosheston, then at the village crossroads continue northwards for about 1 km to Rosehill Cottage. On the west side of the road is a wooden gate that gives access to a track leading down through the woods in Mill Cwm. This is a permissive path that is closed to the public during December and January. It is best to approach Mill Bay at low tide in order to gain access to the rocks in safety.

The most interesting geological aspects of this locality are the soft sediment deformation structures in the Cosheston Group of the Lower Old Red Sandstone. On reaching the river

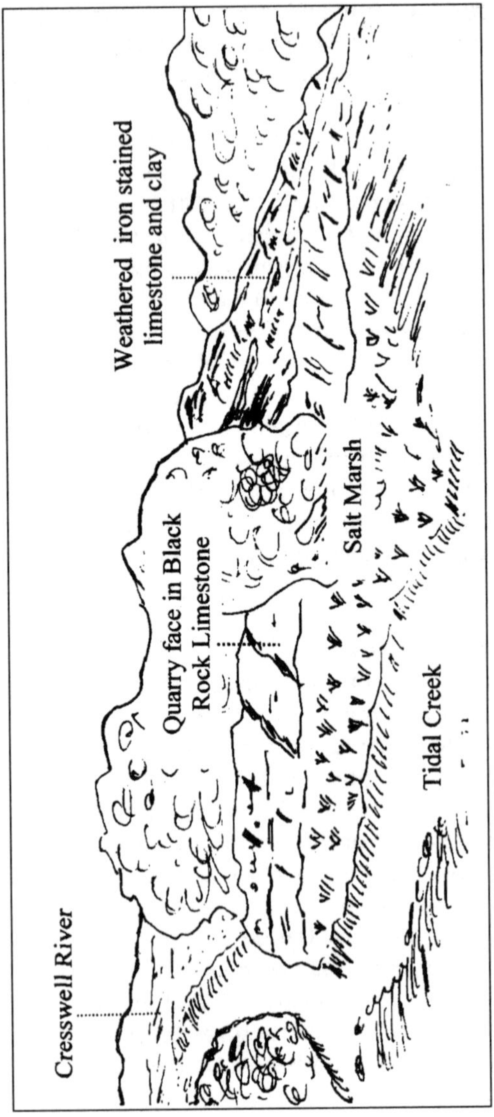

Fig. 12.3: Point Quarry at West Williamson

take the path to the left and walk for about 300 metres to where a set of steps leads down to the rocky foreshore at SN 999050. Look carefully at the low cliff face and you will see classic ball and pillow structures at the base of a sandstone bed. This occurs where rounded masses of sandstone have sunk into the underlying mudstone when it was still soft and unconsolidated. It has also been argued that seismic shocks may convert overlying sediments into quicksand that then founders into the mud. There are more examples on the rock foreshore of sandstone pillows enclosed in slumped sediment. About 200 metres to the west there is a beautiful example of an anticlinal fold that has been cut by a reverse fault whilst the whole structure is underlain by slumped mudstones.

Return to Mill Cwm and cross over the stream to the east side of Mill Bay to examine the founder folds (slump folds) on the foreshore at SN 003050. It is important to recognise that these folds are not produced directly by earth movements but rather by the gravity-induced collapse of overlying wet sediment that slumped down a depositional slope. Walk further to the east of the folds and look for channels that cross-cut the bedded strata. You should see where a curved erosion surface is overlaid by channel fill deposits.

Finally, it is worth considering what these sedimentary structures at Mill Bay can tell us about the environment of deposition when the beds of the Cosheston Group were deposited. It is generally considered that by early Devonian times braided/meandering rivers crossed the floor of a large east-west graben (rift valley) bounded by the Benton and Ritec faults. These rivers laid down repeated fining-up cycles of conglomerate, sandstone and mudstone. Shifting of distributaries during floods would result in the sediments being cross-cut by new channels.

6. Pembroke Castle [SM982016]

Many tourists come to Pembroke to visit the Norman castle, which dates from the early twelfth century when Robert de Montgomery first established a fortified settlement at the head of the tidal Pembroke River. However, it was not until around 1200 that the first limestone walls and the round keep were built by William Marshall, Earl of Pembroke. In 1457 it became the birthplace of Henry Tudor, Earl of Richmond, who later became Henry Vll. The building was a Royalist stronghold during the Civil War and it was partially destroyed in 1648 when Cromwell laid siege to it.

The castle is built on an outcrop of steeply bedded Carboniferous Limestone that is best seen in Westgate Street below the castle walls. Here we are standing approximately in the centre of the Pembroke syncline which trends WNW–ESE. The youngest rocks preserved within the synclinal structure are equivalent in age to the Stackpole Limestone. A small outlier of gash breccia rests on the eroded limestone surface on Castle Hill, and if you look carefully you will see evidence of the reddish-coloured breccia in Westgate Street. It is a pleasant walk around the mill pond where you can look over the sluice gates to the Pembroke River, alongside which are several old limestone quarries that were used to provide building stone for the town.

7. Caled Quarry [SR 959951]

This is a large disused quarry that is owned by the local authority and maintained in good condition so that the flooded workings can be used by schools and other groups for supervised canoeing. The quarry can be approached from Pembroke along the B4319. At Sampson Cross take the minor road signposted to Bosherston and the quarry entrance will be found on the right immediately before entering the village. Park near the gates and walk up the track, which is a public right of way, then enter the quarry on your right.

Caled quarry was opened during the 1960s to provide aggregate for the construction of the Texaco oil refinery and Pembroke power station. It worked the Carboniferous Limestone (Black Rock Limestone) in the crest of the E–W trending Bosherston anticline. The strata dips to the north at 60–70°, whereas to the south the dip is much more gentle. The beds on the north-east face of the quarry display superb Variscan structures with some folds having an amplitude of about 20 metres [Fig.12.4]. The bioclastic limestones contain chert bands and nodules that are well-displayed on some of the large blocks alongside the quarry road. These blocks also contain crinoidal debris, brachiopod shells and the single coral *Zaphrentis* which is a zone fossil. You may see some beds that are intensly bioturbated with both horizontal and vertical burrows.

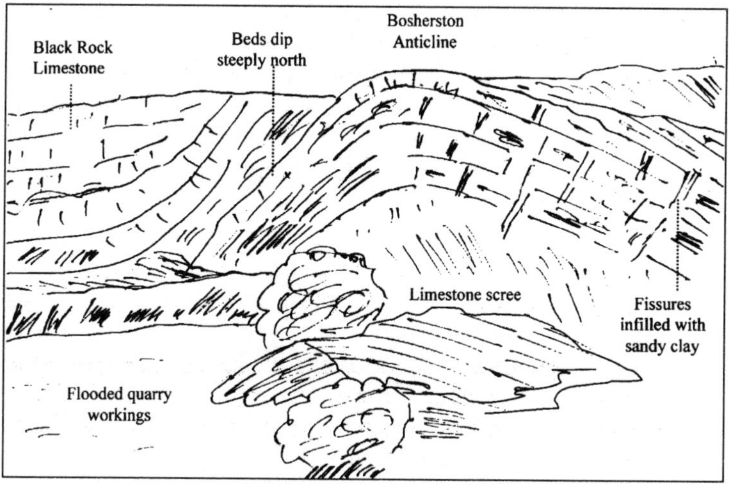

Fig. 12.4: The north-east face of Caled Quarry

On the eastern side of the quarry the well-bedded limestone is cut by strong vertical joints, some of which have been widened by solution into fissures that are filled with a sandy clay. This may be the same pipe clay that is preserved in pockets on the limestone plateau near Flimston and which is thought to be of Oligocene age. On the other hand, the deposit may have been formed as a result of chemical weathering of the limestone under tropical conditions to produce an insoluble clay residue.

8. Stepaside Ironworks [SN 141074]

Turn off the A477 near Kilgetty and follow the tourist signs through Stepaside village to the ironworks. This site is not in the strict sense a geological one, nevertheless its industrial archaeology reflects the importance of economic geology in the nineteenth century in south Pembrokeshire. All the materials for iron making were available locally – anthracite, iron ore and limestone – and the Saundersfoot Railway had already been extended to Stepaside when the ironworks opened in 1849. However, supplies of bedded iron ore from the coalfield were limited; as economic conditions declined, the ironworks was forced to close in 1874. Today the ruined buildings have been consolidated and you can walk safely around the site.

The stone casting house with its three arched doorways and circular openings stands as a monument to solid Victorian engineering [Fig.12.5]. The two blast furnaces originally stood in front of the furnace wall, one to each pair of arches. The furnaces were loaded by overhead bridges leading from the upper platform where the raw materials were assembled. Before the furnaces were charged, the anthracite was converted into coke in the coke ovens and the iron ore was roasted in the calcining kilns. Compressed air to aid combustion was provided by the blowing house, which is the

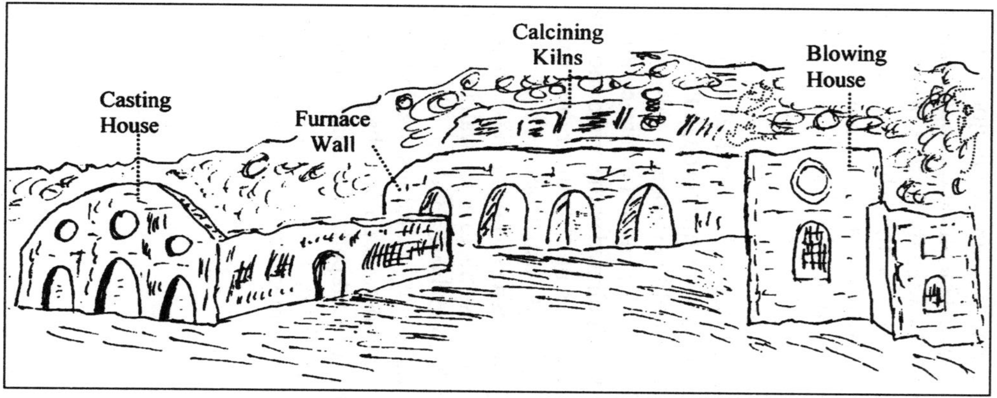

Fig. 12.5: The restored ruins of Stepaside ironworks

tall building to the right of the furnace wall.

After exploring the ironworks, you should climb the pathway leading up the hillside for about 300 metres to the remains of Grove colliery. This mine was opened in 1853 to supply anthracite from the Kilgetty Vein. A branch line from the Saundersfoot railway linked the colliery to the ironworks. Today you can still see the ruins of the winding engine house that lifted the cages up and down the shaft, and the Cornish pumping house that contained a 274 hp beam engine that raised water from the mine.

Finally, it is a good idea to take a walk along the route of the former Saundersfoot railway line through Pleasant Valley. The name of the valley would have been a misnomer during the industrial heyday of the Pembrokeshire coalfield. Then the area would have been polluted with smoke and noise from the blast furnaces, collieries and steam trains. Huge tips of slag from the ironworks and waste from the coal mines would have been visually intrusive. Nature has reclaimed the wasteland, and it is now possible to enjoy walking through the quiet wooded valley down to the sea and the pub at Wiseman's Bridge (see Chapter 8, Locality 4). After suitable refreshment, you can continue to Saundersfoot along the old track, which now forms part of the coastal path. The route runs alongside the sea as far as Coppet Hall, and there are some impressive sections through the coal measure strata on the foreshore.

A GEOLOGICAL FIELDWORK CODE

1. Follow the Country Code and observe local byelaws. Remember to shut gates and leave no litter.
2. Avoid undue disturbance to farm animals, wildlife or natural vegetation. Keep clear of nesting birds particularly on coastal cliffs.
3. Always seek permission before entering private land.
4. Observe and record; make field sketches and photograph geological sections, but do not damage the outcrop by hammering indiscriminately.
5. Restrict the collecting of specimens to a minimum and do not remove in situ specimens.
6. Leave the site in as good a condition as possible for those who come after you.
7. Beware of dangerous cliffs, and rock faces, taking care not to dislodge loose rocks.
8. In coastal localities make sure that you consult tide timetables and warning notices. It is always best to work on a falling tide.
9. When visiting isolated places make sure that someone knows where you are going and your estimated time of return. It is best to go with a companion, rather than alone.
10. Always wear suitable footwear and outdoor clothing. Wear a safety helmet where advisable. Carry a mobile phone, but remember that it may fail to get a signal below cliffs or in remote country.

A more complete code is published by:
The Geologists' Association,
Burlington House,
Piccadilly,
London,W1V 9AG

GLOSSARY OF GEOLOGICAL TERMS

Alkali feldspar Group of silicate minerals containing potassium and sodium.

Alluvial fan Fan-shaped accumulation of sediment deposited where a river gradient decreases rapidly at the foot of a mountain range.

Anoxic Deficient in oxygen as in sediments deposited on deep ocean floor.

Anticline Arch-shaped upfold in strata with the oldest rocks in the core of the anticline.

Auto-brecciation This is the process in which cooled lava crust is fragmented by the continued movement of the underlying molten lava.

Axial planar cleavage Cleavage having a strike direction that is parallel to the axial plane of the fold.

Basalt Dark-coloured fine-grained volcanic rock rich in ferro-magnesian minerals.

Bioclastic Grains in limestone that are formed of organic remains such as shell fragments.

Bioturbation Churning of sediment by burrowing organisms.

Boulder clay Glacial deposit of clay containing ill-sorted sub-angular fragments laid down beneath a glacier or ice sheet. The term glacial till is now more commonly used.

Bouma sequence Idealised fining-upward sequence of sedimentary layers laid down by submarine turbidity currents.

BP Abbreviation meaning 'before present'.

Brachiopod Sessile marine invertebrate with a bivalved shell. Found in Palaeozoic rocks.

Braided river River that splits into many channels separated by sand/gravel bars.

Breccia Coarse-grained fragmental rock containing angular clasts set in a finer-grained matrix. Examples include fault breccia and volcanic breccia. Brecciation is the process by which a rock is fragmented.

Calcrete Carbonate horizon formed by evaporation in a semi-arid climate.

Caledonian orogeny Major earth-building episode that began in late Silurian times with the closure of the Iapetus Ocean.

Carbonate platform Shallow marine shelf where carbonate sediments are deposited.

Chert Fine-grained form of silica precipitated from solution to form nodules and bands.

Chevron fold Fold where the hinge angle is acute. Also referred to as a zig-zag or accordion fold when occurring in sequence.

Clast Fragment or particle of rock varying in size from silt-sized grains to boulders.

Cleavage Planes of weakness caused by the alignment of platy minerals during low-grade metamorphism.

Concretion Rounded rock body that has been cemented within a sediment at an early stage.

Conglomerate Coarse-grained fragmental rock containing rounded clasts set in a finer-grained matrix.

Contact metamorphism Recrystallisation of rocks surrounding of an igneous intrusion as a result of the increase in temperature due to the intrusion.

Crinoid Type of sea lily, the stem of which is commonly found in Carboniferous limestones.

Cross stratification Layers of sediment that are inclined at an angle to the surface on which the sediment was laid down. Usually seen in shallow marine, deltaic or windblown deposits.

Cyclothem A sequence of beds deposited in a single cycle of sedimentation.

Dextral Describes a wrench fault in which the sense of movement is to the right as viewed across the fault plane.

Diorite Coarse-grained intrusive igneous rock of intermediate chemical composition.

Discordant A wall-like igneous intrusion cutting across the strata at right angles (or nearly so) to the bedding. Concordant describes an intrusion that is parallel to the bedding.

Distributary channel Branching channels into which the main river splits as it crosses a delta plain.

Dolerite Medium-grained, mafic, intrusive igneous rock often forming dykes or sills.

Downthrow/upthrow The vertical movement along a fault plane. If the land on one side of a fault moves down relative to the land on the other side, then it said to be downthrown. Conversely, if the land is pushed upwards, then it is upthrown.

Ductile deformation Deformation that takes place in shear zones where the rock is permanently deformed but does not fracture.

Duplex Structure containing a series of fault segments bounded by roof and floor thrust planes.

Dyke Sheet-like igneous intrusion that cuts vertically and discordantly through the country rocks.

En echelon The parallel alignment of tension fractures (filled with quartz or calcite) which are arranged obliquely to the axis of a shear zone.

Erratic Rock boulder that has been transported by ice and deposited far from its original location.

Esker Winding, sinuous ridge of sand and gravel deposited by a sub-glacial stream, i.e. stream flowing below an ice sheet that is melting.

Eustatic Worldwide change in sea level caused either by tectonic movements or by the expansion or melting of ice caps.

Evaporite Mineral produced by the evaporation of highly saline water.

Feldspar Group of rock forming silicate minerals. Alkali feldspars occur in felsic igneous rocks (eg.granite) whilst plagioclase feldspars occur in mafic igneous rocks (eg.basalt). Also found in sedimentary rocks such as arkose and greywacke.

Felsic Term used to describe igneous rocks that are rich in silica, alkali feldspar and mica

Ferruginous Rich in iron minerals.

Flexural slip Movement between parallel layers of rock as they are folded.

Flute cast Tongue-shaped scour cut into mud by water flowing strongly over soft mud. The cast is formed when the scour is infilled by sediment.

Fluvial Describes actions of a river.

Fluvioglacial Describing sediments and landforms produced by streams from melting ice.

Fold axis	Hinge line of a folded bed.
Footwall	Rock layers underneath an inclined fault plane.
Foraminifera	Marine microfossils used for stratigraphical correlation.
Gabbro	Coarse-grained mafic, igneous rock usually forming deep-seated intrusions.
Goniatite	Sub-class of Ammonoidea with simple suture pattern.
Graben	Structure formed when a block of country is downthrown between two parallel faults.
Granophyre	Medium-grained intrusive igneous rock of felsic composition.
Graptolite	Extinct marine organism with simple branching skeleton. Found in some Ordovician shales.
Gash Breccia	Irregular assortment of clasts set in sandy clay matrix thought to be of Triassic age; found in the Carboniferous Limestone of Pembrokeshire.
Glaciation	The process of ice working on a land surface; includes glacial erosion as in glaciers and glacial deposition, as when a melting ice sheet lays down debris such as boulder clay or erratic boulders.
Graded bedding	Sedimentary layers that show a vertical gradation in grain size.
Gutter cast	An elongated sediment infill deposited on the base of a bed in a river channel. This eroded depression in the channel bed is later filled with sand/mud which forms a gutter cast at the base of the overlying sediment (bed).
Hanging wall	Rock layers above a dipping fault plane.
Harmonic folds	Multilayered folds that show a general correspondence in wavelength and symmetry.
Head	Poorly-sorted angular rock debris moved downslope by solifluction under periglacial conditions.
Hornfels	Hard splintery rock produced by contact metamorphism.
Horst	Structure formed when a block of country is upthrown between two parallel faults.
Iapetus ocean	Ocean that existed between Laurentia and Avalonia/Baltica from late Precambrian to Silurian times.
Imbrication	Structure resulting from the stacking of rock clasts so that they overlap like tiles and lean in the direction of the current.

Inlier Outcrop of older rock entirely surrounded by younger strata.

Isostacy State of balance where the earth's crust rests on the mantle (underlying denser material). For example, during an ice age the crust is held down out of isostatic balance by the weight of overlying ice. Hence the western side of Britain (including Wales) is still recovering from the Ice Age and is gradually rising in order to regain isostatic equilibrium.

Kame A mound of sand and gravel deposited by a supra-glacial water

Karst Landscape developed on limestones subjected to solution-weathering.

Lag gravel Accumulation of gravel and pebbles at the base of a point bar in a meandering channel.

Lapilli Pyroclastic fragments ranging in size from 2 mm to 64 mm.

Law of superposition When strata are deposited sequentially so that each layer is younger than the layer beneath it.

Lenses Lens-shaped deposits of sediment that have accumulated in depressions in the land surface.

Liquefaction Process by which sediments are liquefied by rapid deposition which causes water to escape upwards under pressure.

Lithification Process that transforms unconsolidated sediments into sedimentary rocks.

Load cast Depression formed on the base of a bed of sediment that is denser than the bed below so that the heavier material sinks into the underlying bed.

Loess Windblown unconsolidated dust.

Ma Abbreviation meaning 'million years'.

Mafic Term used to describe igneous rocks that are rich in ferromagnesian minerals such as amphibole, pyroxene and olivine.

Marine band An horizon formed of marine sediment in a succession of terrestrial beds. eg. Gastrioceras subcrenatum marine band.

Mass movement	Transfer of surface material down slope; includes rock fall, rock slide, mud flow and soil creep.
Matrix	Fine-grained material separating the clasts in a sedimentary rock.
Microtonalite	Igneous rock of intermediate grain size consisting of quartz, plagioclase feldspar and ferro-magnesian minerals.
Monocline	Fold with one steep limb and one almost horizontal limb.
Moraine	Accumulation of rock debris produced by the melting of a glacier or ice sheet.
Monadnock	Isolated hill standing above the general level of an erosion platform.
Normal fault	Dip slip fault in which the displacement of the hanging wall is downwards relative to the footwall.
Orogeny	Mountain-building process in which sediments are compressed, uplifted and folded as plates converge.
Outlier	Outcrop of younger rocks surrounded entirely by older strata.
Oolitic	Describes limestones that are made up of tiny sub-spherical calcareous grains or ooliths.
Palaeokarst	Fossilized limestone surface that has been subjected to solution weathering in the past and displays karstic features.
Pegmatic	Having large well-formed crystals as in pegmatite
Pericline	An elongated dome, the shape of an upturned rowing boat. Looked at from above the strata dips away from the central axis in all directions.
Periglacial	Area on the margins of an ice sheet where permafrost exists.
Phenocryst	Large crystal in an igneous rock set in a finer-grained groundmass.
Pillow lava	Basalt lava that is erupted under water, producing a pillow-like structure.
Plagioclase feldspar	Rock-forming aluminium silicate mineral ranging in composition from sodium to calcium-rich.
Plinian eruption	Explosive volcanic eruption of pyroclastic material. The eruption column may be up to 55 kms high.
Plunge	Inclination of a fold axis.

Podsol An acidic, sandy, infertile soil that develops typically under coniferous forest.

Point bar Sediment deposited on the inside bend of a river meander.

Porcellanite Fine-grained siliceous airfall tuff, similar in texture to porcelain.

Productid Type of large brachiopod found in Lower Carboniferous rocks.

Proglacial Describes a meltwater glacial lake located between the ice front and adjacent high ground.

Pseudo-anticline Gentle upfold produced when internal pressure builds up during calcrete formation. Literally a 'false anticline' since it is not a tectonic structure.

Pseudobreccia Recrystallised limestone in which irregular growth of coarse crystals gives the rock an apparently broken texture.

Pyroclastic Describes fragmented volcanic rocks produced by explosive volcanic action.

Raised beach Former beach that is now several metres above present sea level as a result of either a fall in sea level or uplift of the land.

Recumbent fold Fold where the axial plane is almost horizontal.

Regolith General term for all unconsolidated material lying on the bedrock.

Reverse fault Dip slip fault in which the hanging wall moves upwards relative to the footwall.

Rheic ocean Ocean that existed between Gondwana and Laurentia, Avalonia and Baltica during Devonian and Carboniferous times.

Rhyolite Light-coloured fine-grained volcanic rock rich in quartz and alkali feldspar.

Ria A 'drowned' river estuary, such as at Milford Haven, caused by a post-glacial rise in sea level which floods the pre-existing tributary valleys.

Scoriaceous Describes the frothy cindery appearance of vesicular lava.

Seat Earth Clay soil layer containing rootlets immediately below a coal seam.

Septarian nodule Large concretion of clay ironstone characterised by internal mineral-filled cracks.

Shear zone Fault-like structure in which ductile deformation occurs with no brittle fracture.

Siliciclastic Term applied to sediments formed of silicate mineral grains such as mudstones and sandstones.

Sill Horizontal sheet-like igneous intrusion that is concordant with surrounding strata.

Sinistral Describes a wrench fault in which the sense of movement is to the left as viewed across the fault plane.

Sinusoidal ripples Ripple beds that have the shape of a sine curve. In simple terms, symmetrical wavy ripples.

Slickensides Grooves on a fault plane aligned in the direction of fault movement.

Slump Where soft sediment slides down a slope. When hardened the soft sediment often appears as a melange of contorted beds.

Solifluction Slow downslope movement of water-saturated surface material.

Solution hollows Depressions in a limestone surface that have been formed by the chemical weathering of the limestone, i.e. the calcium carbonate has been removed in solution by rainwater on the surface.

Stratigraphical From the word 'strata'; refers to the order in which the strata have been deposited. A stratigraphical column shows the strata in the order of formation, with the oldest rocks at the base.

Strike direction Direction of a horizontal line on a dipping bed at right angles to true dip. Also describes general trend of a bed outcrop.

Stylolite Irregular zig-zag surface often seen in limestones where the carbonate minerals have been removed by pressure solution.

Subaerial On the earth's surface, usually describing weathering or erosion.

Subduction zone Where an oceanic plate descends at a destructive plate boundary. Characterised by seismic and volcanic activity.

Suspension deposit Fine particles that stay in suspension in water until the velocity slows sufficiently for the material to be deposited.

Syncline U-shaped fold in strata with the youngest rocks in the core of the syncline.

Tectonic Describes the forces of deformation within the earth's crust.

Tension gash Rock fracture that propagates at right angles to the direction of maximum extension. Often occurs in an échelon pattern.

Till Glacial deposit containing ill-sorted boulders of various sizes in a clay matrix, laid down beneath a glacier or ice sheet.

Thrust Fault Low angle reverse fault.

Trace fossil Structure in sediment produced by an early life form. eg. burrow, footprint or faecal material.

Trilobite Extinct class of arthropods having three body sections. Found in some Palaeozoic rocks.

Tuff Ash ejected from a volcano solidifies to form a tuff. When deposited in water ash forms a volcanoclastic sediment.

Turbidite Sediment deposited by a turbidity current. Complete graded succession is known as a Bouma sequence.

Unconformity Break in the stratigraphical record, usually marked by an erosion surface. The unconformity may represent a gap of several million years or more between two rock formations.

Variscan orogeny Major earth-building movement that began in late Carboniferous times with the closure of the Rheic Ocean. The Variscan Front is the leading edge of the earth movements.

Vesicle Gas-filled cavity in lava.

Wrench fault Fault where the major displacement is horizontal and parallel to the strike of the vertical fault plane. Also known as a tear fault or strike slip fault.

Zone fossil Distinctive fossil chosen to represent a particular biostratigraphical zone.

BIBLIOGRAPHY

General Reading

Allaby, A and Allaby. M., *A Dictionary of Earth Sciences* (Oxford, 1999).

Brenchley, P. J. and Rawson, P. F. (eds), *The Geology of England and Wales* (London, 2006).

Connop-Price, M. R., *Pembrokeshire: The Forgotten Coalfield.* (Ashbourne, 2004).

George, G. T., *The Geology of South Wales* (www.geoserv.co.uk, 2008)

George, T. N., *South Wales, British Regional Geology* (London, 1970).

Howells, M. F., *Wales, British Regional Geology* (Nottingham, 2007).

John, B. S., *The Geology of Pembrokeshire* (Aberteifi, 1979).

John, B. S., *Pembrokeshire Coast Path* (London, 2001).

Owen, T. R., *Geology explained in South Wales* (Newton Abbot, 1973).

Roberts, J. L., *Geological Structures* (London, 1989).

Toghill, P., *The Geology of Britain* (Shrewsbury, 2000).

Research Articles

Chapter 1: Geological History

Brenchley, P. J. and Rawson, P. F., England and Wales through geological time. In Brenchley, P. J. and Rawson, P. F. (eds), *The Geology of England and Wales* (London, 2006) 1-7.

Hunter, A., (ed) *The Geological History of the British Isles* Open University SXR260 (Milton Keynes, 2001).

Palmer, D., *The Atlas of the Prehistoric World* (London, 2000) 12-47.

Powell, C. M., Inversion Tectonics in S.W.Dyfed. *Proceedings of the Geologists' Association* (London, 1987) 98, 193-203.

Chapter 2: Precambrian & Cambrian

Baker, J. W., The Precambrian of South West Dyfed. In Bassett, M. G. (ed), *Geological excursions in Dyfed, South West Wales* (Cardiff, 1982) 15-25.

Birch, R., Tracking Trilobites. *Natur Cymru* (Bangor, 2009) 30, 18-21.

Carney, J. C. Horak, J. M., Pharaoh, T. C., Gibbons, W., Wilson, D., Barclay, W. J., Bevins, R. E., Cope, J. C. W. and Ford, T. D., *Precambrian Rocks of England and Wales*, Geological Conservation Review Series No 20, (Peterborough, 2000) 129-136.

Cowie, J. W., Cambrian. In Duff, P. McL. D. and Smith, A. J. (eds), *Geology of England and Wales* (London, 1992) 35-61.
McIlroy, D. and Horak, J. M., Neoprotozoic: the late Precambrian terranes that formed Eastern Avalonia. In Brenchley, P. J. and Rawson, P. F. (eds), *The Geology of England and Wales* (London, 2006) 9-23.
Owens, R. M., *Trilobites in Wales* (Cardiff, 1984).
Lowman, R. D. W. and Bloxam, T. W., The petrology of the Lower Fishguard Volcanic Group and associated rocks east of Fishguard, North Pembrokeshire (Dyfed), South Wales, *Journal of the Geological Society* (London, 1981), 138, 47-68.
Stephenson, D., Bevins, R. E., Millward, D., Highton, A. J., Parsons, I., Stone, P. and Wadsworth, W. J., *Caledonian Igneous Rocks in Britain*, Geological Review Series, No.17. (Peterborough, 1999) 247-251, 256-264, 342-344.
Thomas, G. E. and Thomas, T. M., The volcanic rocks of the area between Fishguard and Strumble Head, Pembrokeshire. *Quarterly Journal of the Geological Society* (London, 1956) 112, 291-311.
Rushton, A. W. A., Owen, A. W., Owens, R. M. and Prigmore, J. K., *British Cambrian to Ordovician Stratigraphy*, Geological Conservation Review Series No 18, (Peterborough, 1999) 53-67, 137-149.
Williams, B. P. J. and Stead, T. G., The Cambrian Rocks of the Newgale-St David's area. In Bassett, M. G. (ed), *Geological excursions in Dyfed, South West Wales* (Cardiff, 1982) 27-49.

Chapters 3, 4 & 5: Ordovician

Bassett, M. G., Wright, A. D. and Duff, P.McL. D., Ordovician. In Duff, P. McL. D. and Smith, A. J. (eds), *Geology of England and Wales* (London, 1992) 63-125.
Bevins, R. E. and Roach, R. A., Ordovician Igneous Activity in South West Dyfed. In Bassett, M. G. (ed), *Geological excursions in Dyfed, South West Wales* (Cardiff, 1982) 65-79.
Brenchley, P. J., Rushton, A. W. A., Howells, M. and Cave, R., Cambrian and Ordovician: the early Palaeozoic tectonostratigraphic evolution of the Welsh Basin, Midland and Monian Terranes of Eastern Avalonia. In Brenchley, P. J. and Rawson, P. F. (eds), *The Geology of England and Wales* (London, 2006) 26-74.

Davies, J. R., Waters, R. A., Wilby, P. R., Williams, M. and Wilson, D., *The Cardigan and Dinas Island district – a brief explanation of the geological map*. Sheet Explanation of the British Geological Survey.1:50,000 Sheet 193 (including part of Sheet 210) Cardigan and Dinas Island (Nottingham, 2002).

Evans, W. D., The Geology of the Prescelly Hills, North Pembrokeshire. *Quarterly Journal of the Geological Society*, (London, 1944).101, 89-110.

Hughes, C. P., Jenkins, C. J. and Rickards, R. B., Abereiddy Bay & Adjacent Coast. In Bassett, M. G.(ed), *Geological excursions in Dyfed, South West Wales* (Cardiff, 1982) 51-63.

John, B. S. *The Bluestone Enigma*. (Newport, Pembs. 2008)

Lowman, R. D. W. and Bloxam, T. W., The petrology of the Lower Fishguard Volcanic Group and associated rocks east of Fishguard, North Pembrokeshire (Dyfed), South Wales, *Journal of the Geological Society* (London, 1981), 138, 47-68.

Stephenson, D., Bevins, R. E., Millward, D., Highton, A. J., Parsons, I., Stone, P. and Wadsworth, W. J., *Caledonian Igneous Rocks in Britain*, Geological Review Series, No.17. (Peterborough, 1999) 247-251, 256-264, 342-344.

Thomas, G. E. and Thomas, T. M., The volcanic rocks of the area between Fishguard and Strumble Head, Pembrokeshire. *Quarterly Journal of the Geological Society* (London, 1956) 112, 291-311.

Chapter 6: Silurian

Aldridge, R. J., Siveter, D. J., Lane, P. D., Palmer, D. and Woodcock, N. H. (eds), *British Silurian Stratigraphy*, Geological Review Series, No.19. (Peterborough, 2000) 96-101, 227-234, 447-451.

Bassett, M. G., (1982) Silurian Rocks of the Marloes and Pembroke Peninsulas. In Bassett, M. G.(ed), *Geological excursions in Dyfed, South West Wales* (Cardiff, 1982) 103-122.

Cantrill, T. C., Dixon, E. E. L., Thomas, H. H. and Jones, O. T., *The Geology of the South Wales Coalfield. Part XII. The Country around Milford*. Memoir of the Geological Society of Great Britain (London, 1916) 51-81.

Cherns, L., Cocks, L. R. M., Davies, J. R., Hillier, R. D., Waters, R. A. and Williams, M., Silurian: the influence of extensional tectonics and sea-level changes on sedimentation in the Welsh Basin and

on the Midland Platform. In Brenchley, P. J. and Rawson, P. F. (eds), *The Geology of England and Wales* (London, 2006) 75-102.
Hillier, R. D., Depositional environment and sequence architecture of the Silurian Coralliferous Group, Southern Pembrokeshire, UK. *Geological Journal* (London, 2002) 37, 247-268.
Hillier, R. D. and Williams, B. P. J., Sedimentation and tectonics: the marine Silurian-basal Lower Old Red Sandstone transition in South West Wales. *Geological Journal* (London, 2004) 39; 237-256.
Hillier, R. D. and Williams, B. P. J., The Ridgeway Conglomerate Formation of SW Wales, and its implications. The end of the Lower Old Red Sandstone? *Geological Journal* (London, 2007) 42, 55-83.
Thorpe, R. S., Leat, P. T., Bevins, R. E., and Hughes, D. J., Late orogenic alkaline/subalkaline Silurian volcanism of the Skomer Volcanic Group in the Caledonides of South Wales. *Journal of the Geological Society* (London, 1989) 146, 125-132
Ziegler, A. M., Silurian marine communities and their environmental significance. *Nature* (London, 1965) 207, 270-272.

Chapter 7: Old Red Sandstone

Allen, J. R. L. and Williams, B. P. J., Sedimentology and stratigraphy of the Townsend Tuff Bed (Lower Old Red Sandstone) in South Wales and the Welsh Borders. *Journal of the Geological Society* (London, 1981) 138, 15-29.
Allen, J. R. L., Thomas, R. G. and Williams, B. P. J., The Old Red Sandstone north of Milford Haven. In Bassett, M. G. (ed), *Geological Excursions in Dyfed, South West Wales* (Cardiff, 1982) 123-149.
Barclay, W. J., The Anglo Welsh Basin. In Barclay, W. J., Browne, M. A. E., McMillan, A. A., Pickett, A. E., Stone, P. and Wilby, P. R., *The Old Red Sandstone of Great Britain*, Geological Conservation Review Series No 31. (Peterborough, 2005) 211-221, 281-312.
Dineley, D. L., Devonian. In Duff, P. McL. D. and Smith, A. J. (eds), *Geology of England and Wales* (London, 1992) 179-205.
Hancock, P. L., Dunne, W. M. and Tringham, M. E., Variscan structures in SW Dyfed. In Bassett, M. G. (ed), *Geological Excursions in Dyfed, South West Wales* (Cardiff, 1982) 221-239.

Hillier, R. D. and Williams, B. P. J., The alluvial Old Red Sandstone: fluvial basins. In Brenchley, P. J. and Rawson, P. F. (eds), *The Geology of England and Wales* (London, 2006) 155-171.

Hillier, R. D. and Williams, B. P. J., The Ridgeway Conglomerate Formation of SW Wales, and its implications. The end of the Lower Old Red Sandstone? *Geological Journal* (London, 2007) 42, 55-83.

Marshall, J. D., Sedimentology of a Devonian fault bounded braidplain and lacustrine fill in the lower part of the Skrinkle Sandstones, Dyfed, Wales. *Sedimentology* (London, 2000) 47, 325-342.

Marshall, J. D., Fault bounded basin fill: Fluvial response to tectonic controls in the Skrinkle Sandstones of SW Pembrokeshire, Wales. In Friend, P. F. and Williams, B. P. J. (eds), *New Perspectives on the Old Red Sandstone*, Geological Society, Special Publications (London, 2000) 180, 401-416.

Morrisey, L. B. and Braddy, S. J., Terrestrial trace fossils from the Lower Old Red Sandstone, South West Wales. *Geological Journal* (London, 2004) 39, 315-336.

Williams, B. P. J., Allen, J. R. and Marshall, J. D., Old Red Sandstone Facies of the Pembroke Peninsula, south of the Ritec Fault. In Bassett, M. G. (ed), *Geological Excursions in Dyfed, South West Wales* (Cardiff, 1982) 151-174.

Chapter 8: Lower Carboniferous

Adams, A. E., Wright, V. P. and Cossey, P. J., South Wales – Mendip Shelf. In Cossey, P. J., Adams, A. E., Purnell, A. E., Whiteley, M. J., Whyte, M. A. and Wright, V. P. (eds), *British Lower Carboniferous Stratigraphy*, Geological Conservation Review Series No 29. (Peterborough, 2005) 395-430.

Dixon, E. E. L., *The Geology of the South Wales Coalfield. Part XIII. The Country around Pembroke and Tenby*. Memoir of the Geological Society of Great Britain (London, 1921) 138-144.

John, B. S., Valiant Cliffs of Pembrokeshire. *Geographical Magazine* (London, 1978) 50, 467-470.

Kelling, G. and Williams, B. P. J., Deformation structures of sedimentary origin in the Lower Limestone Shales (Basal Carboniferous) of South Pembrokeshire, Wales. *Journal of*

Sedimentary Petrology (London, 1966) 36, 927-939.
Leeder, M. R., Dinantian. In Duff, P. McL. D. and Smith, A. J. (eds), *Geology of England and Wales* (London, 1992) 207-238.
May, V. J., South Pembroke Cliffs. In May, V. J. and Hansom, J. D., *Coastal Geomorphology of Great Britain*. Geological Conservation Review Series, No.28, (Peterborough, 2003).
Thomas, T. M., Gash Breccias of South Pembrokeshire: fossil karstic phenomena? *Transactions of the Institute of British Geographers* (London, 1971) 54, 89-100.
Walsh, P., Batteau-Queney, Y., Howells, S., Ollier, C. and Rowberry, M., The gash breccias of the Pembroke Peninsula, SW Wales. *Geology Today* (London, 2008) 24, 137-145.
Waters, C. N. and Davies, S. J., Carboniferous:extensional basins, advancing deltas and coal swamps. In Brenchley, P. J. and Rawson, P. F. (eds), *The Geology of England and Wales* (London, 2006) 173-203.
Williams, B. P. J., ((1971) Sedimentary features of the Old Red Sandstone and Lower Limestone Shales of South Pembrokeshire south of the Ritec Fault. In Bassett, D. A. and Bassett, M. G. (eds), *Geological Excursions in South Wales and The Forest of Dean* (Cardiff, 1971) 222-239.
Wright, V. P., The evolution of the early Carboniferous limestone province of S.W. Britain. *Geological Magazine* (London, 1987) 124, 477-480.

Chapters 9 & 10: Upper Carboniferous

Cleal, C. J. and Thomas, B. A., *British Upper Carboniferous Stratigraphy*. Geological Conservation Review Series, No.11, (Peterborough, 1996) 59-78.
George, G. T., Sedimentology of the Upper Sandstone Group (Namurian G1) in South West Dyfed: A case study. In Bassett, M. G. (ed), *Geological Excursions in Dyfed*, South West Wales (Cardiff, 1982) 203-214.
George, G. T. and Kelling, G., Stratigraphy and sedimentology of the Upper Carboniferous sequences in the Coalfield of South West Dyfed. In Bassett, M. G. (ed), *Geological Excursions in Dyfed, South West Wales* (Cardiff, 1982) 175-201.
Hancock, P. L., Dunne, W. M. and Tringham, M. E., Variscan

structures in SW Dyfed. In Bassett, M. G. (ed), *Geological Excursions in Dyfed, South West Wales* (Cardiff, 1982) 239-248.
Kelling, G., and Collinson, J. D., Silesian. In Duff, P. McL. D. and Smith, A. J. (eds), *Geology of England and Wales* (London, 1992) 239-273.
Powell, C. M., Inversion tectonics in S.W.Dyfed. *Proceedings of the Geologists' Association* (London, 1987) 98, 193-203.
Smallwood, S., A thin skinned thrust model for Variscan Pembrokeshire, Wales. *Journal of Structural Geology* (London, 1985) 7. 683-687.
Waters, C. N. and Davies, S. J., Carboniferous:extensional basins, advancing deltas and coal swamps. In Brenchley, P. J. and Rawson, P. F. (eds), *The Geology of England and Wales* (London, 2006) 203-223.
Williams, P. F., The Sedimentation of Westphalian (Ammanian) Measures in the Little Haven-Amroth Coalfield, Pembrokeshire. *Journal of Sedimentary Petrology* (London, 1968) 38, 332-362.

Chapter 11: Quaternary

Bowen, D. Q., Dating Pleistocene Events in South West Wales. *Nature* (London, 1966) 211, 475-476.
Bowen, D. Q., The Pleistocene History of Wales and the Welsh Borderland. *Proceedings of the Geologists' Association* (London, 1973) 84, 249-272.
Bowen, D. Q., Pleistocene Deposits and Fluvioglacial Landforms of North Preseli. In Bassett, M. G. (ed), *Geological Excursions in Dyfed, South West Wales* (Cardiff, 1982) 289-295.
Bowen, D. Q. and Lear, D. L., The Quaternary Geology of the Lower Teifi Valley. In Bassett, M. G. (ed), *Geological Excursions in Dyfed, South West Wales* (Cardiff, 1982) 297-302.
Campbell, S. and Bowen, D. Q. *Quaternary of Wales*, Geological Conservation Review Series, No. 2, (Peterborough, 1989) 9-94.
Catt, J. A., Gibbard, P. L., Lowe, J. J., McCarroll, D., Scource, J. D., Walker, M. J. C. and Wymer, J. J., Quaternary: ice sheets and their legacy. In Brenchley, P. J. and Rawson, P. F. (eds), *The Geology of England and Wales* (London, 2006) 430-467.
Charlesworth, J. K., The South Wales End Moraine. *Quarterly Journal of the Geological Society* (London, 1929) 85, 335-358.

Dixon, E. E. L., *The Geology of the South Wales Coalfield. Part XIII. The Country around Pembroke and Tenby*. Memoir of the Geological Society of Great Britain (London, 1921) 198-200.
Jehu, T. J., The glacial deposits of Northern Pembrokeshire. *Transactions of the Royal Society* (Edinburgh, 1904) 41, 53-87.
John, B. S., Pembrokeshire. In Lewis, C. A., (ed), *The Glaciations of Wales and adjoining regions* (London, 1970) 229-265.
John, B. S., Glaciation and the West Wales Landscape. *Nature in Wales* (Haverfordwest, 1971) 12, 138-155.
McCarroll, D., The glacial geomorphology of West Wales. In Walker, M. J. C. and MaCarroll, D., *The Quaternary of West Wales: Field Guide* (London, 2001) 9-16.

Chapter 12: Additional Localities

Connop-Price, M. R., Pembrokeshire: *The Forgotten Coalfield.* (Ashbourne, 2004) 128-135.
Thomas, R. G., Williams, B. P., Morrisey, L. B., Barclay, W. J. and Allen, K. C. Enigma variations: the stratigraphy, provenance, palaeoseismicity and depositional history of the Lower Old Red Sandstone Cosheston Group, South Pembrokeshire, Wales. *Geological Journal* (London, 2006) 41, 481-536.

Ordnance Survey and British Geological Survey Maps

		Sheet	
Ordnance Survey	1:50,000	145	Cardigan
Landranger Series	1:50,000	157	Pembroke and Tenby
	1:50,000	158	St David's and Haverfordwest
Outdoor Leisure Map	1:25,000	35	North Pembrokeshire
	1:25,000	36	South Pembrokeshire
British Geological Survey	1:50,000	193	Cardigan and Dinas Island
	1:50,000	209	St David's
	1:50,000	210	Fishguard
	1:50,000	226/7	Milford
	1:50,000	228	Haverfordwest
	1:50,000	229	Carmarthen
	1:50,000	244/5	Pembroke and Linney Head
	1:25,000	SM72	St David's
	1:250,000		Geological Map of Wales